2004

INSIDE THE
SHADOW GOVERNMENT

Inside the Shadow Government © 2003
by Harry Helms

All rights reserved.

website: www.the-shadow-government.com

ISBN: 0-922915-89-X

Feral House
PO Box 39910
Los Angeles, CA 90039

www.feralhouse.com
info@feralhouse.com

Send SASE for free catalogue

INSIDE THE
SHADOW GOVERNMENT

National Emergencies and the Cult of Secrecy

Harry Helms

CONTENTS

INTRODUCTION

ON MARCH 1, 2002 the *Washington Post* reported in a front-page story that a "shadow government" had been activated in the wake of the September 11, 2001 terrorist attacks. According to the *Post*, President Bush had put it into operation in the first hours after the attacks, sending over 100 senior civilian managers of the federal government by helicopters to secret underground shelters outside of Washington. The purpose of this "shadow government," according to the *Post's* sources, was to allow continued functioning of federal authority in the event of a catastrophic terrorist attack—such as one involving an atomic weapon upon Washington. While not commenting on the specifics of the *Post* story, officials of the Bush administration did confirm its substance.

"We take this issue extraordinarily seriously, and are committed to doing as thorough a job as possible to ensure the ongoing operations of the federal government," said Joseph Hagin, the White House deputy chief of staff. "In case of the use of a weapon of mass destruction, the federal government would be able to do its job and continue to provide key services and respond.

The *Post* story said the activation was intended to be a temporary measure lasting only a few days, but the continued threat of terrorist attacks had made it an ongoing operation. "Teams of federal executives were being rotated at 90-day intervals, to live and work in the underground facilities," said the *Post*. The executives were not allowed to take their families, and could not, under penalty of federal prosecution, tell anyone where they are going or why; they were instructed to simply say they are going on a business trip. Once at the shelters, they remained inside them for the duration of their assignment. Each underground installation contained food, water, medicine, electric generators, and other necessities to allow it to function for several weeks while completely sealed off from the outside world. These activities were still continuing as these words were written in late 2002, and may well have been expanded.

But, as the *Post* story noted, the concept of a "shadow government" did not originate after the September 11 attacks. The initial plans were made during the Truman administration in response to the Soviet Union's emerging nuclear threat, and were greatly expanded during the Eisenhower and Kennedy administrations as the Soviets developed intercontinental missile capabilities. Much of the "shadow government" infrastructure, such as the underground shelters used after September 11, was constructed during the Eisenhower and Kennedy years.

However, the *Post* story failed to convey the true scope and awesome potential of what we will refer to in this book as the Shadow Government, which is much more than just some underground shelters for senior federal officers. It also includes plans for detention and arrest—without probable cause or a warrant —of American citizens, government control of all radio and television stations, seizure of private property (including cars) and bank accounts, and the use of the U.S. military to impose martial law and conduct combat operations in American cities if the president declares a "national emergency." And who determines if a situation constitutes a national emergency? The President.

Perhaps the most incredible aspect of the Shadow Government is the President's ability to suspend Constitutional government (including the Bill of Rights) and rule like a dictator through a little-known procedure called an "executive order." For example, with a stroke of the pen the President could order all American citizens of a certain racial group to be held indefinitely in detention camps under military guard. Sound far-fetched? That, as we'll see in the coming pages, actually happened during World War II (and the presidential action was upheld by the Supreme Court).

Much of the Shadow Government was not created by a single law or master plan. Instead, it unintentionally came about as the product of numerous national security and defense laws passed during World War II and the Cold War. Individually, none of these laws posed a significant threat to Constitutional government or American liberties, but their cumulative impact was not only huge but also largely unrecognized by the public, the media, and Congress. Another key factor in the creation of the Shadow Government was the tendency for Congress during World War II and the Cold War to delegate increasing responsibility to the President often through vaguely worded legislation open to multiple interpretations. Finally, the expanded use of classified information following World War II made it possible to keep the existence of many programs secret from Congress and the public. Combined, these factors made it possible for the Shadow Government to grow with almost no oversight or accountability.

Since the September 11 attacks, several new items of Congressional legislation have added to the powers of the Shadow Government. The federal government can now eavesdrop on attorney-client communication if there is a "reasonable suspicion" that such communications would "facilitate acts of terrorism." A program called "Total Information Awareness" was proposed within the Department of Defense to keep track of all banking and credit card transactions, phone records, travel data, e-mail, and even prescription drug purchases by each person in the United States — all in the name of fighting terrorism. An advisory committee created by Congress to recommend domestic responses to terrorist threats has recommended the creation of a domestic intelligence agency comparable to the CIA. And on December 1, 2002, the *Washington Post* reported the Bush administration was planning to create a second, parallel legal system for terrorism suspects — for U.S. citizens as well as non-citizens — that would allow persons to be investigated, interrogated, arrested, tried and punished without the legal protections guaranteed by the U.S. Constitution.

No rational person could deny in the wake of the September 11 attacks that new, innovative measures were necessary to combat terrorism. Yet most initiatives of the Shadow Government since September 11 seem more designed to fight the civil liberties and privacy of American citizens than they do terrorism. For example, how would a national database of the prescription drugs purchased and used by American citizens have helped prevent the September 11 attacks? How exactly would knowing which single women use birth control pills or which men have prescriptions for Viagra prevent future terrorist attacks?

As with much of the Shadow Government, the proposed Total Information Awareness program would not solve the problem (terrorism) it supposedly addresses. Instead, it would give more information and more power to a secret, nonelected and unaccountable group operating outside normal Constitutional checks and balances. In the hands of the unscrupulous, or just the merely incompetent, such power and knowledge could cause lasting damage to American democracy.

What could have happened on September 11, 2001, if the full powers of the Shadow Government had been unleashed? Turn to Chapter One for a possible scenario.

WHAT COULD HAVE HAPPENED

AT 8:51 ON THE MORNING of 11 September 2001, President George W. Bush was visiting Emma E. Booker Elementary School in Sarasota, Florida, when his chief of staff whispered in his ear that a large civilian airliner had hit the north tower of the World Trade Center.

This was American Flight 11, reported hijacked to NORAD twenty minutes earlier. A few minutes later, while the president listened to schoolchildren reading, air traffic controllers watched another large jet disappear from their radar screens, a 757 that had failed for some minutes to respond to radio calls. Just as Flight 11's had, United Flight 175's transponder, the signaling device that helps ground controllers track planes, failed or was switched off just before a sharp turn away from course. A few minutes later, radar operators in Indianapolis saw yet another large airliner, American Flight 77, disappear from their screens shortly after the 757 crossed the West Virginia/Ohio state line. That meant that this plane's onboard radar transponder had also failed or been shut off. Indianapolis ATC called the American Airlines operations center about American 77 and learned that American 11 had been hijacked earlier that morning. While they discussed the situation with American 77, United 175 flew down into central New Jersey, headed east to the Jersey shore, and then over New York Bay toward lower Manhattan. Millions watched it crash into the south tower of the World Trade Center at 9:03. The first fighter jets from Otis Air National Guard Base were about seventy miles away.

By 9:09, Indianapolis ATC had given up trying to contact American 77 and instead contacted the American Airlines flight operations center and learned that a second jet had struck the World Trade Center. For the next several minutes, Indianapolis ATC contacted its various ground radar sites to see if they had been able to locate American 77, realizing that it could not have reached New York in time to have struck the south tower and that it was probably seeking another target. NORAD was notified of the hijacking at 9:24. At 9:25 the Federal Aviation Administration ordered all flights nationwide to land at the nearest suitable airport and banned all takeoffs until further notice.

At the same time, Washington ATC radar picked up an object with no transponder signal moving fast toward the capital. Three F-16 fighters took off toward Washington from Langley Air Force Base in Virginia at 9:27.

At 9:31, President Bush made a statement at the elementary school in which he called the crashes into the World Trade Center "an apparent terrorist attack." He then immediately departed for nearby Sarasota/Bradenton International Airport to board Air Force One.

At 9:33, the same ground control tower at Dulles that had cleared American 77 for takeoff at 8:19 that morning, spotted a fast-moving blip on their radar screens. They alerted their counterparts at Reagan National Airport, where radar showed the airplane heading into the restricted airspace over the White House, the Capitol, and the Pentagon. The Dulles operators also alerted the Secret Service, who whisked Vice President Dick Cheney down to a bunker under the White House.

The control tower at Reagan National Airport asked a C-130 military cargo plane that had just taken off from Andrews Air Force Base in Maryland to intercept and identify the unknown object. At 9:36, the C-130 crew reported that it was a Boeing 757 with the markings of American Airlines, traveling low and fast.

By then observers on the ground could see American 77 swoop low over the White House and then begin to climb again. The airplane climbed to over five thousand feet and then executed a sharp turn (later estimated to have been in excess of 270 degrees) into a steep descent to its target. At 9:37, American 77 dropped below the minimum altitude ground radar could track.

Terrified visitors to the Lincoln Memorial watched the jet pass a few hundred feet over their heads, so close that many believed it would crash into the Memorial. Barely clearing the top of the Washington Monument, with witnesses scattering in panic or paralyzed with fear under its flight path, it clipped a few treetops and slammed into the center of the United States Capitol at 9:38 a.m.*

The bottom of the 757 scraped along the top steps of the Capitol, releasing jet fuel that was instantly ignited by engine exhaust. As the bulk of the plane thrust into the portico, under the dome in the center of the Capitol, the igniting fuel triggered a gigantic explosion, its blast wave contained by the dome to echo through the interior, a hurricane of metal fragments and burning fuel. Windows along the side of the Capitol blew out in fast succession as the firestorm spread through the hallways toward the House and Senate chambers. Most of the few survivors of the impact and explosion inside the building were trapped inside and quickly burned to death. Viewers of the two live congressional television networks were able to hear the explosion and see members who were standing in both houses knocked off their feet by the impact before the transmission ended. Everyone inside the House and Senate chambers died.

At 9:49, the president received word that the Capitol had been struck by a hijacked plane and that damage would be great and casualties high. He spoke in whispers with his national security advisor and was able to confirm that the vice president was safe in the White House emergency bunker; secure communications between them would be possible when they reached the airport. The president stared out the window of his limousine as Air Force One loomed ahead, surrounded by security forces. F-16 fighters were already airborne to escort Air Force One to its next stop, when a safe place to land could be determined. The president thought back to the briefings he had received on contingency plans and options in the event of a national disaster. The example of disaster in those briefings had been a nuclear attack. But, the president thought, this nonnuclear and yet unconventional blow was surely a national disaster.

The Capitol burned furiously, its dome hidden by flames and smoke. At the nearby Senate and House office buildings, staffers frantically called the cell phone numbers of legislators and other colleagues scheduled to be at the Capitol that morning. In a few cases, people had not made it to the Capitol and answered; in the vast majority of cases, there was no answer.

---

*Everything in this chapter before the preceding paragraph has factually recounted events of September 11, 2001; the remainder of the chapter explores possible consequences of a different turn of events, as described by the preceding paragraph.

Within a few minutes of the Capitol attack, the Senate and House office buildings were evacuated. Evacuees wandered in shock, staring at the Capitol and trying to comprehend what was happening.

Air Force One took off at 9:54 a.m. toward the northwest. It was agreed that to return to Washington would be too risky until the situation there stabilized. The reports coming in rapidly from Washington were grim. The Capitol was destroyed, and only eleven members of the Senate and fifty-two members of the House could be accounted for. To contain the awful news, members of the press aboard Air Force One were restricted to their seats, and Secret Service agents confiscated their cell phones and other communications devices, from laptop computers to ballpoint pens. Those who protested were told the president was operating under the authority of the National Security Act of 1947. In the back, the president was discussing the situation via a conference call involving the vice president, military aides, and national security staff in Washington as well as his on-board staff. They all agreed that the standby executive orders should be signed and implemented as soon as possible. They still needed to determine the nationality of the hijackers before issuing all the executive orders, although the passenger lists for the doomed aircraft were showing several Arabic names. Information already in hand was enough to put several contingency plans in motion.

At 10:38, an hour after the attack, the fire at the Capitol was still out of control. The District of Columbia fire department had the equipment and training to handle house and apartment fires, not thousands of gallons of burning jet fuel. The temperature of the fire was approaching two thousand degrees Fahrenheit in places, and the crowded Washington streets delayed the arrival of men and equipment. The Capitol exterior was black with soot, and flames had burst through the roofs of the Senate and House chambers. As word spread that the twin towers of the World Trade Center had collapsed, many feared that the Capitol dome, with its old-fashioned cast iron undergirding, would also fall.

At approximately 11:00, the president learned that a fourth hijacked airplane, United Flight 93, had crashed in rural Pennsylvania after leaving Newark for San Francisco and turning toward Washington. The president was told that that passengers aboard the plane had phoned loved ones and said that they were going to try to overpower the hijackers; apparently the plane had crashed during the ensuing struggle. There was an urgent message for the president from the director of the FBI: some of the passengers with Arabic names on the doomed jets had been on "watch lists" of persons connected to terrorist groups. Somehow they had entered the country legitimately, overstayed their visas, and eluded the Immigration and Naturalization Service's notice. How many others in this country had helped them, or were waiting to commit further terrorist acts? The director of the FBI told the president that certain areas of Brooklyn, New York, Hudson County in New Jersey, greater Los Angeles, and the Detroit metropolitan areas had the highest concentrations of Arab immigrants, both legal and illegal, in the United States. Given the current emergency, the Director told him, it must be assumed that persons connected to the day's terrorist attacks are in those areas, and that other terrorists are hiding in those areas, preparing to launch more attacks. "What sort of attacks?" asked the president.

"Nothing can be ruled out," said the Director. "It could be anything from truck bombs to biological, chemical, and nuclear weapons. We don't have time to do this by the usual rules. If there is any hesitation, thousands more people may die in the coming hours."

"Yes," he said, "I know what I have to do. Get ready," the president told the FBI Director. The president ended the call by asking the FBI director about the situation at the Capitol and for his estimate of the casualties among members of Congress. The FBI director was blunt: "The death toll will be very high, and we no longer have a functioning Congress."

At 11:22 a.m., huge cracks began to grow over the blackened dome of the Capitol. Chunks of stone began to break off and crash to the ground. The dome rippled with a loud metallic screech as its eight million pounds of supporting ironwork, weakened by the flames, abruptly sagged. The top crumbled first, raining stone nearly three hundred feet down into the Capitol's gutted interior as flames erupted through the resulting hole. The rest of the Capitol dome then slowly collapsed. Flames roared into the space where it had stood and within a few seconds turned to black smoke. It was 11:24 a.m.

Air Force One communications officers had managed to intercept the CNN downlink feed of the Capitol fire, and the president and his advisors watched in silence as the building collapsed. CNN went to a split-screen view of the smoking wreckage of the World Trade Center and the burning, decapitated Capitol. The president stared intently at the screen for a couple of minutes and then asked his staff and aides for a few minutes of privacy. As they left his private cabin, the president turned to the manila folder in front of him. Upon confirmation that the Capitol had been hit, a military attaché had unlocked the briefcase that always accompanies the president. The attaché had removed the folder and handed it to the president's national security advisor, who glanced at the contents and passed it to the president. The briefcase, code-named "the football," contained the launch codes for America's nuclear missile arsenal. But it also contained something else: documents, ready for the president's signature, that would implement a draconian set of measures in the event of a national emergency. Another document, ordering the detention of a certain group of persons, had been hastily prepared at FBI headquarters and faxed to Air Force One. The president knew he needed a few private moments to think what he was about to do.

He thought back to the national security briefings he had received before he was inaugurated, and how he first learned about the Continuity of Government program. It had seemed like something dreamed up by a hack writer imitating Tom Clancy. COG, as they called it, was a set of extraconstitutional plans designed to keep the U.S. government running in the event that everyone in the presidential line of succession specified in the Constitution died, or if the majority of Congress died. COG even included a "parallel" civilian government housed in an underground bunker in the Virginia mountains, ready to take over control of the United States should in the elected government be struck down by a surprise attack. COG was conceived in the 1950s, when the big threat was an attack by Soviet nuclear missiles. The notion that the United States government could be brought to its knees by a small group of Islamic fundamentalists would have seemed laughable back then. But it had just happened. The president began working through the papers that awaited his signature.

The first document was a declaration of a state of national emergency as defined under Title 50, Chapter 34 of the United States Code. In the first few hours after the declaration was signed, few understood the chain of events it set in motion. The president knew, however, that his signing it effectively suspended the U.S. Constitution.

The next document, the one from the FBI, was an executive order to relocate and detain all persons of a Middle Eastern background, including Arab Americans, living in the greater metropolitan areas of New York, Detroit, and Los Angeles. This was the order's point, although its vague language meant that such implications would not be readily understood by the public. The president read the order one last time before signing.

"By virtue of the authority in me as President of the United States, and Commander in Chief of the Army, Navy, and Air Force, I hereby authorize and direct the Secretary of Defense, and the Military Commanders whom he may from time to time designate," it read, "whenever he or any designated Commander deems such actions necessary or desirable, to prescribe military areas in such places and of such extent as he or the appropriate Military Commanders may determine, from which any or all persons may be excluded, and with such respect to which, the right of any person to enter, remain in, or leave shall be subject to whatever restrictions the Secretary of Defense or the appropriate Military Commander may impose in his discretion." The order sounded innocuous, the president thought, but it conveyed all the authority necessary to detain anyone—without a warrant, hearing, or trial—for any reason and for as long its executors thought necessary. The president knew that signing would mean that thousands of innocent people would be arrested in the next few hours and detained for months or even years, but there was no other choice. The reports of Arab-looking men along the waterfront in Brooklyn and New Jersey who cheered as the hijacked planes hit the World Trade Center could not be ignored. Maybe they had helped the hijackers, or maybe they were terrorists who were even now preparing the next strike. He signed the executive order, and within minutes copies were transmitted to high-ranking military commanders around the nation.

Naturally, those targeted for detention could not be expected all to turn themselves in quietly. The president knew the probability of civil disobedience and violence was high. Signing the next document would activate the U.S. Army's Special Operations Command, based at Fort Bragg, North Carolina, to secure urban areas with large populations of persons of Arab descent and take such persons into custody. Since the mid-1990s, Special Forces teams had been conducting urban warfare training exercises in such cities as Chicago, Atlanta, Los Angeles, New Orleans, Miami, Dallas, Seattle, and Detroit. The president remembered reading about such exercises back in 1997 and wondering then if the exercises had any value because American cities were so different from cities in Europe, Africa, and Asia. It was during his pre-inaugural security briefings that he learned the truth: those Special Forces teams were training to take action in American cities, not foreign ones.

The Special Forces teams would occupy New York City, Hudson County in New Jersey, Wayne County in Michigan (including Detroit), and the cities of Los Angeles, San Diego, and Atlanta. Civilian authority, including law enforcement, would yield in those areas by the Special Forces teams' authority, derived from the order before him. The teams would coordinate simultaneous, unannounced arrivals in all the areas to be occupied. The first wave of troops would travel by Black Hawk helicopters to seal off all roads and other routes out of the affected areas and to seize control of key communications and public utilities, such as electric power. Martial law and curfew would be imposed. The Special Forces would be carrying full combat gear, including explosives, and would have "shoot to kill" orders in case of any resistance. In the following hours, more troops and ground transportation would arrive to round up all persons believed to be of a Middle Eastern background for removal to temporary detention centers. Door-to-door searches would employ explosives and other tools to enter any home where a knock went unanswered.

In each city, a Special Forces psychological operations team would take control of all broadcast and cable television and radio stations, from local affiliates such as Fox News Channel 7 in Detroit to bases of network operation such as CNN in Atlanta and NBC in New York. One reason for this was that it was the fastest, surest way to communicate precisely the message they wanted to the public about the state of emergency and the operations in the militarized areas. Another reason was to give the impression of overwhelming power and control, to intimidate any opposition or resistance. It was a step unprecedented in American history, but today's unprecedented events made it necessary. The president signed the order.

The next document troubled the president. He looked at the list of several hundred names attached to it. He knew some of the persons named; a few he even considered friends. But their names were on the sweeping arrest warrant he now held. Compiled over the years with regular input from the FBI and various intelligence agencies, the list included political commentators, business and labor leaders, professional athletes, political activists, obscure academics, journalists and publishers, entertainers, and even website operators. Some were liberals, others were conservatives, and many had no identifiable political orientation. But all had fame and influence and could easily sway public opinion with sound bites. Even with control over the broadcast networks and cable news channels, the president knew, there would still be numerous outlets for dissenting voices to be heard. And those dissenting voices would carry far more weight if they were well-known voices. As he looked over the names, none of those he recognized struck him as likely supporters of terrorism. Maybe they would object to some of the techniques he was authorizing, particularly the detentions and martial law, but they were evidently loyal Americans who were probably horrified by the day's events. This was a time of clear and present danger to the nation, however, and extreme and distasteful actions were sadly necessary.

Besides, thought the president, the people on the master arrest warrant were not going to be packed off on crowded trains to concentration camps. They would not even know that they were being arrested. Instead, they were to be told that they were the objects of terrorist threats and were being temporarily moved to military bases for their own safety. They would be housed in officers' quarters on bases around the country and receive excellent care and food. They would not be kept behind barbed wire by armed guards. Many would probably think they were only to be kept on the bases overnight, or for a few days at most. Only when they were told they could not make or receive telephone calls might the truth dawn on them. But they would still be treated well; at most bases, they would even be able to play tennis and golf. That would not be too bad given the emergency facing the nation, the president thought. He signed the warrant.

There were no more documents in the folder, although the president knew several more would be prepared for his signature in the next few hours. He pressed the button of his intercom, and asked his national security advisor and military attaché to return to his cabin. He told both that he had signed all the orders and that COG should be considered active. The president then invited the rest of his key staff back into his cabin. Since many of them were unaware of the details of COG, he gave them the same overview he would later give the American people. He had declared a state of national emergency, the president said. Heads nodded in his cabin; clearly this was a national emergency. To keep order, prevent panic, and help apprehend associates of the terrorists, he was ordering the U.S. Army and some of its Special Forces teams into certain urban areas where the terrorists may have operated and may have received assistance. This was a step unseen in America since the Civil War, the president noted, but there was reason to believe that further terrorist attacks, possibly involving chemical, biological, and even nuclear weapons, might be planned, and local police forces, not equipped to cope with such challenges, would need the assistance of the military. Again heads nodded in agreement. To inform the public accurately about what was happening in those areas, the president continued, he was using his authority under the National Security Act of 1947 and the Communications Act of 1934 to make use of radio and television stations in the affected areas. Heads again nodded, and the president decided not to mention his plans to take over control of network broadcasting headquarters. Because he had been advised that several prominent Americans could be targets for assassination by terrorists, he continued, they would be moved to U.S. military bases for their safety until the crisis had passed.

Finally, the president announced his decision that spending the coming night in Washington would be too dangerous. Instead, everyone aboard Air Force One except the press would retire to the emergency facility at Mount Weather, Virginia. The press, said the president, would be moved for their own safety to a military base as soon as Air Force One landed. He wondered which of the Pulitzer Prize aspirants in the press section of Air Force One would be the first to realize what was really going on.

While the exact plans of the September 11 hijackers are unknown at this writing and may never be known, the last plane to crash, United Flight 93, is widely believed to have been aimed at the Capitol. Its departure from Newark was delayed, however, for over half an hour, enough to throw off the hijackers' plans and timing (for example, the hijackers did not seize the plane as soon after takeoff as on the other three flights). A combination of luck, hijacker incompetence, and brave actions by Flight 93's passengers and crew may have spared the Capitol on September 11. Congress was in session that day, and the crash of a large jetliner into the Capitol would have killed many, if not most, members of the House and Senate, effectively amputating the legislative branch of the U.S. government.

The developments out of the fictional catastrophe of that paragraph are hypothetical consequences and realizations of known government powers and plans for dealing with catastrophic national events.

Many of them have historical analogs; for example, during World War II, Japanese Americans (including a young Norman Mineta, Secretary of Transportation at the time of the September 11 attacks) were forcibly relocated to detention camps for the duration of the war. None were charged with or suspected of crimes; their ancestry sufficed to warrant their detention. (Most of those detained had never been to Japan, and many could not even speak or write Japanese.) In effect, they were treated as prisoners of war. The instrument was Executive Order 9066, issued by President Franklin Roosevelt on February 19, 1942. The text of the fictional order above was simply the result of substituting the current title "Secretary of Defense" for the older term "Secretary of War" in Executive Order 9066. After World War II, the U.S. Supreme Court ruled this detention to have been legal and justified by the requirements of national security, and held that the president could even issue such an order without a formal declaration of war by Congress. In a future national emergency, Arab Americans could be just as easily and legally detained as Japanese Americans were in World War II—as could blacks, Jews, or members of political groups.

The president also has the power to take control of all radio, television, and broadcasting facilities in case of a national emergency. The Communications Act of 1934 created the Federal Communications Commission and is the basic law governing electronic communications in the United States. Here is section 606(c) of the Act: "Upon proclamation by the President that there exists war or a threat of war or a state of public peril or disaster or other national emergency, or in order to preserve the neutrality of the United States, the President may suspend or amend, for such time as he may see fit, the rules and regulations applicable to any or all stations within the jurisdiction of the United States as prescribed by the Commission, and may cause the closing of any station for radio communication and the removal therefrom of its apparatus and equipment, or he may authorize the use or control of any such station and/or its apparatus and equipment by any department of the Government under such regulations as he may prescribe, upon just compensation to the owners."

Over the years, presidents have accumulated enormous powers to deal with national emergencies. Some of these powers, like those authorized in Section 606(c) of the Communications Act, have been granted (perhaps unwittingly) by Congress. Others, like the detention of Japanese-American citizens by Executive Order 9066, have been, in effect, appropriated by various presidents through the issuance of executive orders justified by a national emergency (executive orders are discussed in the next chapter). Using executive orders, presidents have suspended the constitutional right to a writ of habeas corpus, spent money without Congressional authorization, created entirely new federal agencies, forced banks to close, demonetized gold, seized mines, and control wages and prices.

Just what is a "national emergency"? That term does not appear in the Constitution, nor does it have a precise legal definition. In practice, a national emergency is whatever the president deems to be a national emergency. The result has been that the United States has been in an almost continual state of national emergency since March 6, 1933, when President Franklin Roosevelt declared a state of national emergency to deal with the Great Depression. When President George W. Bush was inaugurated in January, 2001, he inherited thirteen national emergencies declared by his predecessors. Declaring a national emergency enables the president to do everything the fictional president did in this chapter, and much more.

If anything constitutes a national emergency, a nuclear attack surely does. But the Constitution was written in a time when the near-instantaneous annihilation of the majority of Congress (or the executive branch) was unthinkable. As a result, contingencies for such a possibility were not included by the framers of the Constitution. At the end of World War II, however, the simultaneous death of everyone in the constitutional line of presidential succession and the simultaneous death of almost every member of Congress suddenly had to be countenanced as possibilities. Nuclear weapons could wipe out an entire city, such as Washington, in milliseconds. Jet bombers and rockets could deliver such weapons with little warning.

In response to this new threat, several new laws were passed, such as the National Security Act of 1947, which contained sweeping (but little noticed) new powers for the president. Various continuing national emergencies brought about the issuance of ever more expansive executive orders. New systems of classification and official secrecy (many springing directly from the National Security Act of 1947) resulted in increasing government secrecy; eventually billions of dollars in annual federal spending would be kept secret from all but a few members of Congress. Secret plans were drafted for the U.S. military to take over most of the functions of civilian government in case of a national emergency. A huge secret infrastructure was built to protect and shelter the president and other key government leaders in case of a nuclear attack.

Many have never heard of these measures. Rather than have a complete and open debate about the new perils facing constitutional government after World War II, and the proposing of constitutional amendments to deal with those dangers, the whole matter was largely handled off the books. There were several reasons for this, but the strongest seems to have been an obsessive concern for a vaguely defined "national security."

Given the fresh memories of World War II in the late 1940s, that national security seemed to trump all other concerns is understandable. Pearl Harbor demonstrated the dangers of being unprepared, while the development of the atomic bomb showed how secrecy could render a potential enemy defenseless against American force. Certainly no one wanted a potential enemy to understand fully what American reactions would be to an attack or threat of attack; a certain level of secrecy in such cases was both a legitimate and rational response to the rising Soviet threat.

But there was a less healthy reason for the concerns about national security. In the aftermath of World War II, national leaders—civilian and military alike—seem to have developed a strong distrust of the American people. Perhaps it was the paranoia over real and imagined spies that culminated in the Rosenberg trials and McCarthy hearings of the 1950s. Maybe it was a paternalistic belief that the will and morale of the American people would collapse if they had to ponder the horrific implications of a sudden nuclear attack. Or perhaps, more sinisterly, national leaders began to view the constitutional rights of Americans as placing the United States at a serious disadvantage in case of any conflict with the Soviet Union and its allies. Regardless of the reason(s), a consensus developed that plans for handling future national emergencies were not only necessary but also best kept secret from the public.

The result was COG, a sprawling plan to allow the United States government to survive a sudden nuclear attack. As might be expected, its main focus was on the survival of key civilian and military leaders instead of the general public. Most of the details, including the exact costs involved, were not only kept secret from the public but also from most members of Congress by including them as general "black budget" items identified only by code names or hidden in other appropriation items. A huge infrastructure, including secret shelters and operating facilities for key surviving civilian and military leaders, was built. And COG would be implemented by presidential executive orders, not by an act of Congress.

In early March, 2002, the *Washington Post* broke the story that President George W. Bush had activated several elements of COG in the wake of the September 11 attacks, including relocating approximately one hundred senior managers of the civilian government to live and work at "secret" facilities outside Washington. (The locations of such facilities have been known for decades; while the *Post*, at the government's request, did not identify them, this book will.) According to the *Post*, within hours of the September 11 attacks, the first groups of relocated managers were transported to the facilities, allowed only to tell their families they were leaving on a "business trip." The facilities have their own generators and are stocked with food, water, medical supplies, and other consumables. Computer networks and phone, video, and data links allow each facility to communicate with other civilian and military facilities. According to the *Post*, each civilian agency of the government had contingency plans for keeping essential government and civilian activities—such as food production and railway transportation—functioning in case of a national emergency.

The *Post* called this "the Shadow Government." In this book that term will refer to the collection of facilities, plans, people, presidential emergency powers, hidden budgets, and classifications systems used to shield the U.S. government's emergency plans from potential enemies, the American public, and even Congress.

The Shadow Government is nothing new and is strictly bipartisan. Its roots stretch back to the presidencies of Abraham Lincoln, Woodrow Wilson, and Franklin Roosevelt; its later architects include John Kennedy, Jimmy Carter, and Ronald Reagan. The Shadow Government includes secret facilities, presidential orders that create law without Congressional approval, classified projects and budgets, and numerous obscure provisions of various laws that give the president awesome powers in case of national emergency. Many elements of the Shadow Government might seem to violate the U.S. Constitution, but several of those same elements—such as the detention for any length of time of persons not charged with any crime—have been upheld by the U.S. Supreme Court. Much of the Shadow Government is unknown and classified; each year, Congress approves money for various projects whose very existence is unknown to all but a handful of Congressional leaders (and even those Congressional leaders know only the most cursory details of those projects and exercise virtually no oversight).

The Shadow Government is not controlled by any secret cabal—indeed, it is uncertain whether anyone or anything controls it. Wrapped in secrecy, it has been able to grow and mutate without scrutiny or accountability; perhaps even the president is unaware of its scope.

This book scrutinizes the Shadow Government's origins, legal foundations, powers, structure, facilities, and potential for abuse (inadvertent or intended). Most importantly, this book considers whether the Shadow Government can preserve American constitutional government in the event of catastrophe (the lessons of 11 September 2001 are not encouraging on the latter point).

Because of the highly classified nature of the Shadow Government, parts of this book must rely upon unconfirmed reports, rumors, and outright speculation. In all such cases, however, the information will be identified as unconfirmed, rumors, or speculation. Since September 11, 2001, much of the information that was freely available about the Shadow Government from the agencies themselves (such as the Federal Emergency Management Agency) or from reputable third parties (such as the Federation of American Scientists) has been withdrawn from public circulation because of security concerns. Work on this book began months before the September 11 attacks, however, and information collected before September 11 is included. Given that this information was freely available (often on the internet) for years before the September 11 attacks, it is highly unlikely that any information in this book is news to any potential terrorists as sophisticated as those attackers. In no case has any information known to be covered by any government security classification been included in this book.

Some may argue with the wisdom or propriety of a book of this nature, since the events of September 11 demonstrated beyond any doubt that the United States is threatened by those willing to slaughter thousands of average Americans without any hesitation or regret. But it is important to remember that it is those groups (and their sponsoring states) that threaten the United States and its citizens. American citizens—along with the U.S. Constitution and the Bill of Rights—were not the perpetrators of the September 11 attacks. They are not the danger facing the country. It is not unpatriotic to ask whether the Shadow Government in its present form safeguards or endangers American liberty; in fact, it might be more unpatriotic not to ask that question.

Few would dispute that America needs contingency plans for certain emergencies—such as the sudden, simultaneous deaths of almost every member of Congress or of the president and everyone in the line of presidential succession—that were not contemplated by the authors of the Constitution. Many would also agree that standby plans are needed for handling catastrophic situations such as the detonation of an atomic weapon in an American city. But keeping the plans for handling such events secret will do nothing to prevent those events. If anything, uncertainty over what the United States government could or would do in response might actually serve to embolden future terrorists or other enemies. And advance public knowledge of how the government would react to such situations would doubtlessly help to reduce panic and breakdown of civil order if such a catastrophic event actually did happen.

A secret, well-funded, and ill-defined segment of the U.S. government, backed by deadly force and outside constitutional restraints, can be as dangerous to the United States as a foreign enemy. For example, what constitutes a "national emergency" for COG purposes largely depends upon presidential discretion. Most people would agree that attacks on the scale of September 11 constitute a national emergency. But could a president facing impeachment—say for lying under oath about a sexual affair with a young intern—declare a national emergency and invoke sweeping extraconstitutional powers to prevent his conviction by the Senate and silence his enemies? Or could a president likewise declare a "national emergency" to remain in office indefinitely should the election for his successor be disputed?

The answer is, apparently, "yes." Therein is the danger of the Shadow Government. Because it was developed and funded largely in secrecy without adequate inputs from the Congress, courts, and the public, there are few checks and balances on the enormous powers that a president can assume during a national emergency.

This book contends that the United States has no need for a Shadow Government. We already have a "Sunshine Government" defined by the Constitution and implemented by laws passed by elected representatives of the American people. The legitimate need to prepare for unexpected emergencies and catastrophic events can easily be accommodated within the framework of constitutional, not shadow, government.

CHAPTER TWO

EXECUTIVE ORDERS: "KINDA COOL"

"Stroke of the pen. Law of the land. Kinda cool."
—Presidential aide Paul Begala as quoted in the
New York Times, July 5, 1998

ONE OF PRESIDENT George W. Bush's responses to the September 11 attacks was the creation on October 8, 2001 of the Office of Homeland Security and the Homeland Security Council. The Office's mission is "to develop and coordinate the implementation of a comprehensive national strategy to secure the United States from terrorist threats or attacks." Its functions include coordinating the collection and analysis of terrorist threats against the United States, monitoring the activities of terrorists and terrorist groups within the United States, preparing responses to terrorist threats and attacks, ensuring protection of critical national infrastructure, coordinating recovery efforts, and planning Continuity of Government (COG) programs. President Bush appointed Pennsylvania governor Tom Ridge as the first Director of Homeland Security, a Cabinet-level rank. By the end of 2001, over eighty employees were part of the new office.

Article I, Section 1 of the United States Constitution says, "All legislative Powers granted herein shall be vested in a Congress of the United States, which shall consist of a Senate and House of Representatives." But no member of Congress voted to create the Office of Homeland Security. So how did it come into being?

Although not mentioned in the Constitution, executive orders issued by the president have the same legal effect as laws passed by Congress. In effect, then, they allow the president to legislate independently of Congress. For example, Lincoln's Emancipation Proclamation was an executive order, as was his suspension of habeas corpus during the Civil War. Franklin Roosevelt used executive orders in 1933 to close all American banks and force citizens to turn in their gold coins and, in 1942, to intern American citizens of Japanese descent for the duration of World War II. In 1951, Harry Truman used an executive order to seize strike-threatened steel mills to prevent shortages that would endanger "national security." Richard Nixon used executive orders to impose wage and price controls in 1971. The Federal Emergency Management Agency (FEMA) was created not by Congress, but by an executive order of Jimmy Carter. George W. Bush's Executive Order 13228 created the Office of Homeland Security.

Many of the Shadow Government's formative orders were issued in the early 1960s by President John F. Kennedy. Updated and consolidated by their successors, they still form the foundations of the Shadow Government and are key to understanding it.

What Is an Executive Order?

Article II of the United States Constitution defines the powers of the president. Accustomed as we are today to the impression that the president is the United States government, the seemingly weak powers given to him by the Constitution may come as a shock. Section 1 of Article II gives the president a vaguely defined "executive authority"—the authority to carry out the laws passed by Congress and as interpreted by the courts—and Section 3 of Article II charges him to "take Care that the Laws be faithfully executed." Section 2 of Article II gives him command of the armed forces. Many historians and constitutional scholars have argued that the intent of making the president commander in chief was not to give him wide-ranging powers but to ensure civilian control of the armed forces and prevent military leaders opposing the civilian government, as had happened in Europe.

In order to "take Care that the Law be faithfully executed," the president must order members of the executive branch to implement laws and act in ways that conform to the law. While the Constitution is silent on the president's authority to issue such orders, Supreme Court rulings have declared the president has implied powers to issue those orders to the executive branch necessary to discharge his constitutional responsibility to execute the law faithfully. Orders ostensibly of this type are what "executive orders" means in this book.

Since executive orders must purport to carry out the law, a president must cite some legal basis for them. Some of these have been very inventive, but only two types of legal basis have generally withstood review by the Supreme Court:

1) The U.S. Constitution. A president can cite the powers and responsibilities assigned to him in Article II of the Constitution to justify an executive order. The most often cited basis of this kind is the president's position as commander in chief of the armed forces (cited by Clinton, for example, in his executive order establishing a "don't ask, don't tell" rule for gays in the military).

2) Powers delegated to the president by acts of Congress. The Supreme Court has ruled that Congress may delegate various powers and decisionmaking responsibilities to the president through legislation. This is the most common basis for presidential executive orders.

Other legal justifications for executive orders have enjoyed varying degrees of success. One type is the executive agreement, an agreement made between the U.S. president and a foreign leader without the advice and consent of Congress. In effect, executive agreements are unratified treaties. The Constitution does not mention them—in fact, they contradict Article II, Section 2, which requires approval by a two-thirds vote of the Senate of all treaties. Yet the Supreme Court ruled in Dames & Moore v. Regan that executive orders issued by Presidents Carter and Reagan to honor their executive agreements made to end the 1979–1981 Iranian hostage crisis were legal and binding, although they had not been ratified by Congress and entailed the expenditure of public funds. And in 1953, President Truman issued an executive order directing U.S. government agencies to give the United Nations information about U.S. citizens applying to work for the U.N. Truman cited the U.N. Charter, arguing that the United States had accepted the Charter when it joined the U.N. No one challenged this in court, so no one knows whether the Supreme Court would accept the U.N. Charter as a legal basis for an executive order.

Presidents since Washington have issued executive orders, although they have had other names. Washington's first executive orders were "proclamations." After the passage of the National Security Act in 1947, presidential orders relating to that act and other national security matters were "national security directives." During the Kennedy and Johnson administrations, these were called "national security action memoranda," and, during the Carter and Reagan years, "presidential directives." During the Clinton years, "presidential determinations" meant orders dealing with foreign policy matters. These days "presidential decision directives" often applies to executive orders dealing with classified matters. While these various types of order are not included in most counts of executive orders, they have the same legal authority and differ only nominally.

Not until 1907 did the Department of State first began to identify, track, and consecutively number executive orders since the presidency of Lincoln. In 1946, Congress passed the Administrative Procedures Act, which required publication of the number and text of all executive orders in the Federal Register (with exceptions for executive orders dealing with national security matters—only their numbers need be published). Keeping track of which executive orders are in effect is a challenge because many of them modify or supersede previous ones (for example, Reagan's Executive Order 12553 modified or replaced 385 previous orders dating back to 1909) and because of the terminological variety noted above. In testimony on October 28, 1999 before the House Judiciary Committee, Professor Phillip Cooper of the University of Vermont estimated that over 13,000 executive orders were then in effect.

Thirty days after publication, executive orders become as binding upon all affected parties as a law passed by Congress. Congress can overturn an executive order in the same way it can repeal a law, but by far the most common Congressional action is to approve retroactively the actions taken under executive orders. Federal courts also can overturn executive orders but rarely do. The most famous such cases took place in 1952, when President Truman issued an executive order to seize the nation's steel mills, then shut down by strikes, to prevent a shortage of steel to make weapons for the Korean War, and in 1980, when President Carter attempted to impose a fee on imported oil without Congressional action. In both cases, federal courts ruled the executive orders to be outside the president's constitutional or statutory authority.

The potential for presidential mischief through executive orders might seem limited, since almost all are based upon either the Constitution or a law passed by Congress. But problems arise because so many laws passed by Congress are vague and ambiguous, putting the president in a position analogous to a traffic cop's. All states have laws prohibiting driving too fast for conditions (rain, snow, etc.). As many drivers know, however, the definition of "too fast for conditions" varies from one police officer to another. One may ticket a driver going ten miles per hour under the speed limit during a heavy rain while another ignores a driver going five miles per hour over the limit in the same conditions. The clear tendency over the past century has been for presidents of both parties to use the most generous possible interpretations of their constitutional and statutory authority when issuing executive orders.

Congress has delegated so much authority to the president over the years that determining the exact scope of presidential discretion is almost impossible. But it is clear that an astonishing amount of authority has been transferred to the president, especially in cases of "national emergency." Chapter One described a scenario under which the president could seize control of all broadcasting facilities. Actually, the president has the authority to seize any radio transmitting equipment, including cell phones. Here again is the relevant text, section 606(c), of the Communications Act of 1934:

> Upon proclamation by the President that there exists war or a threat of war or a state of public peril or disaster or other national emergency, or in order to preserve the neutrality of the United States, the President. . . may suspend or amend, for such time as he sees fit, the rules and regulations applicable to all stations. . . within the jurisdiction of the United States as prescribed by the Commission, and may cause the closing of any station for radio communication. . . and the removal of its apparatus and equipment, or he may authorize the use or control of any such station. . . and/or its apparatus and equipment by any department of the Government under such regulations as he may prescribe, upon just compensation to the owners.

That short section conveys breathtaking authority to the president in the event of a national emergency, authorizing him to take control of all radio and television stations in the United States, satellite communications, hobby radio stations such as ham radio and CB, and even pagers and cell phones—all fall under the legal definition of "radio communication." And there are similar "emergency" provisions, hidden in a multitude of laws enacted by Congress over the past several decades, which can be activated if the president declares a national emergency.

A trend in executive orders after World War II is to be as vague as possible in citing the legal basis for the order. Before World War II, presidents commonly cited a specific piece of legislation or section of the Constitution as justification for an order. Today, such justifications as "the authority vested in me as President by the Constitution and the laws of the United States" are common, making it difficult or impossible to ascertain whether the order has a valid legal basis.

THE ORIGINS OF EXECUTIVE ORDERS

George Washington issued the first executive order on June 8, 1789, when he directed the officers held over from the previous American government under the Articles of Confederation to prepare reports for him about the general status of the United States. But Washington was also the first president who tried to legislate through an executive order. In 1793, war had broken out in Europe between England, France, Prussia, and the Netherlands, and Washington was anxious to preserve the neutrality of the United States. On April 22, 1793, he issued an order that contained the following language:

> . . . the duty and interest of the United States require, that they should with sincerity and good faith adopt and pursue a conduct friendly and impartial toward the belligerent powers. . . I have therefore thought fit by these presents to declare the disposition of the United States to observe the conduct aforesaid towards those powers respectively; and to exhort and warn the citizens of the United States, carefully to avoid all acts and proceedings whatsoever, which may in any manner tend to contravene such disposition. . . I do hereby also make known, that whosoever of the citizens of the United States shall render himself liable to punishment or forfeiture under the law of nations, by committing, aiding, or abetting hostilities against any of the said powers, or by carrying to any of them those articles, which are deemed contraband by the modern usage of nations, will not receive the protection of the United States against such punishment or forfeiture; and further, that I have given instructions to those officers, to whom it belongs, to cause prosecutions to be instituted against all persons, who shall, with the cognizance of the Courts

of the United States, violate the law of nations, with respect to the powers at War, or any of them.

Washington's order is remarkable for being based not upon the Constitution or an act of Congress, but upon "the law of nations." Reaction to it was swift and overwhelmingly negative, most prominently from Thomas Jefferson and James Madison. According to Madison, the effect of Washington's order was that "no citizen could any longer guess at the character of the government under which he lives." Troubled by such criticism, Washington asked his Cabinet whether he should call Congress into session to pass laws implementing his order. The majority of his Cabinet said it was not necessary, so Washington did not convene Congress. Shortly thereafter, however, a citizen went on trial by jury for violating Washington's neutrality order, but he was acquitted after the defense argued that Washington's proclamation overstepped presidential authority in an attempt to create law, which was the exclusive function of Congress. When Congress opened its next session, a chastened Washington asked for new laws to replace his order, and Congress complied.

For the rest of his term Washington was far more circumspect in issuing orders. Indeed, with rare exceptions, his successors before Lincoln were also reluctant to use executive orders. A study by the Congressional Research Service found only 143 executive orders in the seventy-two years from the Washington administration to that of Buchanan. (Perhaps the most notable use of executive orders in this period was by Andrew Jackson, who used them, based upon his authority as commander in chief, to relocate the Cherokees to Oklahoma.) But Washington's order did establish a precedent followed repeatedly with future executive orders, that of Congress subsequently passing laws that in effect "ratified" presidential executive orders with dubious legal foundations.

Abraham Lincoln first demonstrated the creative potential of executive orders. On February 15, 1848, Lincoln wrote in a letter to William H. Herndon, "The provision of the Constitution giving the war-making power to Congress was dictated, as I understand it, by the following. Kings had always been involving and impoverishing their people in wars, pretending generally, if not always, that the good of the people was the object. This, our Constitution understood to be the most oppressive of all Kingly oppressions; and they resolved to so frame the Constitution that no one man should hold the power of bringing this oppression upon us."

Lincoln apparently changed his mind by the time he became president. On April 15, 1861 — six weeks after his inauguration — Lincoln called for a militia of 75,000 to assemble in response to the secession of southern states. He also called Congress into session beginning July 4, 1861. On April 19 and 27, he ordered the blockade of Southern ports "until Congress shall have assembled and deliberated" on the secession crisis. As authority for his orders, Lincoln made reference to United States law and, as Washington had, "the law of nations." On April 20, Lincoln ordered the building of nineteen warships to enforce the blockade and the payment of $2 million to three private citizens for "meeting such requisitions as should be directly consequent upon the military and naval measures necessary for the defense and support of the government." He followed this on May 3 with another order increasing the size of the Army and Navy by tens of thousands of men. These orders contradict Article I, Section 8 of the Constitution, which states "The Congress shall have Power. . . To raise and support Armies" and Article I, Section 9, which states "No Money shall be drawn from the Treasury, but in Consequence of Appropriation made by Law." Defenders of Lincoln claim that he had to act expeditiously to respond to the impending Civil War; critics point out that he could have reconvened Congress long before July 4 and that his delay in doing so was part of a deliberate plan to present Congress with a fait accompli they could not reject or substantially modify without endangering the lives of American troops already committed to armed conflict. As in Washington's case, Congress passed legislation retroactively validating Lincoln's actions and expenditures.

Lincoln's most controversial and wide-ranging action was his suspension of the right to a writ of habeas corpus, which prevents a person being arrested and held unless formally charged with a crime and brought to trial. Article I, Section 9 of the Constitution reads, "The Privilege of the Writ of Habeas Corpus shall not be suspended, unless when in Cases of Rebellion or Invasion the public Safety may require it." The inclusion of this right in the main body of the Constitution indicates its importance to the framers when compared with others (such as the rights to freedom of speech and freedom of religion) spelled out in the Bill of Rights as afterthoughts. This reflects the colonists' long and unhappy experience with English kings who suspended this right whenever they wanted to keep opponents and dissenters behind bars indefinitely.

Lincoln revoked the right to a writ of habeas corpus on April 27, 1861, in the following order to Winfield Scott, then General-in-Chief of the Army: "You are engaged in suppressing an insurrection against the laws of the United States. If at any point on or in the vicinity of the military line which is now used between the city of Philadelphia via Perryville, Annapolis City and Annapolis Junction you find resistance which renders it necessary to suspend the writ of habeas corpus for the public safety, you personally or through the officer in command at the point where the resistance occurs are authorized to suspend the writ." This order gave Lincoln and his military commanders unlimited powers to arrest and detain anyone they wanted; persons detained had, as a practical matter, no legal rights.

The immediate targets of Lincoln's order were not, as the order implied, rebellious Southerners, but the state legislature of Maryland. Several members were known Southern sympathizers, and there was fear that Maryland might also vote to secede. The fear was justified; the legislature had rejected Lincoln's April 15 order for men from its state militia, calling it unconstitutional. After Lincoln's order of April 27, the first arrests included thirty-one of the legislators along with the mayor of Baltimore and a congressman from the state. The governor of Maryland resigned under threat of arrest, and the Army (presumably with Lincoln's approval) installed a pro-union replacement for him for the rest of the Civil War. Lincoln later extended the order suspending the writ of habeas corpus to the entire United States; its principal targets were not Confederate saboteurs or spies but northerners who opposed the war or the draft (especially newspaper editors and writers).

The most notorious target of Lincoln's order was Clement Vallandigham, a congressman from Ohio who opposed the war and called for a negotiated end to it. He was defeated for re-election in 1862. On May 1, 1863, he made a speech in Mount Vernon, Ohio against "the wicked, cruel, and unnecessary war," charging that "the men in power are attempting to establish a despotism in this country, more cruel and more oppressive than ever existed before." A few days later, soldiers under the command of General Ambrose Burnside raided Vallandigham's farm in the middle of the night, taking him prisoner and charging him with "declaring sympathies for the enemy." Instead of being tried in a civilian court, Vallandigham was tried before a military tribunal and sentenced to prison for the remainder of the war. Lincoln commuted his sentence, and—in a move that had no legal foundation or precedent in American jurisprudence—ordered him banished to the Confederacy. Vallandigham managed to make his way to Canada, and in 1864 received the Democratic nomination for governor of Ohio and almost won. (He is said to be the inspiration for Edward Everett Hale's story "The Man Without a Country.")

Lincoln's suspension of the writ of habeas corpus eventually resulted in his issuing an arrest order for the chief justice of the U.S. Supreme Court. In May 1861 John Merryman was arrested by U.S. troops at his farm near Cockeysville, Maryland. A Southern sympathizer, Merryman was implicated in a plot to burn railroad bridges in Maryland. He was taken to Fort McHenry and held without charge. Roger B. Taney, Chief Justice of the U.S. Supreme Court, was also the sitting federal circuit court judge for the district that included Maryland. He issued a writ of habeas corpus to General George Cadwalader directing that Merryman be either formally charged or released. Using President Lincoln's order as his authority, Cadwalader refused. Taney then found Cadwalader in contempt of court. In his ruling, ex parte Merryman, Taney made the telling argument that the power to suspend habeas corpus is part of Article I of the Constitution, which enumerates the powers and responsibilities of Congress. Article II, which defines the powers and duties of the president, makes no mention of it. As Taney wrote, "A state of rebellion is the only time when Congress could declare the writ removed. . . This Article is devoted to the legislative department of the United States, and has not the slightest reference to the executive branch."

Lincoln, enraged by Taney's ruling, ordered General Cadwalader and other military leaders to ignore it. Taney briefly considered organizing a posse of federal marshals to arrest Cadwalader, but decided against this to avoid massive bloodshed. But Lincoln, suspecting that Taney harbored sympathies for the Confederacy, ordered Federal Marshal Ward Hill Lamon to arrest him. Lamon had misgivings about trying to arrest the nation's top judge, and conveyed those doubts to Lincoln. In his diary, Lamon wrote that Lincoln told him to use his own discretion about making the arrest until he received orders to the contrary. Lamon decided not to arrest Taney until ordered to do so, and Lincoln did not pursue the matter.

Lincoln's suspension of habeas corpus drew international attention. A British publication, *Macmillan Magazine*, editorialized in 1862 that "there is no Parliamentary (congressional) authority whatever for what has been done. It has simply been done on Mr. Lincoln's fiat. At his simple bidding, acting by no authority but his own pleasure, in plain defiance of the provisions of the Constitution, the Habeas Corpus Act has been suspended, the press muzzled, and judges prevented by armed men from enforcing on the citizens' behalf the laws to which they and the President alike have sworn."

Lincoln was not rebuked for his actions until after his death. In 1866, the Supreme Court ruled in ex parte Milligan that it was unconstitutional to suspend the right to a writ of habeas corpus or to establish a system of military detentions and trials anywhere civil courts were still functioning. This Court undermined this decision, however, when it upheld President Franklin Roosevelt's Executive Order 9066 authorizing internment of Japanese Americans during World War II (discussed below).

Lincoln's best known executive order is the Emancipation Proclamation, issued on January 1, 1863 and justified thus: "by virtue of the power in me vested as Commander-in-Chief of the Army and Navy of the United States in time of actual armed rebellion against the authority and government of the United States, and as a fit and necessary war measure for suppressing said rebellion . . ."

After Lincoln, executive orders by presidents in the nineteenth century were comparatively rare and their impact minor. Both Presidents James Garfield and Rutherford Hayes issued no executive orders. But the latter recognized the immense danger posed to constitutional government by a president intent on rule through executive orders. Shortly before his death, Hayes was interviewed by the historian David Watson, whose 1910 book *The Constitution of the United States: Its History, Application and Construction* was a landmark in constitutional scholarship. With remarkable candor, Hayes told Watson, "The executive power is large because it is not defined in the Constitution. The real test has never come, because the Presidents have down to the present been conservative, or what might be called conscientious men, and have kept within limited range. And there is an unwritten law of usage that has come to regulate an average administration. But if a Napoleon ever became President, he could make the executive almost what he wished to make it. The war power of President Lincoln went to lengths which could scarcely be surpassed in despotic principle."

Executive Orders in the Early Twentieth Century

Theodore Roosevelt was the first new president of the twentieth century, sworn in on September 14, 1901 after the assassination of President McKinley. He came into office with the boldest, most expansive view of presidential power since Lincoln. As Roosevelt later explained in his autobiography, he "declined to adopt the view that what was imperatively necessary for the Nation could not be done by the President unless he could find some specific authorization to do it," and he also considered it his "duty to do anything that the needs of the Nation demanded unless such action was forbidden by the Constitution or by the laws." Roosevelt's view—that a president can do whatever he wants unless it is expressly prohibited by law—would become the underlying assumption behind presidential executive orders for the remainder of the twentieth century. Fortunately, Roosevelt's broad interpretation of presidential power was largely restricted to federal land use issues and other matters that did not adversely impact civil liberties or the prerogatives of Congress. Perhaps the most significant executive order he issued was one giving disability pensions to Civil War veterans over sixty-two years of age, which was widely denounced for being in violation of Article I, Section 9 of the Constitution prohibiting expenditure of public funds without Congressional authorization. But, as it had during the Lincoln administration, Congress eventually passed a law validating the order.

It was also during Theodore Roosevelt's administration, in 1907, that the Department of State began to track and number executive orders systematically, including retroactively assigning numbers to orders and proclamations from presidencies before Lincoln's. The accounting of these is flawed, crediting Lincoln, for example, with only three executive orders. Nevertheless, the system gives a good idea of how different presidents used executive orders. For example, Grover Cleveland issued only seventy-seven executive orders in his two terms. William McKinley issued fifty-one orders in the slightly over four years of his presidency. In contrast, Theodore Roosevelt cranked out a whopping 1006 in slightly over seven years as president.

The next president to use executive orders extensively was Woodrow Wilson. Wilson's executive orders were sweeping in their scope and controversial years after their issuance. In 1974, the Senate Special Committee on National Emergencies and Delegated Emergency Powers called Wilson's actions exercises of "dictatorial powers" and concluded that "Wilson's exercise of power in the First World War provided a model for future presidents and their advisors." Wilson was the first president to declare a national emergency (on February 5, 1917, two months before Congress formally declared war on Germany and the Austro-Hungarian Empire) and the first to create entirely new federal agencies (such as the Food Board and the Committee of Public information) through executive orders.

Unlike Lincoln, Wilson based his executive orders upon laws passed by Congress. His interpretation of those laws, however, was broad and creative. For example, Wilson interpreted the Trading with the Enemy Act of 1917, passed to prohibit commerce with belligerent nations, as giving him the right to regulate and censor all foreign communications, including mail, telegraph, and the recently invented radio. He used the Food and Fuel Control Act of 1917 to seize manufacturing, food production, and mining facilities as well as fix prices of various commodities. In fairness to Wilson, many of the acts passed by Congress after war was declared on April 6, 1917, delegated extraordinary powers to him and were, in retrospect, patently unconstitutional. For example, the Selective Service Act of 1917 not only set up the mechanism for drafting men into the armed forces but also made it a criminal offense even to criticize the draft (people were jailed merely for publicly expressing the opinion that the draft was unconstitutional). But Wilson eagerly pushed the powers delegated to him by Congress in radical directions, such as when he directed his attorney general, Thomas Gregory, to work with private organizations including the American Protective League, a group of self-styled patriots, to locate draft resisters and others opposed to American participation in World War I. (League members made over forty thousand citizens' arrests of suspected draft evaders and investigated over three million Americans as possible subversives.) Several of Wilson's acts were challenged before the Supreme Court, but all were upheld. In the opinion upholding the seizure of railroad property by executive order, Chief Justice Charles Evan Hughes wrote, "while emergency does not create power, emergency may furnish the occasion for the exercise of power" and that the Fifth Amendment to the Constitution (". . . nor shall private property be taken for public use, without just compensation") "is not to be read with literal exactness."

Fortunately, Congress and a large segment of the American people realized that excessive power had been granted the president during World War I and vital civil liberties had been denied. On March 3, 1921—the last day of Wilson's presidency—a joint resolution of Congress repealed most of the powers delegated to the president in 1917. The Trading with the Enemy Act was the main piece of legislation that remained intact.

In total, Wilson issued 1791 executive orders. In contrast, Warren Harding issued 484 in the three years before his death, and his successor, Calvin Coolidge, issued 1253 in the five years of his administration. Herbert Hoover issued 1004 in his four years. While none of these three's executive orders had the scope and impact of Wilson's, it is clear that the executive order had become an accepted part of a president's administrative tool kit. Many of Hoover's executive orders came in the aftermath of the October 1929 stock market crash and in response to the deepening economic depression that followed. But Hoover's efforts failed, and he was soundly defeated in 1932 by the man who would use executive orders as no president before or since.

THE EXECUTIVE ORDERS OF FRANKLIN ROOSEVELT

The Democratic Party had a majority of 334 to 89 in the House of Representatives and 75 to 17 in the Senate when Franklin Roosevelt was inaugurated, and the margin of his victory indicated widespread public support for far-reaching measures to fight the Great Depression. But the new president made it clear in his March 4, 1933 inaugural address that he wanted more power:

> It is to be hoped that the normal balance of executive and legislative authority may be wholly adequate to meet the unprecedented task before us. But it may be that an unprecedented demand and need for action may call for temporary departure from that normal balance of public procedure. I am prepared under my constitutional duty to recommend the measures that a stricken nation in the midst of a stricken world may require. But in the event that Congress shall fail to take one of these two courses, and in the event that the national emergency is still critical, I shall not evade the clear course of duty that will then confront me. I shall ask the Congress for the one remaining instrument to meet the crisis—broad executive power to wage a war against the emergency, as great as the power that would be given to me if we were in fact invaded by a foreign foe.

That passage neatly summarizes the attitude toward presidential power and its exercise through executive orders that Franklin Roosevelt repeatedly displayed throughout his presidency. Not even Lincoln legislated (some would say "dictated") through executive orders as Franklin Roosevelt did. Much of the potential for presidential abuse of executive orders arises directly from precedents set by Roosevelt during his twelve years in the White House.

Roosevelt's first official act as president was an executive order that violated federal law. At 1 a.m. on March 6, 1933, he issued Proclamation 2038, declaring a state of national emergency and a "bank holiday" or forced closing of all banks in the United States. As his authority, Roosevelt cited the Trading with the Enemy Act of 1917. But that act gave Roosevelt no authority whatsoever to issue his proclamation, because it covered only transactions taking place between citizens within the United States, and because its various provisions only applied if Congress had declared war. Yet Congress retroactively authorized Roosevelt's proclamation by amending the Act on March 9, 1933. The necessary amendments were part of the Emergency Banking Relief Act, which sped through Congress so hastily that neither house had printed copies of the bill for members to read before voting on it.

Whether by design or coincidence, Roosevelt's use of executive orders followed the pattern of taking actions—such as forcing the nation's banks to close—that would be difficult or impossible even for the Supreme Court to reverse. An example occurred on August 28, 1933, when Roosevelt issued Executive Order 6260, declaring a national emergency due to economic conditions. Citing the Emergency Banking Relief Act and other acts, he demonetized gold by ordering all banks and individuals to turn in their gold coins and declaring the provisions of contracts requiring payment in gold (including U.S. government bonds) null, so that payment would have to be accepted in paper currency instead. His justification of the order interpreted the cited acts very freely. Various legal challenges to Executive Order 6260 appeared in the courts, but by the time the first case reached the Supreme Court in 1935, the Court's ability to act was greatly constrained. All gold coins had been removed from circulation, melted down, and stored as bars in Fort Knox. Contracts and other instruments specifying payment in gold had instead been settled for the past two years with currency payments. Ruling against Roosevelt would have invited severe economic consequences. (Would parties to affected contracts be forced to pay yet again, this time in gold?) In a 5-4 decision, the Court upheld Executive Order 6260, but in his dissent Justice James McReynolds compared Roosevelt's action to "Nero at his worst." Striking down Executive Order 6260 would have precipitated a constitutional crisis. Roosevelt was prepared; in a speech draft discovered among his papers after his death, he promised to defy the unfavorable ruling.

The Supreme Court was not always so compliant during Roosevelt's first term. Several legislative cornerstones of his program—such as the National Industrial Recovery Act and the Railroad Retirement Act—were ruled unconstitutional by the Supreme Court. Perhaps overly encouraged by his landslide re-election in 1936, Roosevelt submitted his Judiciary Reorganization Bill to Congress on February 5, 1937. This bill would have added six new justices, all Roosevelt appointees, to the Supreme Court. Despite Roosevelt's popularity, his proposal seriously miscalculated the mood of the public, who rejected the court-packing attempt. The Court's sitting justices, however, felt the pressure. One of them, Owen Roberts, wrote after his retirement, "Looking back, it is difficult to see how the Court could have resisted the popular urge," and also wrote darkly of the "tremendous strain and the threat to the existing Court, of which I was fully conscious." As it turned out, Roosevelt did not need to add new justices to the Supreme Court to get his wish. The retirement of Roberts and others allowed Roosevelt to appoint a majority of the Court by the midpoint of his second term. For the rest of his presidency, Roosevelt's executive orders were never questioned by the Supreme Court.

As World War II loomed, Roosevelt expanded his use of executive orders and declared new states of national emergency in 1939 and 1941. On March 19, 1941, citing his authority as commander in chief of the armed forces, he established the National Defense Mediation Board, a labor-management dispute resolution agency empowered to seize private businesses with defense-related contracts in case of labor disputes. Roosevelt did just that on June 7, 1941, when he ordered a North American Aviation plant seized to end a strike. (This practice gave labor unions a powerful advantage over management in the affected industries.) Once World War II was underway, Roosevelt even claimed the right—by virtue of being commander in chief of the armed forces in wartime—to act contrary to statutory law. In 1942, he objected to a provision of the newly-passed Emergency Price Control Act and demanded that Congress repeal the offending provision. Roosevelt warned, "In the event that Congress should fail to act, and act adequately, I shall accept responsibility, and I will act." Congress did as Roosevelt demanded, and he never had to make good on his threat.

But none of Roosevelt's other executive orders equaled the impact of Executive Order 9066. No other better illustrates the awesome power of executive orders, their potential for abuse, and how seemingly innocuous text can have fearsome applications.

EXECUTIVE ORDER 9066

Appendix A reproduces Executive Order 9066, issued on February 19, 1942. Its language gives little reason to suspect that it would entail the internment of over 110,000 persons of Japanese descent, including 77,000 American citizens, for the duration of World War II. That is no accident; Executive Order 9066 was expressed vaguely to avoid provoking organized resistance. And, in the now traditional pattern of executive orders, Congress later passed legislation validating it.

Executive Order 9066 originated in the rabid anti-Japanese hysteria that followed the bombing of Pearl Harbor. In the first few days following the attack, General John L. DeWitt, commander of the Western Defense Command, sent a report to President Roosevelt accusing Japanese Americans of engaging in espionage and disloyal conduct. His suspicion of Japanese Americans was purely racist, and his report the work of a bewildered mind; he took the total lack of evidence of such Japanese-American disloyalty or sabotage as proof of their guilt. In DeWitt's convoluted words: "[t]he Japanese race is an enemy race and while many second and third generation Japanese born on United States soil, possessed of United States citizenship, have become 'Americanized,' the racial strains are undiluted. . . The very fact that no sabotage has taken place to date is a disturbing and confirming indication that such action will be taken." Newspapers also did their part to feed mass racist hysteria. The *Los Angeles Times* editorialized, "[a] viper is nonetheless a viper wherever the egg is hatched, so a Japanese American—born of Japanese parents—grows up to be a Japanese, not an American."

The implementation of Executive Order 9066 was draconian. Posters headlined "INSTRUCTIONS TO ALL PERSONS OF JAPANESE ANCESTRY" appeared in Los Angeles, San Francisco, and other cities with large Japanese-American populations, ordering Japanese Americans to report to "control stations." They were forbidden more than two suitcases per person, and permitted only such necessities as clothing, toiletries, and food. Those who reported to the control centers were then relocated to various internment camps. The most famous of these was Manzanar, located on Highway 395 along the eastern slopes of California's Sierra Nevada Mountains. Nine other camps were scattered through the western United States. Most Japanese Americans interned at the various camps did not have time to close their businesses, store their property, or otherwise settle their affairs. As a result, most internees incurred significant financial losses.

The sole criterion for internment under Executive Order 9066 was race. Most affected Japanese Americans were born in the United States and had never been to Japan. Even Japanese Americans who had been adopted and raised by white families — and who could not speak or write a word of Japanese — were swept up by Roosevelt's order.

While it did not single out Japanese Americans explicitly, in practice it applied only to them. German and Italian nationals were interned during World War II, but never any German-American or Italian-American citizens. If President Roosevelt and General DeWitt had any reason for their apparent belief that German Americans and Italian Americans were less prone to disloyalty than Japanese Americans, it must have been simple racism.

Life in the detention camps was hard, and the accommodations Spartan. Manzanar stood on the poor and arid soil in the eastern rain shadow of the Sierra Nevada Mountains, almost directly underneath 14,375-foot Mount Williamson. Summer temperatures often top 100 degrees Fahrenheit there, while snow and freezing temperatures are common in winter; violent storms and high winds happen year-round with little warning. Pneumonia was common in Manzanar and killed several internees. Most internees were housed in one-room barracks measuring twenty by twenty-five feet and shared by four persons (when possible, families were housed in a single barracks). The internment camps closed in September 1945, and cemeteries are all that remain of most of them.

Fred Korematsu, a welder in San Francisco who was born in the United States to Japanese parents, challenged Executive Order 9066. He had twice tried to enlist in the Army, which rejected him because of physical disabilities. When the detention orders appeared, Korematsu decided to defy it and try to remain unnoticed in the San Francisco Bay area. He was arrested in May 1942. When his case reached the Supreme Court in 1944 the Court upheld the legality of Roosevelt's order. The Court's language was chilling: "The adoption by Government, in the crisis of war and threatened invasion, of measures for the public safety, based upon the recognition of facts and circumstances which indicate that a group of one national extraction may menace that safety more than others, is not wholly beyond the limits of the Constitution and is not to be condemned merely because in other and in most circumstances racial distinctions are irrelevant." Justice Hugo Black, generally thought of as a liberal justice and civil libertarian, wrote in his opinion, "We are not unmindful of the hardships imposed [by the president's order] upon a large group of American citizens. But when under conditions of modern warfare our shores are threatened by hostile forces, the power to protect must be commensurate with the threatened danger." In a dissenting opinion, Justice Frank Murphy—normally considered a conservative—said the order "falls into the ugly abyss of racism." The government was represented before the Supreme Court by Tom C. Clark, who was later appointed to the Supreme Court by President Harry Truman. Writing after his retirement from the Court, Clark said "Despite the unequivocal language of the Constitution of the United States that the writ of habeas corpus shall not be suspended, and despite the Fifth Amendment's command that no person shall be deprived of life, liberty, or property without due process of law, both of these constitutional safeguards were denied by military action under Executive Order 9066."

In a symbolic gesture, President Ford withdrew Executive Order 9066 in 1976, and internees and their survivors later received payments. Nevertheless, this order was found constitutional, and a future president could use a similar one to detain any number of persons on the basis of race, national origin, or almost any other criterion. Since Executive Order 9066's linguistic stealth is a model for many subsequent executive orders, the criteria need not even be explicit.

Franklin Roosevelt was president for a little over twelve years. In that time, he issued 3,723 executive orders, a figure greater than the total issued by all succeeding presidents through the end of the Clinton administration.

EXECUTIVE ORDERS FROM TRUMAN TO NIXON

Many of the laws expanding presidential power passed by Congress during World War II remained on the books after the war, when Congress also passed several new laws (such as the National Security Act of 1947) that increased governmental secrecy and enabled the president to react quickly to an entirely new threat, nuclear weapons delivered by jet bombers or missiles. The result was more grounds for increasingly sweeping executive orders as well as the first executive orders whose content was classified. And while Roosevelt's pre-World War II declarations of national emergency in 1939 and 1941 were rescinded, his 1933 declaration of national emergency (rationalizing the national bank closing and recalling of all gold coins) was not. Indeed, the United States was to remain in a state of presidentially declared national emergency from 1933 to 1975.

President Harry Truman used a World War II law, the War Labor Disputes Act, as the basis for Executive Order 9728, issued on May 21, 1946, to seize most of the nation's coal mines. Labor disputes were threatening to shut down almost all coal mining, and Truman's order allowed the Secretary of the Interior to negotiate a contract with mine workers. Truman used other executive orders to seize oil refineries, rail yards, and factories where workers were on strike or threatening to strike. Given Truman's heavy backing by organized labor, it is no surprise that the settlements imposed by the government after such seizures were far more generous to labor than those reached in similar situations where the government did not intervene. But Truman's interventions in labor-management relations earned him a rare rebuke by the Supreme Court. In Executive Order 10340, Truman seized most of the nation's steel mills and granted workers a $0.26 per hour pay increase. One of the affected companies challenged the validity of the order in federal court, and in the 1952 Youngstown Sheet & Tube v. Sawyer case the Supreme Court found the executive order to be unconstitutional. Concurring, Justice Hugo Black wrote that the president's role as commander in chief did not convey "the ultimate power to take possession of private property in order to keep labor disputes from stopping production" and also found that the president's constitutional duty "to see that the laws are faithfully executed refutes the idea that he is to be a lawmaker." Also concurring, Justice Robert Jackson noted, "The executive action we have here originates in the individual will of the President and represents an exercise of authority without law." Jackson continued, "With all its defects, delays and inconveniences, men have discovered no technique for long preserving free government except that the executive be under the law, and that the law be made by parliamentary deliberations."

In many ways, the Youngstown Sheet & Tube v. Sawyer decision remains the strongest judicial restraint upon presidential executive orders, and is one of only three instances of hte Supreme Court voiding one. It would be almost three decades before another challenge to an executive order even reached the Supreme Court.

Despite the setback in Youngstown Sheet & Tube v. Sawyer, Truman used executive orders aggressively, especially in conducting the Korean War. He declared a state of national emergency in 1950 in response to the North Korean invasion of South Korea, and followed that with a series of executive orders mobilizing American troops (including ending segregation in the armed forces) and establishing various controls over the American economy. Truman also used a variation of an executive order called a "National Security Council intelligence directive" to create the National Security Agency (NSA) secretly on October 24, 1952. The NSA, created to intercept and analyze all international communications to and from the United States, was for years one of the most secret of government agencies—the directive that created it was kept secret for over two decades, and even the agency's name was classified. Large segments of the NSA budget are still classified.

In a little over seven years as president, Truman issued 905 executive orders. In contrast, his successor, Dwight Eisenhower, issued only 452 executive orders in his two terms. Like Truman, however, Eisenhower used a directive to create a new agency, the National Reconnaissance Office (NRO), to coordinate the nation's spy satellite programs. The very existence of the NRO was officially still a secret (although widely rumored) until September 18, 1992; many aspects of the NRO, including its total operating budget, are still classified.

John F. Kennedy issued several influential executive orders during his short presidency. The Soviet Union had deployed intercontinental ballistic missiles by the time Kennedy took office, and his response to the very real possibility of sudden nuclear attack was to issue a series of executive orders concerning "emergency preparedness." These orders directed the heads of various departments to develop plans to cope with national emergencies—plans that would be put into action, if necessary, by future presidential executive orders. The texts of the orders issued by Kennedy give clues as to what any additional orders might involve:

Executive Order 11000: Assigning Emergency Preparedness Functions to the Secretary of Labor

This order directed the Secretary of Labor to develop plans for emergency mobilization and use of the civilian labor force in case of national emergency. Section 2 directs the Secretary to develop "procedures for translating survival and production urgencies into manpower priorities to be used as guides for allocating available workers." Much as the broad language of Executive Order 9066 admitted interpretation as sanctioning the detention of Japanese Americans, that phrase opens the door to mandatory work assignments for civilians during a national emergency.

Executive Order 11003: Assigning Emergency Preparedness Functions to the Administrator of the Federal Aviation Agency

This order directed the Administrator of the Federal Aviation Agency to develop plans for control of civilian aviation in time of national emergency. Section 2(b) of this order called for the Administrator to "formulate plans for the development, utilization, expansion and emergency management of the Nation's civil airports, civil aviation ground facilities and equipment," and Section 2(c) directed him to "develop plans and procedures for controls, allocations and priorities concerned with the utilization of aircraft other than air carrier aircraft in an emergency."

Executive Order 11051: Prescribing Responsibilities of the Office of Emergency Planning in the Executive Office of the President

This order created an Office of Emergency Planning within the executive branch. Its director, who reports to the president, is responsible for "development of policies and procedures to determine the relationship between available supplies of the nation's resources and the requirements of military, foreign, and essential civilian programs," "planning for the emergency mobilization of telecommunications resources," and "the development of policies, programs, and control systems designed to deal with supply deficiencies and to meet effectively the most urgent requirements for those resources in the interests of national defense."

The director was also required to provide "advice and guidance to the States with regard to preparations for the continuity of State and local civilian political authority in the event of nuclear attack on the United States which shall include, but not be limited to, programs for maintaining lines of succession to office, safekeeping of essential records, provision for alternate sites of government, the protection and effective use of government resources, personnel, and facilities" and to "develop policies and plans to assure the continuity of essential Federal Government activities through programs to provide for lines of succession to office, safekeeping of essential records, alternate sites for Government operations, and the protection and effective use of Government resources, personnel, and facilities." Finally, the director was to "provide for the prompt exercise of Federal emergency authority through the advance preparation of such proposed legislation, Executive orders, rules, regulations, and directives as would be necessary to put into effect operating programs appropriate to the emergency situation." These sections lay the foundations for the Continuity of Government programs discussed in the next chapter. Several of Kennedy's 214 executive orders resemble these examples, directing departments of the executive branch to develop contingency plans to protect everything from electrical power and petroleum distribution to public warehouses.

Kennedy's successor, Lyndon Johnson, issued only 324 executive orders. Surprisingly (for such a controversial administration), none of them were very controversial, and most were based either on legislation, such as the Civil Rights Act of 1964, or on constitutional authority, such as Johnson's role as commander in chief, used for orders expanding American military involvement in Vietnam. In fact, Johnson sought Congressional backing in the form of the 1964 Gulf of Tonkin Resolution before launching his massive escalation of American involvement after the 1964 elections.

Richard Nixon issued a modest number of executive orders, 346, but some of them had far-reaching effects. Executive Order 11490, issued on October 28, 1969, consolidated and replaced the emergency planning executive orders issued by President Kennedy and was, in effect, the blueprint for the Shadow Government. As Kennedy had, Nixon directed the heads of various executive branch agencies to develop national emergency contingency plans to be implemented, if necessary, by presidential executive orders ("Plans so developed may be effectuated only. . . by an order or directive issued by the President pursuant to statutes or the Constitution of the United States"). The plans required of various agency heads by these orders again indicate what sort of presidential executive orders might be issued during a national emergency:

- Section 201: "The Secretary of State shall prepare national emergency plans and develop preparedness programs to permit . . . documentary control of persons seeking to enter or leave the United States." [emphasis added]

- Section 301: "The Secretary of the Treasury shall develop policies, plans and procedures for the performance of emergency functions with respect to (1) stabilization aspects of the monetary, credit, and financial system; . . . (4) regulation of financial institutions; . . . (9) regulation of foreign assets in the United States . . ."

- Section 401: "[T]he Secretary of Defense shall perform the following emergency preparedness functions . . . (3) Advise and assist the Office of Emergency Preparedness in developing a national system of production urgencies . . . (6) Assist the Department of Commerce and other appropriate agencies in the development of the production and distribution controls plans for use in any period of emergency . . . (17) Advise on existing communications facilities and furnish military requirements for commercial communications facilities and services in planning for and in event of an emergency, including an attack on the United States . . . (18) Furnish military requirements for all forms of transportation and transportation facilities in planning for and in the event of emergency, including an attack upon the United States . . . (19) Assist the Office of Emergency Preparedness in preparation of legislative programs and plans for coordinating nonmilitary support of emergency preparedness programs . . . (20) Develop plans and procedures for the Department of Defense utilization of nonindustrial facilities in the event of an emergency in order to reduce requirements for new construction and to provide facilities in a minimum period of time . . . (22) Develop plans and procedure to carry out Department of Defense responsibilities stated in the National Censorship Agreement between the Department of Defense and the Office of Emergency Preparedness . . . (27) Develop with the Federal Communications Commission and the Office of Telecommunications Management (OEP) plans and programs for the emergency control of all devices capable of emitting electromagnetic radiation."

• Section 501: "The Attorney General shall perform the following emergency preparedness functions . . . Develop emergency plans for the control of alien enemies and other aliens within the United States, and in consultation with the Department of State and Department of the Treasury, develop emergency plans for the control of persons attempting to enter or leave the United States . . ."

• Section 502: "In consonance with national civil defense programs developed by the Department of Defense, the Attorney General shall . . . assist the States in preparing for the conduct of intrastate and interstate law enforcement operations to meet the extraordinary needs that would exist for emergency police services . . ."

• Section 601: "The Postmaster General shall prepare plans and programs for emergency mail service and . . . (a) Censorship of international mails."

• Section 901: "The Secretary of Commerce shall prepare national emergency plans and develop preparedness programs covering . . . (1) The production and distribution of all materials, the use of all production facilities (except those owned by, controlled by, or under the jurisdiction of the Department of Defense or the Atomic Energy Commission), the control of all construction materials, and the furnishing of basic industrial services . . ."

• Section 1001: "The Secretary of Labor shall have primary responsibility for preparing national emergency plans and developing preparedness programs covering civilian manpower mobilization, more effective utilization of limited manpower resources . . ."

• Section 1101: "[T]he Secretary of Health, Education, and Welfare shall prepare national emergency plans and develop preparedness programs covering health services, civilian health manpower, health resources, welfare services, social security benefits, credit union operations, and educational programs . . ."

• Section 1301: "The Secretary of Transportation . . . shall prepare emergency plans and develop preparedness programs covering . . . (2) Movement of passengers and materials of all types by all forms of civil transportation . . . (4) Develop systems for the control of the movement of passengers and cargo by all forms of transportation . . ."

• Section 1802: "The Federal Communications Commission shall develop policies, plans, and procedures . . . covering . . . (5) Electromagnetic radiation. Closing of any radio station or any device capable of emitting electromagnetic radiation or suspension or amending any rules or regulations applicable thereto, in any emergency, except for those belonging to, or operated by, any department or agency of the United States Government."

The preceding is just a sample of the contents of Executive Order 11490; the complete text of this lengthy document is Appendix B. Nixon's intent is obvious: he was telling the various departments of the executive branch to draw up plans to control virtually every aspect of American life in the event of "any national emergency type situation that might conceivably confront the nation"—a remarkably broad description of the conditions under which the resulting plans might be implemented.

During 1970–1971, Nixon twice demonstrated that his definition of "national emergency" included situations far short of nuclear war. Responding to scattered strikes among postal workers in the northeast, Nixon declared a national emergency and issued a proclamation (not an executive order) in April 1970 that mobilized the National Guard to process and deliver mail. The main impact of this was to pressure striking postal workers to return to their jobs, which they did in less than a week. The following year, rising inflation and a deteriorating balance of payments situation, with pressure on the dollar, caused Nixon to issue Executive Order 11615 on August 15. Declaring that economic conditions constituted a national emergency, Nixon, using the same Trading with the Enemy Act employed by Wilson and Franklin Roosevelt, froze wages and prices for 90 days, ended the gold standard by making the U.S. dollar no longer redeemable in gold, and created a Cost of Living Council empowered to ask the Department of Justice to bring action "whenever it appears to the Council that any person has engaged, is engaged, or is about to engage in any acts or practices constituting a violation of any regulation or order issued pursuant to this Order." The wage and price freeze was abandoned soon after the order was issued, but the end of the gold standard now appears permanent.

To some, one surprise about the Watergate crisis was that Nixon never attempted to declare a state of national emergency during it. One reason may have been that he little or no support for such a move even among members of his administration and Republicans in Congress. But another reason may have been Alexander Haig, his chief of staff. According to numerous (but unconfirmed) press reports, Haig made sure in the final days of Nixon's presidency that all written communications from the president, especially to the military, had to cross his desk first.

THE NATIONAL EMERGENCIES ACT OF 1976

Nixon's declaration of a national emergency in order to impose wage and price controls managed to offend both the political right (who were philosophically opposed to any wage and price controls) and the left (because lower-paid employees suffered most from a wage freeze). In 1973, the Senate created Special Committee on the Termination of the National Emergency to address the presidentially declared states of national emergency the United States had been under since 1933.

Its final report to the Senate castigated Congress for transferring extraordinary power to the president through its own sloppiness and inaction. The committee identified 470 instances since 1933 of Congress transferring what were constitutionally and traditionally congressional powers to the president; most such transfers pertaining to emergency powers had been passed by Congress during times of crisis and with little debate or committee review. Almost no consideration was given to possible impacts on civil liberties or the potential for presidential abuse of such powers. Such transfers of power were constitutional, however, since Congress had effected them in due process of its constitutional authority, even in those cases where presidents had acted first and sought congressional approval later. The result, the committee concluded, was "an imperial presidency" with powers far beyond those enumerated in the Constitution.

The committee was also concerned with how many executive orders were classified. According to the committee report, the "legal record of executive decisionmaking has thus continued to be closed from the light of public or congressional scrutiny through the use of classified procedures which withhold necessary documents from Congress, by failure to establish substantive criteria for publication, and by bypassing existing standards."

Distracted by the Watergate scandal, Congress did not attend to the report again until 1975. Testifying before the House Judiciary Committee that year, Senator Charles Mathias (R-Maryland), one of the members of the Senate special committee, said, "Under the authority delegated by these statutes, the President may seize property, organize and control the means of production, seize commodities, assign military forces abroad, institute martial law, seize and control all transportation and communication, regulate the operation of private enterprise, restrict travel, and in a plethora of ways control the lives of all American citizens."

The result was the National Emergencies Act of 1976, which canceled all national emergencies then in effect. It required presidents declaring future national emergencies to specify the provisions of the Constitution or statutory law supporting the declaration, which must be immediately transmitted to Congress and published in the Federal Register. Congress would have the right to terminate any declaration of national emergency after six months, and all such declarations would automatically expire after one year unless explicitly extended by the president. The Act also required the president and executive branch to maintain files on all actions taken in response to a declaration of national emergency.

In 1977, Congress enacted a companion law known as the International Emergency Economic Powers Act to curb the authority of presidents to impose restrictions on economic activities, such as Nixon's use of wage and price controls in 1971.

The National Emergencies Act did little to curb presidential declarations of national emergency and their potential for abuse. The Act was vague in many ways. For example, it offered no criteria to qualify a situation as a national emergency, leaving that determination wholly to the judgment of the president. The Act seemed to suggest that only the president may declare a national emergency, not Congress (whether Congress may do so has never been definitely established). While the Act attempted to limit the duration of national emergencies to no more than a year, it gives presidents the right to renew them indefinitely each year (and they have done so). The requirement to publish executive orders in the Federal Register also had a large loophole. The president could declare that an executive order pertained to national security, and in such cases only the number of the order need be published. In effect, the Act did nothing to address the concerns expressed by Senator Mathias and other critics; the president retained the same emergency powers as before.

Only a brief respite in the state of national emergency followed the passage of the National Emergencies Act. In 1979, President Carter declared national emergencies in the wake of oil shortages and the seizing of the U.S. embassy in Iran. From then until this writing, the United States has been under one or more presidentially declared states of national emergency.

RECENT PRESIDENTIAL EXECUTIVE ORDERS

Perhaps the most notable executive order issued by Jimmy Carter was 12148, issued on July 20, 1979. This created the Federal Emergency Management Agency (FEMA), now the best known element of the Shadow Government. While ostensibly established to coordinate federal responses to such events as earthquakes, floods, hurricanes, and other natural disasters, FEMA's charter incorporated many earlier executive orders dealing with responses to nuclear war (or the threat of such war) and national security. FEMA was assigned responsibility for the continuity of government (COG) program, and quickly grew into a sprawling agency with a multi-billion dollar annual budget, much of it classified. Chapter Four discusses FEMA in detail. The text of Executive Order 12148 is Appendix C.

As mentioned earlier, Carter suffered a rare judicial reversal of an executive order in 1980 when he attempted to impose a fee on imported oil. The result was a jump in the retail price of gasoline of approximately $0.10 per gallon. A federal district court, ruling that Carter had attempted to legislate with his order, voided it. Yet both Carter and Ronald Reagan were vindicated in the courts when their executive orders dealing with resolution of the Iranian embassy hostage crisis were upheld. For example, Reagan's Executive Order 12294, issued in February 24, 1981, prohibited the filing of private claims against Iran in federal courts and mandated the mediation of any such claims by a special tribunal, in apparent violation of the Seventh Amendment to the Constitution. Reagan's order was upheld by the Supreme Court on the grounds that Congress had delegated such authority to the president by "acquiescence" as determined by "the general tenor of Congress' legislation in this area," in the words of Justice William Rehnquist, who wrote the majority opinion. Judicial rulings on other executive orders have not appealed to this "acquiescence theory," but it seems greatly to expand the president's ability to issue executive orders without specific statutory authority.

Reagan issued 381 executive orders, including national security directives that increased military support of traditionally civilian law enforcement matters (such as drug law), expanded the scope of FEMA's responsibilities and operations (including "Rex 84," discussed later in this book), and enhanced government secrecy and covert operations.

His successor, George Bush, issued 166 executive orders in his four years, but they (at least the public ones) were unremarkable. It was widely reported, however, that Bush came very close on two occasions—the 1991 Gulf War and the 1992 Los Angeles riots—to declaring a national emergency and activating the plans developed under Executive Order 11490. Unconfirmed reports said that the 1992 situation was the nearest miss, with Bush ready to act if rioting on a similar scale had broken out in other cities.

As the opening quote to this chapter indicates, Bill Clinton was an enthusiastic believer in executive orders. Most of the Clinton executive orders that attracted the ire of conservatives dealt with environmental issues, creating new national monuments and prohibiting the introduction of "invasive species" into public lands. His "don't ask, don't tell" policy on gays in the military was also accomplished by executive order. Clinton did suffer a significant legal setback in his use of executive orders, however, when a federal appeals court overturned a 1995 order prohibiting federal contractors from hiring permanent replacements for strikers in February, 1996.

Clinton also suffered another serious setback when he issued Executive Order 13083 in May, 1998. In this order, Clinton directed federal agencies to determine if they had the "constitutional and legal authority" to impose various federal mandates, regulations, and standards upon "state governments, including units of local government and other political subdivisions established by the states." The effective date of the order was to be August 12, 1998, but it met with swift opposition from state and local officials for being an attack on the concept of federalism and in violation of the Tenth Amendment to the Constitution. Legislation was introduced in Congress to overturn the order. Faced with a storm of criticism and a likely defeat in Congress, Clinton suspended his order on August 5, 1998; on that same day, the House of Representatives voted 417–2 to prohibit any federal expenditures to implement Executive Order 13083. The margin of the vote indicates the pressure members of Congress were receiving from constituents against the order.

A little noticed but potentially far-reaching Clinton executive order was 12919, issued on June 6, 1994. This order concerned emergency industrial resource preparedness and was, in effect, an extension of Nixon's Executive Order 11490. Clinton's order gave FEMA a large role in "central coordination of the plans and programs incident to authorities and functions delegated under this order" and in establishing a "National Defense Executive Reserve, composed of persons of recognized experience from various segments of the private sector and from government (except full-time federal employees) for training in employment in executive positions in the Federal Government in the event of an emergency."

Clinton's use of executive orders provoked two Republican congressmen, John Metcalf of Washington and Ron Paul of Texas, to introduce a proposed "Separation of Powers Act" in 1999. It would have given Congress the sole right to declare states of national emergency, terminated all existing national emergencies, and greatly restricted the scope of presidential executive orders. Their proposed legislation did not pass in either 1999 or 2000, and with the election of George W. Bush most Republicans lost interest in restricting presidential executive order authority.

At the time this book was written, George W. Bush has issued several executive orders in response to the September 11 attacks. In addition to Executive Order 13228, which created the Office of Homeland Security, Bush issued executive orders to freeze assets of organizations linked to terrorist groups and to prohibit future financial transactions that might support terrorism. It is likely that many other executive orders will be issued in response to future terrorist threats and attacks.

SECRET PRESIDENTIAL EXECUTIVE ORDERS

Some critics have claimed that executive orders are not serious threats to American democracy. They point out correctly that none of the presently known executive orders (such as Nixon's 11490) say anything about suspending the Constitution, detaining people indefinitely, confiscating private property, or other actions executive orders supposedly authorize. Executive orders such as 11490 merely direct the heads of various agencies to develop plans that the president could activate with additional executive orders. But those plans remain secret, and so do the texts of any executive orders that the president would use to put such plans into action.

While the protocol for implementing emergency plans is not precisely known, it has been reported that a set of emergency executive orders ready for signature accompanies the president and vice president at all times. There is always someone near the president with a briefcase containing the codes necessary to launch a nuclear strike. It stands to reason that some similar system allows the president (and presumably the vice president, in case the president is killed) ready access to prepared executive orders that could be issued in the event of nuclear war or other catastrophe (such as the fictional scenario in Chapter One).

Executive orders are the glue that holds the Shadow Government together. Almost everything described in the remainder of this book will have one or more executive orders as its foundation.

CHAPTER THREE

THE SCARIEST AGENCY IN THE ENTIRE GOVERNMENT

"Are you familiar with FEMA? What the Federal Emergency Management Agency's real power is? FEMA allows the White House to suspend constitutional government upon declaration of a national emergency. It allows creation of a non-elected national government. Think about that, Agent Mulder!"
> —Dr. Al Kurtzweil to Special Agent Fox Mulder in the movie
> *X-Files: Fight the Future*

PEOPLE WHO SAW the 1998 movie *X-Files: Fight the Future* did not panic when they heard one of its characters say these words. They assumed it was just another part of a fictional plotline.

But the people at FEMA took it seriously.

The June 24, 1998 Washington Post reported that Maurice Goodman, FEMA's director of communications, issued a memo to FEMA employees to guide their response to the portrayal of FEMA in the movie. "While [the film is] entertaining and humorous to the employees of FEMA, some moviegoers may not understand they are watching a fictional portrayal of the agency," wrote Goodman, who complained that, as a result of the movie, some Americans may "believe we have a somewhat sinister role . . . it is not realistic to think that we can convince them otherwise and it is advisable not to enter into debate on the subject." He continued, however, "you may emphatically state that FEMA does not have, never has had, nor will ever seek, the authority to suspend the Constitution."

Goodman was not advising FEMA employees to lie, for FEMA does not have and has never had the authority to suspend the Constitution, declare martial law, confiscate private property, or do any of the things widely but mistakenly attributed to it. Those are things that only the president can do, and only by declaring national emergency and issuing executive orders. If the president ever does so act, however, it will be FEMA that carries out his orders. If there had been a FEMA when President Roosevelt issued Executive Order 9066 in 1942, FEMA would have been responsible for rounding up Japanese Americans and running detention camps. FEMA is not the Shadow Government, but the muscle behind it.

FEMA: CHILD OF THE COLD WAR

President Jimmy Carter created the Federal Emergency Management Agency with Executive Order 12148 on July 20, 1979 (it is Appendix C). According to FEMA's official history of itself, the new agency "absorbed the Federal Insurance Administration, the National Fire Prevention and Control Administration, the National Weather Service Community Preparedness Program, the Federal Preparedness Agency of the General Services Administration, and the Federal Disaster Assistance Administration activities from HUD." Almost as an afterthought, the FEMA web site adds, "Civil defense responsibilities were also transferred to the new agency from the Defense Department's Defense Civil Preparedness Agency."

FEMA understandably wishes to downplay its having absorbed the tasks of this last agency. "Defense Civil Preparedness Agency" was the final name for the Office of Civil and Defense Mobilization created after World War II with a mandate to plan America's domestic responses to nuclear war. The resulting plans covered relocation of key government leaders to secure shelter, relocation of civilians, control of all aspects of the economy, control of the civilian population in case of panic or riots, control of all communications media and transportation systems, and detention of groups of civilians to be designated—in short, plans for control of nearly every aspect of life in the United States if nuclear war threatened or occurred. FEMA assumed these responsibilities.

Some insight into these planning efforts appeared in the December 1998 *Reason* magazine, where Jodie Allen, former editor of the "Outlook" section of the *Washington Post*, wrote of his experiences in the 1960s as a planner with FEMA's predecessor agencies. As an example of fine detail in the planning, Allen described calculating livestock breeding rates achieved by different strategies in different scenarios, including attacks mostly by air explosions of nuclear bombs (lighter fallout) and mostly by ground explosions (heavier fallout). (The best strategy he discovered was to reduce herds to the sustainable minimum proportion of males, to conserve feed.) While Allen's article said that many claims about FEMA are "preposterous" and that the agency's aims were "ultimately benign," he did admit, "Though it didn't occur to me much at the time, we were indeed planning to 'take over' the country, in a manner of speaking."

Just exactly what FEMA and its predecessor agencies planned for America in the event of a nuclear attack remains classified. Until the collapse of the Soviet Union, a substantial portion of FEMA's budget was not only classified but also dwarfed spending for such "non-national" disasters as earthquakes, hurricanes, and floods. A 1992 study by the Cox Newspapers Group found that during 1982–1992 FEMA's budgets included only $243 million for disaster relief but $2.9 billion for "black" and classified operations. The Cox study also estimated that one-third of FEMA's employees during that period worked on classified projects. Even after the collapse of the Soviet Union, much of FEMA's budget remained "black"; in 1993, for example, approximately 27% of FEMA's budget was for classified projects.

The imbalance of spending left FEMA poorly prepared for natural disasters, a shortcoming dramatically illustrated in August 1992, when Hurricane Andrew smashed into south Florida and caused more damage than any other natural disaster in American history. The city manager of Homestead, an especially hard-hit city south of Miami, asked to borrow about one hundred hand-held radios from FEMA to replace the destroyed radio system of Homestead's police and fire departments. It turned out that FEMA did not have any such portable radio systems in its inventory, but did have—and sent—several radiation-resistant vans with communications gear capable of sending encrypted messages via satellite or shortwave radio to military aircraft or ships anywhere in the world. Ready to spring to Florida's aid with this impressive technology, FEMA was slow to provide such basics as temporary housing, water purification, sanitation systems, and other critical supplies.

After the Hurricane Andrew fiasco, the National Academy of Public Administration (NAPA) reviewed FEMA's operations and released a report early in the Clinton administration. NAPA recommended spinning off as many of FEMA's classified and national security operations as possible to the Department of Defense. The Clinton administration quickly adopted this recommendation, and in 1994 only $7.5 million of FEMA's budget was classified.

In 1995–1999 the FEMA budget more than doubled. Critics charged that FEMA was turning into a dispensary of political pork, and that inconveniences were too easily being declared disasters. For example, before 1993 no snowstorms were disasters, but in the next four years almost fifty snowstorms counted as such, causing FEMA funds to flow to the affected localities. In 1996, FEMA declared seventy-five disasters, roughly one for every five days of the year.

FEMA resumed attack-response planning in 1996 with the passage of the Defense Against Weapons of Mass Destruction Act, which charged it with coordinating the federal response to any terrorist (including biological, chemical, and nuclear) attacks. This role increased during Clinton's second term and more after September 11, 2001. Today FEMA has a presidential mandate to coordinate its activities with the new Office of Homeland Security and develop an "all hazards" approach to homeland security planning.

FEMA is organized into ten geographical districts, with district headquarters at Maynard, MA, New York, NY, Olney, MD, Thomasville, GA, Battle Creek, MI, Denton, TX, Kansas City, MO, Denver, CO, San Francisco, CA, and Bothell, WA. This structure essentially replicates that of the 1950s Office of Civil Defense. FEMA maintains a presence throughout American territory, including Puerto Rico and America Samoa.

CONTINUITY OF GOVERNMENT (COG) PROGRAMS

Most of FEMA's classified spending has probably been for continuity of government (COG) programs—that is, activities deemed essential to survival of the nation in case of nuclear attack, terrorist attack, or any other event that would endanger the functioning of civil government or the lives of national leaders.

The Constitution is silent about COG, probably because its authors did not conceive the possibility of the sudden annihilation of most of the civilian government. World War II, with the introduction of long-range missiles and atomic weapons, made that possibility vivid, motivating two new laws in 1947. The first extended the line of presidential succession to the speaker of the House of Representatives, the president pro tem of the Senate, and various members of the Cabinet. The second, the lengthy National Security Act, created the Department of the Air Force and the Central Intelligence Agency and authorized the creation of the National

Security Agency. It also greatly increased the government's ability to classify information (such as items in the federal budget) for national security reasons.

Responding to the growing Soviet nuclear threat, President Truman issued Executive Order 10346 on April 17, 1952, directing federal agencies to plan for the continuation of their essential operations in case of nuclear war or other catastrophe. The phrase "continuity of government" first appeared in this order, which is the foundation of several 1950s COG projects. Several of these were classified, including the construction of relocation shelters, mostly near Washington, for the heads and key staff of federal agencies. This strategy assumed sufficient warning to evacuate the president, vice president, key federal officials, and most members of Congress before the bombs arrived. Originally managed by FEMA's predecessor agencies (such as the Office of Civil and Defense Mobilization and Office of Civil Defense), these often classified shelters came under the new FEMA's control.

The development of credible Soviet intercontinental ballistic missile (ICBM) systems stimulated an expansion of COG plans toward the end of the Eisenhower administration. For a nervous fifteen months the Soviet Union had ICBM capability while the United States did not: the USSR successfully tested their R-7 ICBM on August 21, 1957, but the US's first successful ICBM launch (of the *Atlas*) was November 28, 1958. This missile gap prompted a flurry of executive orders by President Kennedy in 1961. For example, Executive Order 10952 called for the Director of the Office of Emergency Planning to "develop plans, conduct programs and coordinate preparation for the continuity of governmental operations in the event of attack." Kennedy is also believed to have accelerated construction of emergency command posts and relocation shelters for government VIPs.

Most "essential functions" of the federal government that fall under COG's purview are classified. Preservation of presidential leadership, including of those in the line of presidential succession, is presumably near the top of the list, as are the preservation of military leadership, military retaliatory capabilities, and communications and coordination infrastructure between civilian and military leaders. Beyond these functions things get murky. The Speaker of the House would become president if the President and Vice President died, but who would become the new Secretary of Defense if the incumbent died in an attack that blocked the usual avenues of appointment? Outside the administration of defense and security, most agencies' lines of succession are public information. For other agencies, such as the CIA or NSA, lines of succession are classified.

Even where lines of succession are public, the specific emergency functions of the agency may be classified. For example, Executive Order 11092, Section 1, says:

> The Federal Communications Commission (hereinafter referred to as the Commission) shall, subject to the policy guidance of the Director of the Office of Emergency Planning, prepare national emergency plans and develop preparedness programs covering provisions of service by common carriers, broadcasting facilities, and the safety and special radio services; assignment of radio frequencies to Commission licensees; and the protection, reduction of vulnerability, maintenance, and restoration of facilities operated by its licensees in an emergency. These plans and programs shall be designed to develop a state of readiness in these areas with respect to all conditions of national emergency, including attack upon the United States, and will take into account the possibility of Government preference or priority with common carriers or of exclusive Government use or control of communications services or facilities, when authorized by law.

When Executive Order 11092 appeared, "common carriers" included telephone, teletype, and telegraph providers and networks; today, it could include internet providers and cable television stations. "Broadcasting facilities" are AM, FM, and TV stations, and "safety and special radio services" include all two-way radio services, such as those of police and fire departments, commercial aviation, CB and ham users, delivery trucks, and taxicabs. If there were a national emergency, would broadcasting stations be seized by the government? Would certain types of stations, such as ham and CB radio, be ordered off the air? Would telephone networks be shut down, or internet service providers ordered to shut off their routers?

As is true for virtually every other branch of the federal government, the responses available to the FCC are unknown. Would the Department of the Treasury be able to freeze, or even confiscate, bank accounts? Could the Department of Transportation seize private airplanes, boats, or even cars? Could the Department of Labor order citizens to work in certain jobs? Answers are classified or underdetermined by public information, but Chapter Two presented numerous precedents for such actions legitimized by executive orders.

With the collapse of the Soviet Union, COG programs were scaled back by means of national security directives and presidential decision directives (discussed in Chapter Two). Two of the most significant were National Security Directive #68, "Enduring Constitutional Government," issued by President George Bush on June 2, 1992, and Presidential Decision Directive #67, issued on October 21, 1998 by President Clinton. While the texts of these directives remain classified, their summaries refer to "continuity of government operations" instead of "continuity of government." The significance of the new term "enduring constitutional government" is unclear, although it may be a reaction to fears that such plans could violate constitutional rights if implemented. Since the September 11 attacks, the phrase "continuity of government" has come back into common use, and all areas of the federal government are believed to be pursuing new, intensive planning reminiscent of the Cold War.

"REX 84": A REHEARSAL FOR CIVILIAN INTERNMENT

During the 1987 Iran-Contra hearings, Representative Jack Brooks of Texas, Senator Daniel Inouye of Hawaii, and Brendan Sullivan, attorney for Colonel Oliver North, had the following exchange during North's testimony before Congress:

REPRESENTATIVE BROOKS: Colonel North, in your work at the NSC, were you not assigned, at one time, to work on plans for continuity of government in the event of a major disaster?

BRENDAN SULLIVAN: Mister Chairman?

SENATOR INOUYE: I believe that question touches upon a highly sensitive and classified area so I request that you not touch on that.

REPRESENTATIVE BROOKS: I was particularly concerned, Mister Chairman, because I read in Miami papers, and several others, that there had been a plan developed by that same agency, a contingency plan in the event of emergency, that would suspend the American constitution. And I was deeply concerned about it and wondered if that was the area in which he had worked. I believe that it was and I wanted to get his confirmation.

SENATOR INOUYE: May I most respectfully request that this matter not be touched upon at this stage. If we wish to get into this, I'm certain arrangements can be made for an executive session.

Brooks, a crusty, no-nonsense Texas Democrat, had touched upon what may have been the most worrisome but least discussed aspect of the Iran-Contra investigations: the expansion of FEMA's mandate during the Reagan administration to include capabilities to detain American citizens, as had happened to Japanese-American citizens in World War II. This plan developed during a military exercise known as Readiness Exercise 1984, or "Rex 84."

In April, 1984 President Reagan signed Presidential Directive 54, authorizing FEMA to conduct a simulation of a "state of domestic national emergency" declared as a result of a U.S. military operation in Central America. Rex 84 took place on the fifth floor of the FEMA building in Washington under conditions of especially heavy security, behind newly installed metal doors where participants had to show special identification badges.

The first reports about Rex 84 appeared in the *Miami Herald* on July 5, 1987 (this is the report referred to by Representative Brooks). According to the *Herald*, the plan the Rex 84 group produced called for the detention of up to 400,000 undocumented immigrants in internment centers at military bases around the country. (These would eventually become known as the "Rex 84 camps.") If necessary, U.S. military forces, including the National Guard, would be deployed for domestic law enforcement, and state and local military commanders could assume control of state and local governments if so directed by the president. Rex 84 also included plans for suspension of the Bill of Rights of the U.S. Constitution for the duration of the national emergency. While undocumented immigrants were the only ones targeted for detention during the Rex 84 exercise, the logistics of interning American citizens would essentially be the same.

Oliver North was the principal author of the Rex 84 plan, but a faction within the Rex 84 group led by Attorney General William French Smith vehemently opposed him. As Smith wrote in August 1984 to National Security Council chairman Robert McFarlane, "I believe the role assigned to the Federal Emergency Management Agency in the revised Executive Order exceeds its proper function as a coordinating agency for emergency preparedness. . . This department [of Justice] and others have repeatedly raised serious policy and legal objections to the creation of an 'emergency czar' role for FEMA." Smith's opposition was probably instrumental in convincing President Reagan not to issue new executive orders to support the plan imagined for Rex 84. The *Herald* also reported that twenty-two new executive orders were drafted to realize the Rex 84 internment plan, to be kept ready for a future president's signature in case of a national emergency. The Rex 84 group identified large military bases that have previously sheltered refugees (such as Fort Chaffee in Arkansas, used in 1980 for over 20,000 Cuban boat people) as the primary detention centers.

One aim of the Rex 84 exercise was to determine what types of national emergency would be severe enough to persuade the majority of Americans to accept even a temporary suspension of normal Constitutional government. Among the severe enough situations identified by the Rex 84 group were a nuclear attack, imminent threat of nuclear war, massive terrorist attacks in the United States, simultaneous rioting in major American cities, a widespread natural or environmental disaster, and a devastating economic depression.

So is there a current plan based upon the lessons learned during Rex 84 waiting to be put into effect with a presidential signature? We don't know, but in the wake of the September 11 attacks such a possibility must be taken seriously.

RELOCATION SHELTERS FOR GOVERNMENT LEADERS

On March 1, 2002, the *Washington Post* reported that approximately one hundred senior executives of the federal government were living and working in two special facilities outside of Washington. According to the *Post*, rotating teams of executives had been living and working continuously, away from their families, for intervals of up to three months since shortly after September 11, 2001. An unidentified source told the *Post* that these managers, in the event of a catastrophic attack on Washington, would "contain disruptions of the nation's food and water supplies, transportation links, energy and telecommunications networks, public health, and civil order." Later, the *Post's* source added, they would "begin to reconstitute the government."

A primary responsibility of FEMA and its predecessor agencies was the construction and maintenance of a network of emergency shelters and command posts for managing disasters and "reconstituting" the government.

One of these sits atop a high hill known as Lambs Knoll near Boonsboro, MD, most easily seen from southeast of Boonsboro on Highways 67, 17, or 40 Alternate. The closest public road to it is Reno Monument Road; the unmarked access road begins near a monument to Civil War General Jesse Reno in the area known locally as Fox's Gap. Before September 11, visitors could drive up as far as a tall electric gate. Visitors are probably more strongly discouraged now.

Aerial views show the road from the gate proceeding to a tower like a large farm silo, implausibly identified on U.S. Geological Survey maps of the area as a fire lookout. Besides this tower, several collapsible antenna masts, and a helipad, no other aboveground structure is visible, meaning this facility is either impractically small or mostly underground. Persons of unknown duties in blue jumpsuits have been observed from the air.

Another Maryland retreat is near Hagerstown, in a wooded area between Highways 66 and 17. The gated access road is marked only with "no trespassing" signs. Highways 66 and 17 offer no view of the site, but aerial photos taken before September 11 show strong resemblances to the one at Boonsboro. Another compound reported to be similar to the Maryland ones is a few miles northwest in Mercersburg, PA, on Cove Mountain, at the end of an unmarked road from Highway 456. (Again, security around these sites has probably tightened, and tourism is not recommended.)

Northwest of a fire station off Dry Creek Road near Oakville, CA, another unmarked road leads to a tall electric gate in the Maryland style. Aerial photographs of this thickly wooded spot beyond the end of Oakville Grade show concrete bunkers with large concrete doors, a freshly graded road from Oakville Grade, and several tall satellite and microwave towers. The aboveground part of the site occupies eighty-seven acres. Constructed in the late 1980s shortly before known relocation shelters at Benicia and Ukiah, CA, closed, the Oakville compound is probably a replacement for them.

While those who relocated to such accommodations after September 11 do not talk much about them, evidence indicates Spartan living arrangements. In 1992 a relocation shelter near Culpepper, VA, was decommissioned and auctioned off. The David and Lucile Packard Foundation bought and renovated it and donated it to the Library of Congress for use as a film archive. The Culpepper facility was well suited for film storage, having been built in 1969 as a relocation post for senior managers of the Federal Reserve Bank System and cache for over $1 billion in currency for distribution after a nuclear attack or similar emergency. Reporters took a tour before the renovations. The 140,000 square-foot bunker, built into the side of a hill called "Mount Pony," had steel-reinforced concrete walls over a foot thick surrounded by two to four feet of earth. The few windows had rapid-closing lead-lined shutters. Like the Maryland, Pennsylvania, and California sites, Culpepper was on a road that ended for the unadmitted at a tall electric gate. Culpepper's approach had an extra fortification beyond the gate, though—a guardhouse with "gun ports" and the road in its line of fire.

An entrance reminiscent of *The Andromeda Strain* featured a decontamination room with showers and disposals for contaminated clothing or gear. Culpepper could self-sufficiently support about five hundred occupants for thirty days with its stores of food, water, medicine, fuel, computer and communications gear, and generators. The first floor held the currency reserve, and the second and third held living and working space. Only two hundred beds were provided in the separate male and female dormitories, so that in an emergency most persons inside would have had to "hot bunk"—that is, relinquish their beds to others after sleeping shifts. The most senior executives of the Federal Reserve would have shared small, private rooms with two single beds separated by a wooden storage cabinet. Only the chairman of the Federal Reserve (or his surviving successor) would have had a private room. The living arrangements were very much like those on U.S. Navy submarines.

Culpepper was continuously staffed 1969–1992 by around one hundred employees on rotations; if those designated for relocation to Culpepper in case of an emergency could not get there, the staff on rotation inside were to carry out the emergency plans. In effect, a parallel, "shadow" version of the Federal Reserve System was at Culpepper and ready to assume the Reserve's duties in case of its destruction. Rumors describe similar "shadow" equivalents of various federal agencies at other shelters, and liken the accommodations at Culpepper to those at other relocation sites still in operation.

FEMA itself has an "alternate national warning facility" near Olney, MD. 5321 Riggs Road, off Route 108 between Olney and Laytonsville, backs up FEMA's Washington headquarters and Mt. Weather command post (discussed below) in case of their destruction, and also is the hub for the agency's radio network.

The Olney facility was a Nike missile site before FEMA got it. This means there must be at least two levels underground, because all Nike sites had two underground levels (rumors say there are twenty underground levels at Olney). Many transmitting and receiving antenna towers and satellite dishes are visible from the air. Back-up generators and other power supplies are likely, and workers on an upgrade of the facility in the mid-1980s reported offices and barracks inside. While the facility looks neglected from the road, it is actually a high security installation; trespassers will be stopped and probably arrested.

The Olney post's radio station is WGY903, the network control station for FEMA's national emergency coordination network. Shortwave listeners able to receive upper sideband (USB) transmissions may be able to hear FEMA's periodic nationwide on-the-air drills and exercises during the day (10493 kHz) and night (5211 kHz). WGY903 determines which stations transmit and what messages, if any, they may transmit to other stations. Reception on those two frequencies is often good throughout North America, and they are worth monitoring in the event of a national emergency.

From 1962 to 1995, FEMA and its predecessors operated a massive bunker for Congress under the tony Greenbrier Resort in West Virginia. The 112,000-square-foot steel-reinforced concrete retreat took three years to build. Surrounded by over twenty feet of earth, it had twenty-five-ton steel doors that dwarfed those used in bank vaults and supposedly could withstand the force of nearby nuclear explosions. Inside, separate chambers awaited the two houses of Congress, with a larger room for joint sessions, a radio and television studio, special sleep and work areas for congressional leaders, and bunk-bed dormitories for the rank and file. A dining hall (stocked with military rations), three 24,000-gallon water tanks, communications equipment, shower and decontamination rooms, generators, an infirmary, and a crematorium completed the amenities. False windows with pastoral scenes painted inside their frames aimed to relieve the feeling of entombment. The Greenbrier underground could support the Congress and essential staff (including armed security) for a month.

Remarkably, Greenbrier remained a well-contained secret for almost three decades. Only the very highest ranks of Congressional leadership, such as the Speaker of the House and Senate majority leader, knew about it. Construction and maintenance costs were paid from classified items in budgets passed by Congress, a practice explored in Chapter Four. While senior managers at the Greenbrier Resort knew that some large thing was under their property, they knew almost nothing about what it was. False walls concealed its real architectural features; inside, the House, Senate, and joint meeting rooms were cleverly disguised as exhibition halls.

Maintenance of the Greenbrier facility was done by a government "front" company known as Forsythe Associates. Managers and employees of the Greenbrier were told that the Forsythe employees were there to repair and maintain the resort's television sets and telephone system. To avoid detection and suspicion from Greenbrier employees and guests, the Forsythe people entered the facility usually between 1:00 to 4:00 in the morning.

Greenbrier first came to public attention in an article by Ted Gup in the May 31, 1992 *Washington Post*. In the article, Thomas Foley (then Speaker of the House) and past and present Greenbrier Resort managers declined to comment. Former Speaker of the House Thomas "Tip" O'Neill, however, was not so reticent. "I never mentioned it to anybody," O'Neill told Gup, "but every time I went down to the Greenbrier, and I went there half a dozen times, I always used to look at the hill and say, 'well, that's where we're supposed to live in the event something happens, and that's where we're going to do business, maybe under the tennis courts.'" Gup also talked to former government officials and security guards who had been inside and who gave him what turned out to be an accurate description.

These revelations coincided with the collapse of the Soviet Union and a great reduction in the risk of sudden nuclear war. In July of 1995, it was finally decided that the facility had outlived its usefulness, and it was decommissioned. Today, the Greenbrier Resort offers guided tours of the underground bunker, and the rooms where Congress would have met after a nuclear war are available for special events and parties. If Congress later found a new home in case of emergency or one is being planned, it is a secret.

Mount Weather: Capital of the Shadow Government

The novel *Seven Days in May* by Fletcher Knebel and Charles Bailey II, a bestseller in 1962, imagines an attempted military coup against the United States government. Knebel and Bailey were Washington journalists, and they had heard rumors about a secret installation where government leaders would be sheltered in case of nuclear war. They incorporated it in their book:

> Because of his White House job, Corwin knew something about this road that few other Americans did. Virginia 120 appeared to be nothing more than a better-than-average Blue Ridge byway, but it ran past Mount Thunder, where an underground installation provided one of the several bases from which the President could run the nation in the event of a nuclear attack on Washington.

Most readers assumed that "Mount Thunder" was purely fictional. Instead, it was probably the first print allusion to Mount Weather, FEMA's most important relocation compound. For years, Mount Weather was one of the governmental secrets most carefully guarded from the American public, and even from members of Congress. In 1975, retired Air Force General Leslie Bray told the Senate Subcommittee on Constitutional Rights, "I am not at liberty to describe precisely what is the role, and the mission, and the capability that we have at Mount Weather." Things are different today; FEMA even has a page about Mount Weather on its web site. What really goes on there, however, far outstrips the pedestrian functions publicly attributed to the place.

Mount Weather is beside Virginia Route 601, near the town of Bluemont and the intersection of Loudoun and Clarke counties. Now that Mount Weather has come out of the closet, it has an address (19844 Blue Ridge Mountain Road), and signs on Route 7 and the intersection of Routes 50 and 17 point the way to "Mount Weather EAC" (Emergency Assistance Center). Its hospitable-sounding name notwithstanding, the site is still heavily guarded and off-limits to all unauthorized visitors. There are no parking areas near Mount Weather on Route 601, and walking the no-shoulder highway is dangerous. Local sheriff's deputies are reported to be apt to stop and question snoops.

Mount Weather got its name from the National Weather Bureau, which used it as a launch site for weather balloons from 1893 to 1933. The world's record for altitude achieved by a kite, 23,111 feet, was set there in 1907 by Weather Bureau workers. In 1936 the Bureau of Mines took over the site for experiments of new deep mining techniques in the mountain's hard, thick rock.

Perhaps someone remembered those experiments in 1954 when the government was planning a gigantic shelter to protect the president and other senior officials from a nuclear attack. Mount Weather's combination of proximity to Washington and favorable geology made it the best candidate for such a site. The U.S. Army Corps of Engineers began construction in 1954 under the code name "Operation High Point." Construction of the underground compound apparently continued until 1958 or 1959. Aerial photographs reveal further aboveground construction since then.

FEMA's web site now includes an aerial photo of Mount Weather, remarkable for how unremarkable it looks — like a sprawling administrative compound for an agency such as the Social Security Administration, but in a picturesque wooded setting. FEMA refers to it as the "Mount Weather Emergency Operations Center" and says it is used for conferences and training sessions, computer and communications services, disaster-relief worker management, storage, and other innocuous tasks. But the real action at Mount Weather, unknown even to most FEMA employees, takes place underground.

The first hint that something big was happening at Mount Weather came in the 1974 annual report of the Federal Preparedness Agency, one of the agencies folded into FEMA in 1979. In an apparent blunder, the report stated, "Studies conducted at Mount Weather involve the control and management of domestic political unrest where there are material shortages (such as food riots) or in strike situations where the FPA determines that there are industrial disruptions and other domestic resource crises." (It was this statement that resulted in the questioning of General Bray by the Senate Subcommittee on Constitutional Rights in 1975.) Mount Weather drew more attention when a TWA Boeing 727 crashed near it on December 1, 1974, killing all ninety-two persons on board. Reporters covering the crash noticed the high perimeter fence with numerous warning signs. Asked about the site, the Department of Defense refused to comment. Curious, reporters quizzed residents of the nearby towns of Bluemont and Berryville and learned that the road to Mount Weather was always the first cleared of snow and that there was heavy helicopter and limousine traffic into the site.

Intrigued by such reports and the Senate testimony, Richard Pollack investigated Mount Weather and managed to find people willing to talk with him off the record. His report, "The Mysterious Mountain," appeared in the March 1976 issue of *The Progressive* and sounded like something out a James Bond movie, but other reporters confirmed and expanded upon its essential claims in future investigations (most notably Ted Gup in the December 9, 1991 *Time* and Steve Emerson in the August 7, 1989 *U.S. News & World Report*).

Pollack described an underground city capable of housing over two thousand people deep within the mountain. According to his sources, twenty separate buildings, some three stories deep, were submerged there, all linked by sidewalks in tunnels. There were two 250,000-gallon water reservoirs, a sewage treatment plant, generators, a hospital, a crematorium, and a radio and television studio. Iron reinforcements of the buildings and tunnels reached up to ten feet into the surrounding rock and a thirty-four-ton door, ten feet tall by twenty feet wide and five feet thick, protected the entrance. While the depth of the compound inside Mount Weather is not public information, the Bureau of Mines experiments in 1936 managed to reach over 300 feet, and given refinements in deep drilling technology since then, the shelter complex is probably much further down. From Pollack's description of the door, it seems that the ability to withstand a direct nuclear strike was one design criterion.

According to Pollack's sources and to subsequent reports, Mount Weather has computer and communications equipment for quickly assessing any catastrophe, surveying resources, and communicating with and commanding workers on the outside. Private quarters were reserved for the president, vice president, Congressional leaders, the Cabinet, and members of the Supreme Court; others inside would have to share dormitories or even cots. Duplicate copies of all COG plans and other vital national records are also believed to be in the facility.

The first non-drill full activation of Mount Weather reportedly happened during the Cuban missile crisis. The Cuban-based missiles that could have reached Washington in a few minutes and the state of Soviet-American relations in those days make these reports plausible. Some sources claim that Mount Weather also became operational on November

22, 1963, when President Kennedy was assassinated. This is also credible, since it was unclear during the first few hours after the assassination whether it was an isolated event or part of a larger plan to kill government leaders. Other reported or rumored activations occurred during the 1965 power blackout in the northeastern U.S. and after the 1968 assassination of Martin Luther King, Jr.

Mount Weather certainly became operational on September 11, 2001. A report that day for the Associated Press by James Jefferson said, "House Speaker Dennis Hastert and other top leaders of Congress were taken to the safety of a secure government facility seventy-five miles west of Washington." That points to Mount Weather. Paul Bedard, a reporter for *White House Weekly*, reported in its December 4, 2001 issue that local residents reported "a traffic jam of limos" on Route 601 on the afternoon of September 11, including a motorcade with a motorcycle police escort. A report by Barton Gellman and Susan Schmidt in the March 1, 2002 *Washington Post* told of several government helicopters, with F-16 fighters on patrol overhead, arriving at an unnamed government relocation facility. From their description of the site, it was almost certainly Mount Weather. Mount Weather was probably Vice President Cheney's workplace in the first few weeks after the attacks.

Is There a Parallel, Secret Government in Waiting?

The COG executive orders issued by President Kennedy and refined by his successors have directed agencies of the federal government to develop lines of succession in case their leaders perish in some national emergency. The Constitution and federal law specify the line of presidential succession, and the Constitution provides for the replacement of senators (appointed by the governor of the state) and representatives (by special election in the affected district). All of these methods have worked well in cases of a single vacancy. But what would happen if most of the leadership of the federal government died in a single incident? Consider the annual State of the Union address, during which the President, almost everyone in the line of presidential succession, most or all members of Congress, heads of various agencies, and most or all justices of the Supreme Court are inside the Capitol. What would happen if a terrorist group detonated a nuclear bomb near the Capitol, killing all of these persons among others? (This possibility is not far-fetched; the March 3, 2002 issue of *Time* magazine reported that the highest levels of the federal government were worried in October 2001 that terrorists had obtained a ten-kiloton Russian atomic bomb and were trying to smuggle it into the United States.)

FEMA was apparently working on that problem long before September 11, 2001. A report in the November 18, 1991 *New York Times* said, "Acting outside the Constitution in the early 1980s, a secret federal agency [FEMA] established a line of succession to the presidency to assure continued government in the event of a devastating nuclear attack, current and former United States officials said today. The program was called 'Continuity of Government.' In the words of a recent report by the Fund for Constitutional Government, 'succession or succession-by-designation would be implemented by unknown and perhaps unelected persons who would pick three potential successor presidents in advance of an emergency. These potential successors to the Oval Office may not be elected, and they are not confirmed by Congress.'"

Such plans, if they actually exist, are among the most tightly guarded FEMA secrets, glimpsed by the public only through anonymous reports and speculation. But various sources indicate that FEMA maintains an "Office of the Presidency" at Mount Weather and possibly at other FEMA facilities. If the executive branch of the U.S. government were suddenly and catastrophically eliminated, a person (or persons) on a list of "standby presidents" would be transported to the nearest FEMA COG facility to act as the chief executive of the United States until such time as normal Constitutional government could be restored. Who are these "standby presidents"? A 1992 CNN report on FEMA said that Howard Baker, Richard Helms, Jeanne Kirkpatrick, James Schlesinger, Richard Thornberg, Ed Meese, Thomas "Tip" O'Neill, and Dick Cheney all served in that role during the Reagan and first Bush presidencies. Since none of these persons have spent documented time at Mount Weather or other FEMA posts, they probably would have been transported there should everyone in the line of presidential succession be suddenly killed (or possibly as a precautionary measure in an emergency).

Other reports place teams representing the Departments of Agriculture, Commerce, Defense, Health and Human Services, Housing and Urban Development, Interior, Labor, State, Transportation, and Treasury inside Mount Weather. An executive in charge of each team is ready to assume the functions of the secretary of each department should the secretary die or become incapacitated in an emergency. This person has Cabinet-level rank in the standby government and is addressed by subordinates, in anticipation of any emergency, as "Mr. Secretary." Unlike regular Cabinet members, these standby secretaries serve for an indefinite term; some have served under both Republican and Democratic presidents.

Another possibility, hinted at in Pollack's original 1976 article, is that FEMA maintains a master arrest warrant and lists of persons to be arrested in the event of various emergencies. Rumors of these documents say that a person may be targeted for arrest in some situations and emergencies but not others, and that the lists include such opinion-makers as journalists, television personalities, political activists, entertainers, and others who might be able to influence public reaction to a crisis.

None of this can be reliably confirmed. Any executive orders or presidential directives covering such events would be classified at the highest levels. Such plans may have been scaled back or even abandoned in the 1990s after the collapse of the Soviet Union. New plans, however, have likely been drawn up in the wake of the September 11 attacks, perhaps now including some provision for a standby Congress and Supreme Court that could function until normal constitutional government was restored.

But Would Anyone Go?

If it became necessary—say because of a radiological or chemical attack upon Washington—to relocate the heads of federal agencies and members of Congress to places such as Mount Weather, how many would actually go?

That question is not as silly as it might seem. Thomas "Tip" O'Neill told Ted Gup for his 1992 *Washington Post* article, "I kind of lost interest in it when they told me my wife would not be going with me. I said, 'Jesus, you don't think I'm going to run away and leave my wife? That's the craziest thing I ever heard of.'" According to Gup, other senior government officials (some of Cabinet rank) expressed similar concerns. Like a Navy ship's, the accommodations lack provisions for spouses, children, parents, or any other extra-official companions.

If a national emergency prompted FEMA to activate its relocation plans, the affected officials would face a nightmarish choice: go with FEMA to the designated relocation site and abandon their families, or shirk their duties to face the disaster with loved ones.

But would these officials have the option of ignoring FEMA's plans for them? Would the relocation actually be voluntary, or would those affected be forcibly removed to new quarters? One is reminded of how Vice President Cheney was, quite literally, picked up by two Secret Service agents and carried to the bunker under the White House on September 11 when a hijacked flight was detected heading toward Washington. The Secret Service agents did not discuss options with Cheney, nor was Cheney allowed to decide what to do; he was simply removed. Those whom FEMA plans to relocate would probably receive similar treatment. And, in the rush and shock of an emergency comparable to September 11, most would probably cooperate.

But what would happen after they were in the relocation facility and realized their families were still outside and would not be joining them? How well could such officials function if they had no idea whether their spouses and children were alive or dead? Would some of the relocated officials crack under the strain?

If we're lucky, we'll never have to learn the answers to such questions.

THE MORE THINGS CHANGE . . .

When Bill Clinton became president in 1993, he appointed James Witt, an Arkansas native and longtime friend, as FEMA's director. Witt was the Arkansas director of disaster relief under Governor Clinton, and 1993 seemed like an auspicious time to remake FEMA into an organization more attuned to meeting natural disasters than to responding to a nuclear attack. The Soviet Union was no more, international tensions were decreasing, and nuclear war seemed a very remote possibility. When the National Academy of Public Administration recommended transfer of FEMA's national security operations to the Department of Defense, Witt enthusiastically complied. One of his first acts was to declassify most of FEMA's facilities; the Mount Weather compound was openly acknowledged, and it was admitted that a super fallout shelter for government leaders had been built underground there during the height of the Cold War. The rumors of radiation-resistant vans packed with cryptographic communications gear were confirmed, and their actual mission—to pick up officials and transport them to relocation facilities during an emergency—acknowledged. Witt said that all the secret preparation for nuclear war was past, and that henceforth FEMA would operate in the open, like most other government agencies. And the classified portion of FEMA's budget went from over $100 million during the last year of the first Bush presidency to $7.5 million during the first year of the Clinton presidency.

To most observers, it seemed that FEMA had gotten out of the Shadow Government business. Ted Gup, the reporter who first broke the news about Greenbrier, decided to explore the changes at FEMA. His report, in the January/February 1994 issue of *Mother Jones*, found that things had not changed at FEMA as much as Witt claimed. Gup's conversation with Maurice Goodman, then a FEMA spokesman and later the author of the *X-Files* memorandum quoted above, nicely summarized what he found. "There are, of course, certain areas that can't be discussed or even acknowledged," Goodman told Gup. "That's just the nature of the beast."

The "nature of the beast" included the recommended transfer of classified FEMA programs to the Department of Defense. (While total defense budgets decreased during the Clinton years, the percentage of the defense budgets that was classified actually increased during that period.) Previously classified budget items, like Mount Weather and the radiation-hardened vans, were funded in the "public" portions of the defense budget and were kept operational. The information uncovered by Gup strongly indicated the supposed overhaul in FEMA's mission and capabilities during the Clinton administration was more cosmetic than substantive.

In the aftermath of September 11, it is safe to assume that FEMA is rapidly returning to its original mission. And its mission may be expanding. In late 2001, the government enlarged the aboveground part of the Mount Weather compound by 150 acres. Whether this is to allow more construction or to enlarge the security perimeter is unknown, but it is clear that the Mount Weather and other FEMA operations are here to stay.

CHAPTER FOUR

THE CULT OF SECRECY

THE PREVIOUS CHAPTER'S reports of a secret, unelected government in waiting at Mount Weather, or classified plans to arrest large groups of Americans in case of a national emergency, may seem implausible because—after all—neither the president nor Congress nor other government leaders would approve or tolerate such policies. But that raises a troubling question: *How much do elected officials know about the Shadow Government's activities and plans?*

That is not a flippant question. One would assume that the director of FEMA would have a good overview of that agency's major plans, if not all of their details. But that assumption is wrong. As part of his report on the "new" FEMA that appeared in the January/February 1994 issue of *Mother Jones* magazine, Ted Gup spoke with Wallace Stickney, FEMA's director during the first Bush presidency. With amazing candor, Stickney admitted that, even when he was director, he knew that he was ignorant of some of the things FEMA was doing and planning. "I was aware funding was being passed through [FEMA], but didn't know where it was going, nor did Congress, which demanded to know." When that happened, said Stickney, those within FEMA invoked "national security" as a rationale for declining Congress' demands, and the money was allocated anyway.

Stickney also encountered severe problems in trying to declassify various items after the collapse of the Soviet Union. "Getting that stuff declassified met with the full resistance of the security industry," Stickney told Gup, "as well as what might even be called a 'security cult,' people who believed strongly in what they'd been doing for ten years and longer."

Perhaps Stickney was so open because he felt slighted by FEMA's planners. Most FEMA emergency plans, he learned, called for him to remain at Washington headquarters in case of a nuclear attack, presumably to be incinerated in milliseconds when the incoming missiles arrived. But other FEMA workers, his subordinates, would be safe at locations such as Mount Weather.

Chapter Three contained several examples of critical information about the United States' planned response to a national emergency, including the budgeting for such responses, being withheld from nearly all members of Congress. Those are by no means isolated examples. Each year, Congress allocates billions of dollars for classified projects known only to senior Congressional leaders, precluding any meaningful Congressional oversight of those projects. Do the Congressional leaders receive detailed information or just a cursory overview? Are their opinions and advice solicited in advance, or is the information they receive of the "here's the way it's going to be" variety? How often are Congressional leaders informed of new emergency plans and changes to existing plans? The highly secret nature of much of the Shadow Government prevents the informed few in Congress consulting independent experts or using other public means (hearings, debates, etc.) to assess the effectiveness, practicality, and wisdom of specific Shadow Government policies even when these are known. In practice, most of the Shadow Government operates independently of Congress.

Is the situation better in the executive branch? The president and other key players (such as the vice president and secretary of defense) presumably receive more detailed information than Congress and can impose changes. The problem, as with Congress, is the lack of independent means of verifying what they are told. While no evidence suggests that key players in the Shadow Government have been plotting to deceive the president (or Congress, for that matter), a natural tendency of humans in any organization is to hide bad news from the boss and tell the boss what they think he or she wants to hear. Even without intending to deceive the president, they could misrepresent America's capabilities and plans for a national emergency by overemphasizing the positive, underemphasizing the negative, downplaying mistakes, ad-libbing to conceal ignorance, or many other distortions common among persons reporting to their superiors. The result could be as dangerously misleading as an outright lie.

And of course, it is easy to imagine a situation in which participants in the Shadow Government—who typically come from conservative, often military backgrounds—deliberately mislead a politically liberal president or Congress.

The question was: *How much do our elected officials know about the Shadow Government's activities and plans?*

And the answer is already becoming clear: *Not enough.*

HOW AND WHY INFORMATION GETS CLASSIFIED

While the United States has long had official secrets—military plans, diplomatic codes, and similar items—classifying information did not become a mania until World War II and its aftermath. Many of the decisive developments in the war, such as the planning of the Allied invasion of Normandy and the creation of the atomic bomb, took place in secret and took the Axis powers by surprise. But, as was learned later in the 1940s, spies kept Stalin informed about the United States' atomic bomb program and greatly accelerated the USSR's. This created a mindset by 1950 that information deemed vital to national security had to be kept not just from potential enemies but also from the American people. And while that may sound reasonable, "the American people" included most elected officials (including members of Congress) and the federal judiciary. While such extreme caution makes sense in the context of the times and was justifiable in most cases, it also created components of the executive branch and military that are exempt from normal constitutional checks and balances. While Congress could not pass "secret" laws, nor courts issue "secret" decisions and verdicts, the executive branch and military were allowed to make decisions and undertake projects exempt from normal Congressional and judicial oversight. Some accommodation was made by briefing key Congressional leaders on various secrets and giving security clearances to judges in cases involving classified information, but the net impact was that large sectors of government activity, and spending, simply became invisible to any meaningful review.

The information that any government wants to protect can be divided into two main categories: unique and objective. Unique is information (such as the president's nuclear missile launch codes and a general's battle plans) that cannot be determined independently and must be given by or stolen from its source. Objective information usually concerns new scientific discoveries and technologies; it typically has a limited lifespan because, with enough time and effort, others can discover the same information. Two examples of objective information are the technologies of hydrogen bombs and stealth aircraft. A hydrogen bomb's workings can eventually be learned by potential enemies no matter what steps are taken to protect the information; in contrast, unique information—a hydrogen bomb design's details, the bomb's weight, size, power, and appearance—can, in theory, be kept secret forever. (Some currently classified information dates from World War II.)

There are two main legal authorities for classifying information. The Atomic Energy Act of 1954 allows classifying information about U.S. atomic programs as either restricted data or formerly restricted data; the former is information not known to have been learned by other nations (such as a new nuclear process), while the latter is information believed or known to have been acquired by other nations. The "formerly restricted data" type applies when the United States does not want to alert other nations that we know that they have the information, or when public disclosure of the information is undesirable. The other legal authority for classification, and the one most commonly used, is the National Security Act of 1947. This act authorized classification of almost every type of government information, including diplomatic, scientific, military, and intelligence, as well as a type called "miscellaneous." "Miscellaneous" alone could apparently include anything the government does or knows.

The classification system and terminology used today are refinements of the system used in World War II, with the major differences being the deletions of the "restricted" and "official use only" types in the 1950s. The current guidelines for classification come from Executive Order 12356, issued on April 2, 1982 by President Reagan, and were expanded upon in Executive Order 12958, issued by President Clinton on April 17, 1995 (see Appendix D). Those orders classify three main types of information:

- Top Secret: "information, the disclosure of which reasonably could be expected to cause exceptionally grave damage to the national security."

- Secret: "information, the unauthorized disclosure of which reasonably could be expected to cause serious damage to the national security."

- Confidential: "information, the unauthorized of disclosure of which reasonably could be expected to cause damage to the national security."

Neither executive order clearly defines "exceptionally grave" or "serious" damage. Information eligible for classification includes military plans and weapons, vulnerabilities of defense systems and installations, foreign relations, intelligence-gathering methods, and "other categories of information that are related to the national security." The last category admits almost any information, although the order specifically forbids classification of information "to conceal violations of law, inefficiency, or administrative error; to prevent embarrassment to a person, organization, or agency; to restrain competition; or to prevent or delay the release of information that does not require protection in the interest of national security."

How much information is classified each year, and at which levels, is not generally known, but some idea was made public with the 1992 release of a report to the President by the Information Security Oversight Office. The report said that there were 511,868 original security classifications (that is, of documents containing no previously classified information) and 6,595,149 derivative classifications (that is, of documents containing previously classified information) in 1991. Of the original classifications, 4% were Top Secret, 57% Secret, and 39% Confidential; of the derivative classifications, 8% were Top Secret, 74% Secret, and 18% Confidential.

Given such data, it is no surprise the most commonly held security clearance is Secret. A higher clearance allows access to all lower levels. A holder of a Secret clearance could see Confidential material but not Top Secret, while a holder of Top Secret clearance could see any classified material. It is believed, however, that there are several other classification levels above Top Secret, established according to the needs and requirements of various programs and activities.

Having a Top Secret clearance does not mean that one has access to all material with that classification. The key to management of sensitive information is to restrict that information to those persons who have a "need to know" it in order to do their jobs, and to allow access to the minimum information required to do the job. The September 11 hijackers followed this principle; substantial evidence suggests that only those assigned to pilot the planes knew that they were on a suicide mission. For another example, an engineer working on the guidance system for a new type of missile would likely have no idea of most of the other aspects of the missile, such as its propulsion system, payload capacity, or purpose. Casual shop-talk on classified projects is strongly discouraged, and even married couples working on the same project are warned not to talk about the project at home.

Classification guides for activities that produce or use classified information typically give examples of each level of classification. Nevertheless, deciding whether or at what level to classify information still requires judgment. Unsurprisingly, the tendency is to classify whenever in doubt and to assign the highest classification level permitted.

Information does not necessarily remain classified in perpetuity (although it often seems to). Executive Order 12356 directed that "Information shall be declassified or downgraded as soon as national security considerations permit," although such a broad statement is open to many interpretations. Executive Order 12958 attempts to set a ten-year limit on keeping information classified, but the order provides so many exceptions that the limit is more symbolic than effective. In addition to exceptions for cryptographic and military items, it also exempts information that would "damage relations between the United States and a foreign government," "reveal an intelligence source, method, or activity," or "undermine diplomatic activities that are reasonably expected to be ongoing for a period greater [than ten years]," and "national security emergency preparedness plans."

While doing so seems irrational, the government has tried on several occasions to classify information retroactively that had been released to the public. There were several such cases in the first term of the Reagan administration; information publicly available during the Carter presidency (such as the radio communications frequencies used by American embassies overseas) was suddenly classified. (Radio monitors confirmed that the newly classified frequencies were still in use.) For another example, in 1994 lawyer Jonathan Turley filed suit against the government on behalf of several former employees at Nevada's infamous "Area 51" who claimed they had been exposed to dangerous fumes when chemicals and other debris were burned in open-air pits. Gathering materials for his case, Turley obtained "Det 3 SP Job Knowledge," a document purporting to be a manual for the security guards at Area 51. The document was soon available on the Internet, including some web sites devoted to Area 51 rumor and speculation.

Many thought the "Det 3 SP Job Knowledge" manual a hoax. Several of the code names mentioned in it sounded phony, the design and layout were amateurish, and the map of Area 51 it contained included a casino. When Turley tried to enter the manual as evidence, however, the government (through the Air Force) decided to classify it as Secret, despite its having been widely circulated. Turley's suit eventually failed when President Clinton submitted a statement to the court in September 1995 that disclosure of what Turley wanted to know on behalf of his clients "could reasonably be expected to damage the national security." The biggest outcome of Turley's suit was the government's admission there was an installation at Area 51 and that classified projects were going on there.

Executive Order 12958 also established formal guidelines for a type of classified program used under various names since the 1950s and now known as special access programs (SAPs). In practice, SAPs are beyond Top Secret, and they are how the Shadow Government does business off the books.

SPECIAL ACCESS PROGRAMS

Executive Order 12958 defines a special access program as "a program established for a specific class of information that imposes safeguarding and access requirements that exceed those normally required for information at the same classification level." While this was the first time the term "special access program" appeared in an executive order, SAPs were nothing new. The Manhattan Project that developed the first atomic bomb during World War II was one by a different name. Other SAPs built Mount Weather, the SR-71 spy plane, and the first Stealth aircraft. All of those projects shared the defining characteristic of SAPs: even the existence of such programs is kept secret from almost all of Congress and others in the government with oversight responsibility, even if they have clearances for Top Secret information. The SAP designation on a project frees its managers to ignore the law and to lie whenever or however they wish.

What kind of activities can be covered by a SAP? "Special Access Programs (SAPs)," a document prepared for Headquarters, Department of the Army, October 12, 1998 and declassified in 2000, gives these answers:

(1) A specific technology with potential for weaponization that gives the United States a significant technical lead or tactical advantage over potential adversaries.

(2) Sensitive technology that is especially vulnerable to foreign intelligence exploitation without special protection.

(3) An emerging technology, proposed operation, or intelligence activity risking the compromise of other SAPs.

(4) Exposure of sensitive activities that could jeopardize the lives of U.S. citizens.

(5) A capability that is so unique or sensitive that it requires protection beyond normal procedures.

(6) An extremely sensitive activity requiring special protection from disclosure to prevent significant damage to national security or the reputation or interests of the United States.

(7) Methods used to acquire foreign technology or equipment.

(8) Sensitive support to DOD and non-DOD agencies.

While most items in that list are situations in which an extraordinary degree of security would be reasonable, item (6) opens the door to all sorts of mischief and abuse, especially when the goal of a SAP is to prevent significant damage to "the reputation or interests of the United States." For example, the revelation that the U.S. government was sending funds to a favored political party in a European country would cause significant damage to the reputation of the United States if disclosed; therefore, such a policy would qualify as a SAP. The potential for abuse of SAPs is enormous.

While no reliable details are available about current SAPs, histories of previous SAP programs, like those that created Area 51 in Nevada and the U-2 and SR-71 spy planes, give an idea of the level of security around them. Potential employees of the SAP are drawn from those who already have Top Secret clearances and then heavily vetted, even to a seemingly absurd degree (such as interviewing elementary school teachers). Potential employees generally learn nothing about the nature of the project until the last interview and often have only a day or two to accept the job. Construction workers for any buildings the project requires may ride to work in buses or planes with blacked-out windows, having no idea where they are working. In his book *Dark Eagles*, Curtis Peebles wrote that the pilots of transport planes into what became Area 51 during the U-2 project had no idea where they were flying. All flights were made at night, Peebles said, and pilots were instructed to fly to a point along the California/Nevada border, where they were to contact "Sage Control." "Sage Control" would reply, tell the pilots not to acknowledge further transmissions, and then give the pilots new headings and altitudes. "Sage Control" would steer the plane into the Area 51 site, even telling the pilots when to set the flaps for landing and when to lower the landing gear. They descended into a dark desert area with no landing strip indicated on air navigation charts (had they known where to look). Suddenly runway lights would appear and the pilots would receive clearance to land. When the flight landed, the runway lights would go out, and a truck would lead the plane to taxi to an unloading area.

Family life can be difficult for employees of SAPs. They are forbidden to discuss their jobs with their families in any way, and they may work for months at a time at isolated locations on "bachelor status." Often communication with their family (such as telephone calls) may be limited while working in a remote place, and all such communications (including mail) subject to monitoring and censorship. It is said that divorce and other domestic problems are more common among SAP employees than among the general population.

Since telephones are one of the easiest ways to release information, even if accidentally, about a SAP, they are subject to several restrictions in a SAP program. It is reported that all telephone use in certain SAP programs is monitored and recorded; in other programs, it may be impossible to call outside the facility without going through a central switchboard. A caller to a SAP facility will reach a "hello" phone. The "hello" phone is so named because that is all an outside caller will hear when it is answered. The caller then asks to speak to a specific person; if the person is associated with the SAP and the caller's identity is verified, the caller will be connected. But if the caller tries to initiate a conversation or ask a question, the voice on the other end will ask, "Who do you want to speak to?" If the caller can't give the name of a SAP employee or if the caller's identity can't be verified, the person answering the "hello" phone will hang up.

Unauthorized persons in the military who dial a SAP number, even if by accident, almost always are questioned by security personnel (this happened several times with the U-2 and SR-71 spy plane projects). There have been rumors that civilians who have accidentally dialed sensitive SAP numbers (like the one that connects Mount Weather to the civilian telephone system) have been visited and questioned by FBI agents.

Employees of SAPs have something in common with persons in the federal witness protection program—if they leave the SAP, they are supplied with false but "verifiable" information about their period of employment that can be used on their résumés when looking for other jobs. Their work experience is "sanitized" so that accurate information about their professional competencies can be conveyed to future employers without compromising the SAP in any way.

The most common methods of protecting the security of SAPs, however, are also the simplest: silence and lying. And it is not just the American public who is kept uninformed; it is also members of Congress and the judiciary. If something happens to jeopardize the secrecy of a SAP, numerous measures, many involving deception, will be taken. For example, the F-117 Stealth fighter was still a SAP when one piloted by Air Force Major Ross Mulhare crashed on July 11, 1986 at approximately 1:45 a.m. in the mountains east of Bakersfield, California. The crash was witnessed by several people, including Andy Hoyt, who managed to take a couple of photographs of the mysterious aircraft (reportedly Hoyt thought it was a UFO) seconds before it crashed. Within minutes of the crash, the Air Force had dispatched search and rescue teams from nearby Edwards Air Force Base. The crash site was on public land, in Sequoia National Forest, but the search and rescue teams were the first to arrive and quickly declared the crash site a "national security area." This designation meant that civilian authorities, such as local sheriff's deputies, emergency services workers, and Federal Aviation Administration experts, were barred from entering the site. All civilian aircraft as well as military aircraft not connected with the search and rescue mission were banned from a five mile radius around the site. The only official statement issued by the Air Force was that one of their jets had crashed and a pilot had been killed.

Andy Hoyt had called Edwards Air Force Base after witnessing the crash to report what he had seen. He and other witnesses were interviewed at a command post set up by the Air Force outside the national security area in an effort to learn what they had seen and whether the secrecy of the F-117 had been compromised. The witnesses were told they had seen the crash of a nonclassified aircraft. When Hoyt mentioned they he had photographed the plane before it crashed, the Air Force took his film. Hoyt received two sets of prints and his negatives back from the Air Force a few days later, but there were no prints of the mysterious aircraft, and his negatives of those shots were also missing.

Federal law permits the confiscation of any photographs, videos, audio recordings, drawings, or other materials which might disclose the existence of a SAP or other highly classified activity. Signs forbidding photography and other recording activities are posted on the perimeters of military bases and other facilities where SAPs and other highly classified activities are taking place often attracting attention to otherwise unremarkable locations.

Ordinary citizens and reporters have had film and other media confiscated in cases besides Hoyt's. Perhaps the best known case occurred in July 1994, when a camera crew from Los Angles television station KNBC had their videotapes of the boundary of Nevada's Area 51 seized by local sheriff's deputies responding to a call from the base's security forces. At the time of the seizure, the KNBC crew were all outside the base on public land, but had their cameras pointed toward the base, photographing the inside of the restricted area.

An example of how deception can be used to protect a SAP occurred in 1984. In 1983 several Greenpeace activists had managed to sneak inside the original boundary of what came to be known as Area 51 in a protest against U.S. nuclear policy. In response, the government announced plans to expand the base by 89,600 acres. Doing so required a public notice of several months, and until the expanded boundaries became effective, armed guards were posted along the proposed new boundaries. Hunters, hikers, and drivers heading into the area were "requested" to turn away. In May 1984 a reporter for the *Las Vegas Review-Journal* found the guards polite but firm in their requests that no one go beyond the proposed new boundary; when he asked their supervisor why he was being "asked" to go no further, he got no more answer than "national security." In August 1984, the House Subcommittee on Lands and National Parks held hearings on the proposed new boundaries. The subcommittee chairman, Rep. John Seiberling (D-Ohio), asked John Rittenhouse, an Air Force representative, why people were being turned back by armed guards when the land was still legally open to the public. Rittenhouse replied that he could answer that only in a closed session, and Seiberling exploded. "Shades of Watergate!" he told Rittenhouse. "All I am asking you is under what legal authority this was done. I am not asking you the technical reasons. That certainly is not classified." In response, Rittenhouse admitted, "We had no legal authority, but we asserted our right to request people not to enter the area." Of course, a "request" by uniformed men carrying firearms will not be perceived as such by the "requestees," but the Air Force did not have to perpetrate its legal fiction for long; the expanded Area 51 boundaries were approved.

Congress learns of SAPs only through briefings given to senior members of Congress on a "need to know" basis, such as the chairmen and ranking minority members of committees with budget authority over the SAP. The depth and level of detail of the briefings are unknown. Do lawmakers get details about delays, cost overruns, and operational effectiveness of various SAPs, or just assurances that things are going well? Do they learn enough to make rational decisions about whether to continue funding the programs? Since the informed members of Congress cannot consult independent experts about any technical aspects of SAPs they may know, they must rely on the honesty and good will of those who brief them. Critics such as Tim Weiner, a Pulitzer Prize-winning reporter for the *Philadelphia Inquirer*, have charged that SAPs are frequently used not to protect national security but instead to hide program failures, mismanagement, waste, overly cozy relationships between defense contracts and the military brass, and even outright fraud. Such problems occur throughout government programs that are not classified and subject to public review and investigation; one can only wonder at what happens inside programs of which any meaningful public oversight is impossible.

An example of the lengths to which agencies will go to protect SAPs from Congressional oversight came in 1999, when the House Permanent Select Committee on Intelligence tried to investigate "Echelon," the

National Security Agency's global eavesdropping system. The committee's chairman, Porter Goss (R-Florida), requested that the NSA provide legal opinions, decisionmaking memoranda, and policy guidelines for handling intercepted telephone, fax, and email messages involving U.S. citizens. The NSA rejected the committee's request, arguing that, since the NSA's general counsel had developed the guidelines, the request violated attorney-client privilege, with the general counsel being the "attorney" and the NSA being the "client."

SAPs hide deep within the budgets passed by Congress. They are referred by acronyms only, or by code names such as "Tacit Blue" or terms such as "miscellaneous research" or "special evaluation program," or, in some cases, as simply "miscellaneous" (the 1997 Air Force budget included a single item for "miscellaneous" that totaled $4.67 billion—the largest item in the Air Force budget). The use of SAPs has proliferated over the past three decades, with the result that each year members of Congress approve billions of dollars in funding for programs of which they have no knowledge whatsoever. This appears to violate Article 1, Section 9 of the U.S. Constitution, which says, "No money shall be drawn from the Treasury, but in consequence of appropriations made by law; and a regular statement of account of the receipts and expenditures of all public money shall be published from time to time."

Two SAPs that "came in from the cold"

There have been cases where a SAP eventually becomes public knowledge yet still performs essentially the same functions as when it was classified. Perhaps the two best-known examples are the National Security Agency (NSA) and the National Reconnaissance Office (NRO).

The National Security Agency is the eyes and ears of the U.S. intelligence community, including the Shadow Government. It intercepts nearly all international telephone calls, faxes, and emails that travel by satellite or microwave link over any part of their journey. The same goes for cell phone calls (NSA maintains satellites devoted to intercepting cell phone calls), radio transmissions, and other electronic communications that cross international borders. Domestic communications can be, and have been, monitored with equal ease. NSA has the most advanced computers in the world, and their text and speech recognition software scans all intercepted communications for key words and phrases; if they detect any of these, then the entire communication is analyzed. Email encryption and telephone scrambling offer no security. NSA can easily crack such encryption, and it is reported that using encryption only arouses NSA's interest. In fact, it is safest today to assume that any communication you make via electronic means—by phone, fax, the internet, radio, etc.— may be intercepted and analyzed by the NSA.

In the spring of 1999, reports began to appear in the media about a new system called "Echelon," a network of spy satellites and worldwide listening posts run by the NSA. The May 27, 1999 issues of *Business Week* and *The New York Times* carried stories about Echelon and its sinister ability to intercept telephone calls, faxes, email, and radio signals and then analyze their contents with powerful supercomputers looking for key words or phrases. As *Business Week* told its readers, "Just get used to the fact—Big Brother is listening."

The NSA does not, to the best of public knowledge, actually install wiretaps on phone lines. It does not need to, because most electronic communications today involve wireless links. Cell phone and long-distance calls use satellites; many local calls use microwave relays beyond the local switching office. And when a wireless signal travels, the NSA is listening to it, storing it, and processing it. If something in the communication catches the NSA's interest, the NSA analyzes it to see if it has any "national security" implications. If the analysis yields something suspicious, or if the NSA cannot figure out what the communication is about, the parties involved may be targets of more intensive surveillance, including possible wiretaps authorized by the Foreign Intelligence Surveillance Act (FASA) Court.

While it is the NSA's interception of telephone calls and faxes that disturbs most people who know about it, the NSA also tracks everything sent electronically, including e-mail, financial transactions (such as stock trades and credit card sales), travel reservations, etc. In addition, recent reports have claimed that the NSA is tapping into undersea cables and network access points that local internet service providers (ISPs) use to connect to the Internet.

In addition to its own signal interception operations, the NSA serves as a clearinghouse for all signal intercepts by the military and the various civilian agencies of the federal government. The results of all intelligence-gathering by means of signal interception by the U.S. Army, Navy, Air Force, and Coast Guard go to the NSA for processing and analysis. The same thing happens with signals intercepted by the FBI, Customs Service, Drug Enforcement Administration, Federal Communications Commission, and other civilian agencies. Anything that appears remotely connected to "national security" (or if the intercepting agency cannot figure out what it is) winds up in the NSA's lap.

To keep track of everything it intercepts and receives from other agencies, the NSA houses (at its main headquarters, Fort George Meade, Maryland) what is probably the most powerful combination of physical and human computing resources in the world. The NSA has what is reported to be the second most powerful collection of supercomputers anywhere (and that might be an understatement). Its computer scientists and programmers have developed incredibly sophisticated software such as the speech- and text-recognition software mentioned earlier.

No act of Congress created the NSA, and no statute establishes the agency or defines the scope of its permissible activities (in sharp contrast with the CIA, which was created by an act of Congress and thus has clearly defined missions and accountability). The NSA came into being on November 4, 1952, through a National Security Council intelligence directive issued by President Harry Truman under the authority of the National Security Act of 1947. President Truman's directive consolidated the various signal interception and analysis activities of the U.S. government, including those of the military, under the umbrella of the NSA. The directive itself was classified Top Secret until the 1970s; even the name "National Security Agency" was classified for over two decades. (A joke among NSA employees at the time was that "NSA" stood for "no such agency.")

The NSA's operating authority is to gather "foreign intelligence" for the purposes of "national security." Those terms, however, have never been precisely defined and are open to broad and creative interpretation. No law has ever been enacted by Congress to prohibit the NSA from engaging in any activity; however, Congress has enacted numerous laws prohibiting anyone from divulging information about the NSA or its activities.

Loose definitions of "foreign intelligence" and "national security" let the NSA turn its attention to surveillance of American citizens in the 1960s and 1970s. Senate hearings chaired in 1975 by Idaho Senator Frank Church revealed that the NSA began to compile "watch lists" of American citizens in 1962. The purported intent of snooping on American citizens was to determine if any "foreign powers" were lending support to the civil rights movement. These lists and surveillance efforts against Americans greatly expanded in 1967, as the NSA targeted antiwar groups and more civil rights organizations. Among the Americans whose names appeared on NSA watch lists during that era were Martin Luther King, Jr., Jane Fonda, Joan Baez, Eldridge Cleaver, and Abbie Hoffman. The NSA also began to get requests for surveillance from other government agencies, like the CIA and the Bureau of Narcotics and Dangerous Drugs (forerunner of today's Drug Enforcement Administration) that were prohibited by law from conducting it themselves.

The NSA's program of domestic spying was ended by Attorney General Elliott Richardson in October 1973 as the rapidly unraveling Watergate scandal threatened to expose it. In the wake of Watergate, NSA Director Lew Allen finally revealed the NSA's surveillance efforts against Americans to the Church committee in 1975; these revelations accompanied promises to establish safeguards against such abuses in the future.

But the NSA still fights Congressional efforts to control its activities. As noted earlier, when the House Permanent Select Committee on Intelligence attempted in 1999 to investigate the NSA's handling of intercepted communications involving Americans, the agency claimed an attorney-client privilege between the NSA director and its general counsel to exempt the requested documents from Congressional review (the same tactic President Nixon tried with his counsel John Dean during the Watergate scandal). Even right-wing Republicans on the committee were outraged by the NSA's response. Representative Bob Barr (R-Georgia), a former CIA analyst, called the NSA claim "bogus" and said it was an attempt to "deny the chairman and committee members proper information with which to carry out their oversight responsibilities." Despite such protests, the NSA steadfastly refused to provide the request documents and the committee could only protest in its final report.

A United Press International (UPI) story by Richard Sale, dated February 13, 2001, gave insights into how the NSA operates today. The article concerned the NSA's efforts to locate Saudi exile and terrorist Osama bin Laden through his telephone communications. Sale reported that when UPI wanted to email some information about one of bin Laden's associates to a former CIA official, the official replied, "My God, don't put that in an email." The official explained that such an email would get him placed on one of the NSA watch lists, which he did not want to happen.

The UPI story explained that the NSA maintains computerized "dictionaries" of personal names, political groups, names of criminal organizations, and other expressions. All intercepted communications are checked against these dictionaries. If there is a match between any of the dictionaries and the intercepted communication, both the sender and receiver of the communication are placed on a watch list. All future communications to and from the sender and receiver are then intercepted and analyzed. For example, suppose someone sends you an email with something that matches a name, word, or phrase in one of the dictionaries. You are then placed on a NSA watch list. Anyone to whom you send email joins the list; so does anyone who sends you emails. You get off the watch list when it is determined that you pose no threat to national security. Who determines whether you pose a threat to national security? The NSA. And no, the NSA does not have to tell anyone that you are under surveillance, nor does it need any warrant to monitor your communications.

The main NSA buildings at Fort George Meade and elsewhere in Maryland, reported to occupy over 3.5 million square feet, are two high-rise office complexes and smaller support buildings, including a technical library and engineering laboratories. It is reported that the NSA employs approximately 20,000 persons in Maryland.

NSA maintains two communications satellite interception stations in the continental United States, at Sugar Grove, West Virginia and Yakima, Washington. The Sugar Grove station processes intercepts from communications satellites over the Atlantic, while Yakima does the same for Pacific satellites. Overseas, the NSA and Britain's GCHQ jointly operate a mammoth listening complex at Menwith Hill, near Harrogate in Great Britain. This station mainly intercepts signals from Russia and the rest of the former Soviet bloc. Misawa Air Base at Misawa, Japan, is the NSA's main base for eavesdropping on China. The U.S. and Australia jointly operate a large station at Pine Gap, Australia, that covers southeast Asia. In addition, almost any military site in the United States with communications receiving equipment is a potential source of input for the NSA. U.S. embassies and consulates abroad also have signal interception capabilities; one major intelligence coup of the 1960s by the U.S. embassy in Moscow was interception of calls from the crude radio-telephones in the limousines of Politburo members.

Insights into the NSA's workings are scarce. What purported to be a copy of the agency's employee security handbook was leaked in 1990 and widely circulated on the Internet. The NSA has never confirmed or denied the authenticity of the document. Former NSA employees have stated the handbook is genuine, however, and its language, terms, and stipulations are similar to the security handbooks issued by other government agencies.

In 1999, the NSA sent a memorandum to employees banning the popular Furby toys from all NSA facilities. The Furby, which resembled a big-eyed, cute-faced stuffed owl, could "learn" to speak by recording and repeating words and phrases it heard. The NSA worried that a Furby could overhear sensitive conversations, memorize them, and repeat them to unauthorized persons if taken home. The memo advised any NSA employees who had a Furby in their office or spotted a Furby on NSA premises immediately to "contact their Staff Security Office for guidance."

The National Reconnaissance Office was created on August 25, 1960 to coordinate America's spy satellite activities and the efforts of the CIA, Air Force, and Department of Defense in obtaining and analyzing data from the satellites. President Eisenhower cited the National Security Act of 1947 in his presidential directive establishing NRO, and for over three decades it was one of the most obscure of all SAPs; even the name "National Reconnaissance Office" was classified Top Secret until September 1992, and the location of its headquarters in Chantilly, Virginia remained classified until 1994. While it was common knowledge by the late 1960s that the United States was making extensive use of spy satellites, the scope of the NRO's activities came as a surprise even to most members of Congress.

There were more shocks when the NRO's accounting was examined. In 1994 a General Accounting Office audit of the NRO found that one of its classified projects involved the construction of a $300 million office building easily visible from busy Route 28 near Washington. The same audit found that, since its founding in 1961, NRO spent over $4 billion that could not be accounted for. Some felt that this was a sign of sloppy managerial and accounting practices within NRO, while others speculated that the funds had actually been redirected—as difficult as it may be to conceive—to even more highly classified activities.

How Much Does The Government Spend On Classified Programs?

In all probability, no one really knows. In addition to SAPs, the budgets of several known agencies, such as the Central Intelligence Agency and the National Reconnaissance Office, are classified. With so many budget items classified, the best approximation available is to subtract the nonclassified items from the total amount of the national budget.

In the mid-1990s, Steve Aftergood of the Federation of American Scientists thus calculated that the Pentagon's annual "black budget" was likely in excess of $30 billion. Aviation writer Bill Sweetman analyzed the 1996 defense budget and discovered that, while total defense spending had dropped since the collapse of the Soviet Union, the percentage devoted to SAPs and other secret projects had actually increased. He also found that in the 1997 budget 41% of all Air Force procurement spending was for classified projects, and that President Clinton's proposed budget for the next fiscal year called for a $5.9 billion increase in spending on SAPs and other classified projects. Sweetman also discovered that most "black budget" spending went to a handful of companies such as Lockheed Martin and McDonnell Douglas. The senior managers of these companies were heavily drawn from those who had worked on secret programs while serving in the government in a military or civilian capacity. While this certainly did not establish a quid pro quo relationship—support a SAP while a government employee, get a high-paying private sector job later— the links between those companies and secret projects did raise eyebrows.

Some budget items have abruptly disappeared from the public, nonclassified budget, leading to speculation that the project continues but has become a SAP or similar classified budget expenditure. The legend of the rumored Aurora hypersonic spy plane got started in 1986 when a project code-named "Aurora" appeared in the 1986 defense budget with an entry for $8 million. The next year, the entry for Aurora suddenly jumped to $2.3 billion, indicating a major new program. But Aurora disappeared from the 1988 budget and has not reappeared as an unclassified budget item. The Aurora item may not refer to any new spy plane, but it does appear that some sort of classified activity with that code name was started in 1986 and funding sharply increased for it in 1987 before the project became secret. Tim Weiner presents a similar example in his book *Blank Check:* a budget item identified only as "207248F" that jumped from $885,000 to $20 million in one year before vanishing from the public budget.

Some idea of the spending on an individual project may be obtained after it is declassified. In 1991 the Navy cancelled its previously classified A-12 stealth fighter program because it was late and the fighter was not performing as expected. The contractors for the A-12 sued the Navy for improper contract termination, and financial data became public as a result. The Navy spent $2.68 billion on the A-12 project without producing a working example of the plane. The Navy's inspector general issued a report saying that the program's secrecy precluded the necessary program oversight and management, and even the Secretary of the Navy had not received routine reports on the project's (lack of) progress.

There are indeed cases in which national security justifies keeping projects and activities secret. But stories such as the A-12 fighter's causes one to wonder if the definition of "national security" has been enlarged to include the careers and reputations of bureaucrats within the Shadow Government.

CHAPTER FIVE

OUTPOSTS OF THE SHADOW GOVERNMENT

THERE IS MORE to the Shadow Government than executive orders, FEMA, COG shelters, and SAPs. The military also has its own relocation shelters and plans for continuity of military leadership, and large areas of the American west are, for all practical purposes, occupied territories controlled by the Shadow Government. There are also private companies with close ties to the Shadow Government whose business is to do what would be difficult, illegal, or embarrassing for the Shadow Government to do.

CONTINUITY OF MILITARY LEADERSHIP

There is no reliable evidence of an equivalent to the civilian COG program for America's top military leaders, but emergency relocation shelters for them were built at the same time as Mount Weather and other civilian COG facilities. Some top-level military leaders participate in civilian COG programs (for example, there is a senior military presence at Mount Weather), and vice versa (the president, secretary of defense, persons in the line of presidential succession, and others have spent time at the military relocation installations).

This happened on September 11, 2001, when President George W. Bush went to the U.S. Strategic Command Center (USSTRATCOM) at Offutt Air Force Base near Bellevue, Nebraska. USSTRATCOM is a two-level reinforced concrete and steel building of over 14,000 square feet. Twenty-four hours a day, either an Air Force general or a Navy admiral commands it, ready to direct the deployment of U.S. nuclear forces should the president authorize their use.

USSTRATCOM is home to an airborne command post named "Looking Glass" for use in case an attack incapacitates Offutt. Looking Glass is housed in a rotating set of customized Boeing 707s, one of which is in the air all day, every day. Each flight has an Air Force general or Navy admiral aboard who is in direct communication with the president and other military officers. If an incoming missile is detected heading for Offutt, Looking Glass flies to safety so the counterattack can be directed from aboard it.

The interior of USSTRATCOM includes numerous workstations with video monitors and secure telephones. Eight large wall screens display video and still images. In the event of war, battle information would appear on the wall screens and on individual video monitors. Numerous high-powered computer systems are here, along with an extensive telephone network—the USSTRATCOM commanders have direct telephone access to over two hundred U.S. military sites around the world, including missile silos. Direct lines also go to the president, secretary of defense, and the chairman of the Joint Chiefs of Staff. Satellite and radio communications link USSTRATCOM with military computing and communications centers, and with Looking Glass and other mobile units such as Navy submarines. This communications capability is one reason President Bush went to USSTRATCOM on September 11; from there he could command virtually all of the U.S. military.

Some of President Bush's advisors wanted him to go instead to the Cheyenne Mountain Operations Center near Colorado Springs, Colorado on September 11. Cheyenne Mountain is the military equivalent of Mount Weather. Inside a hollowed-out mountain designed to withstand a direct strike from an atomic bomb are fifteen buildings—eleven of which are three stories tall—keeping track of everything in earth orbit and all planes flying in North American airspace. Large, backlit maps of the world display information received from orbiting spy satellites; a large video screen tracks the president and vice president. In case of a nuclear war, over eight hundred workers could survive in here for more than thirty days completely cut off from the outside world. 1319 springs, each weighing over a thousand pounds, support the buildings inside the mountain and let them rock to absorb the impact of a nuclear strike. If a nuclear attack is imminent, twenty-five-ton blast doors can close in fifteen seconds to seal the installation 1700 feet inside the granite of Cheyenne Mountain.

Perhaps the best known tenant of the Cheyenne Mountain site is the North American Aerospace Defense Command (NORAD), an American and Canadian effort to defend North America from attack by missiles or aircraft. (Since NORAD is a joint effort, several members of the Canadian military work inside the mountain.) Others include the Air Operations Center, which ties together military and civilian radar systems to track aircraft over North America, logging over 2,500,000 flights annually, and the U.S. Space Command, which controls all military satellites, including spy, communications, and navigation satellites. (The main purpose of this command is to detect enemy missiles; it detects all missile launches around the world and then has to decide, in no more than a few hundred seconds, whether the missile is hostile.) Also inside the mountain is the Air Force Space Command, tracking and cataloguing all objects in orbit, ranging from the Space Shuttle to debris the size of a large bolt. (A piece of space junk that size, orbiting the Earth at 17,500 miles per hour, could do severe damage to a satellite or the Space Shuttle.) It also operates the global positioning satellite (GPS) network.

The steel buildings stand in a grid, reminding many visitors of the layout below deck of a large Navy ship, such as an aircraft carrier or destroyer. Besides strength, steel has the advantage of being able to absorb much of the electromagnetic pulse that would be produced by a nearby nuclear explosion. There are no barracks or other living quarters for workers, just a supply of cots and other temporary bedding. Visitors have been surprised at how small the rooms are, especially the command centers. Workers sit close together, and the ceiling is about as high as a typical American house's. Some command center furnishings are like movie set-pieces, though: the generals normally in command have a red telephone that connects them directly to the president. Duty officers responsible for monitoring such developments as missile launches or aircraft intruding from south of the United States have a beige phone at their duty station. If an officer detects something unusual, he or she picks up his or her phone, all the other beige phones ring, and the officers at those stations respond as necessary.

The main command center for Cheyenne Mountain has several large, backlit maps of North America and other areas of the world. One shows the current location of the president, the vice president, the Canadian prime minister, and other senior government and military leaders. Other maps and monitors track moving aircraft (especially those approaching the airspace of North America) and display data from spy satellites and ground-based space radars. According to a 1999 CNN report, Cheyenne Mountain detected over 670 "unknowns" in North American airspace in 1997 and turned that information over to other government agencies, such as the Drug Enforcement Administration. To augment these efforts, balloon-borne radar systems are monitoring the border with Mexico. Which other agencies receive information from Cheyenne Mountain and to what degree it cooperates with civilian law enforcement are not known.

For several years, there was what might be termed a "standby Pentagon" inside Raven Rock Mountain in Adams County, Pennsylvania, near Waynesboro, a few miles north of the Maryland border. It became operational in 1953, when manned Soviet bombers were the main threat. Similar in design to the Cheyenne Mountain facility, although at a lesser depth, it serves now mainly as a communications post and is known as the Alternate Joint Communications Center (AJCC). It could easily be returned to its former role of a standby military command post, however, and the necessary steps to do so may have been taken since the September 11 attacks.

AREAS RESERVED FOR THE SHADOW GOVERNMENT

Large areas, particularly in the western United States, are controlled by the Shadow Government for SAPs and similar activities. The size of these areas is staggering; several are larger than Connecticut. Within them, the laws that apply to the rest of the United States, such as environmental laws, are simply void. Local and state officials have no control over what goes on inside those areas, nor are they informed of possible dangers or problems. Federal officials, such as judges and members of Congress, are equally in the dark. The airspace is closed to all civilian air traffic and even unauthorized military flights. In effect, the Shadow Government is already occupying large territories in the United States.

The largest such area is the Nellis Range Complex (NRC), which occupies over three million acres in central Nevada—in other words, an area almost as big as New Jersey—and has two thousand miles of known roads crisscrossing it. The NRC is bounded on the west by Highway 95, on the north by Highway 6, on the east by Highway 375, and on the south by Highway 93. Very little of what goes on inside can be seen from these roads, however, because the area is mountainous. The NRC is subdivided into areas with different purposes, the most famous of these being the Nevada Test Site (NTS), the Tonopah Test Range (TTR), and the legendary Area 51.

The Nevada Test Site is on the western side of the NRC, about 65 miles northwest of Las Vegas on Highway 95. The exit for Mercury along Highway 95 will take you to the main entrance for the NTS. The "town" of Mercury only exists within the NTS, and there are no services at this exit other than the gate.

The NTS was established in December 1950, and occupies over 1350 square miles, making it larger than Rhode Island. Its eastern boundary is at Area 51. Between 1951 and 1962, 126 atomic bomb tests were conducted above ground within the NTS. In that era, a highlight for many vacationers to Las Vegas was not seeing Frank, Dean, or Sammy at the Sands, but instead driving north on Highway 95 to see an atomic bomb explosion. Here was the scene of the first live telecast of an atomic bomb test; on May 17, 1953, viewers of NBC's *Today* show got to watch the "Annie" test. The television crew were seven miles away on a hilltop later known as "News Knob." Annie exploded just before dawn, entertaining families gathered around their breakfast tables in the eastern and central time zones.

Atmospheric nuclear testing was banned by international treaty in 1962. While trumpeting this at the time as an enlightened move to protect the environment and reduce international tensions, the United States and the Soviet Union actually agreed to the ban because spy satellites were making it impossible to conceal the results of above-ground tests. Underground tests were still permitted, and over eight hundred were conducted here until 1992. Since then, underground subcritical tests (tests using amounts of fissionable material too small to sustain a chain reaction) have occurred at the NTS.

All these tests have left the NTS hot. According to a report in the October 23, 2000 *Las Vegas Sun*, the soil there is contaminated with over four tons of plutonium. In most areas of the NTS, however, the concentration of plutonium is too small to pose a health risk. That is good, because it will still be radioactive for another 500,000 years.

While the NTS may not be doing much nuclear testing these days, it is doing a good bit of testing of other hazardous substances. In fact, the NTS seems to be pitching itself as a place to test things away from the prying eyes of the media and the Environmental Protection Agency.

According to a marketing sheet prepared by the Department of Energy to generate business from private companies, "The Nevada Test Site also serves the nation as a proving ground for alternative energy research and Department of Defense projects that require the isolation, complex infrastructure, and technical expertise we can provide. As a National Environmental Research Park, the Nevada Test Site is home to important environmental activities including technology development, clean up and remediation of contaminated environments, and waste management. The Test Site is a unique outdoor laboratory where federal agencies and private industry conduct large-scale open-air experiments with hazardous and toxic chemicals and test remediation and emergency response techniques . . . The Nevada Test Site offers an enormous amount of space, including more than 1,000 miles of completely undisturbed land available for new projects. The vast site also offers security. The boundary and security areas are guarded, and the area is isolated from population centers." That sounds like an ideal place to do something secret.

More than 1100 buildings and laboratories are located at the NTS, along with four hundred miles of paved roads, three hundred miles of unpaved roads, two airstrips, ten heliports, and power transmitters and generators. There is also housing for 1200 people (although most employees commute from the Las Vegas area via shuttle buses or government aircraft), a hospital, a cafeteria, a post office, a fire station, and a substation of the Nye County sheriff's department (who are there mainly to arrest trespassers and haul them to the county jail). In fact, the population of the NTS makes it the second largest "city" in Nye County; the biggest is Pahrump, home of radio talk show host Art Bell. The NTS is Nye County's biggest "industry," with the second largest apparently consisting of several legal brothels and massage parlors near Pahrump.

The NTS is divided into different areas, and employees are able to enter only those areas for which they have the proper security clearance. The areas visible from Highway 95 require only relatively low-level security clearances, while those bordering Area 51 require very high-level clearances. Immediately adjacent to it inside the Nevada Test Site is Area 15. Area 13 is where plutonium dispersal tests took place in the 1950s. The most isolated region of the NTS, Area 19, is the subject of much speculation; it is actually more remote than the fabled Area 51. Topographic maps show that several large power lines lead into Area 19, but official NTS maps show nothing there. Satellite photos, however, do indicate some buildings. So what is going on there that requires so much electric power? One possibility is high-power lasers or some other form of directed-energy weapon.

Other facilities at the NTS assemble or disassemble nuclear weapons. The Device Assembly Facility (DAF) is a 100,000 square foot building in Area 6 where the atomic bombs to be tested underwent final assembly. Since testing stopped, it is used for disassembly of atomic weapons being withdrawn from America's stockpile. All aboveground portions of the DAF are covered with at least five feet of soil, and the building includes decontamination stations, testing laboratories, bridge cranes, and—even though it is located entirely inside the NTS—its own guard stations and security cameras. Its interior is divided into five assembly "cells." As official NTS literature says, the DAF is "designed to minimize release of nuclear material in the unlikely event of an accidental explosion."

The Hazardous Material (HAZMAT) Spill Center, according once again to official NTS literature, "allows live releases of hazardous materials for training purposes, field-test detection, plume dispersion experimentation, and equipment and materials testing." In other words, laws and regulations to protect the environment do not apply here. The Spill Center is in Area 5 of the NTS.

The U1a Experimental Facility in Area 1 is an underground complex originally built for a nuclear test that never happened. The complex includes a vertical shaft that goes 960 feet below the surface, where it connects to horizontal tunnels over a half-mile long; a mechanical hoist carries equipment and workers down to the tunnels. On the surface, the U1a is marked only by trailers and other temporary structures. What is its purpose? Official NTS literature vaguely says that it permits "scientists to gain more knowledge of the dynamic properties of aging nuclear materials." But, the literature continues, "the complex will provide a high degree of safety for NTS workers and the public and will minimize environmental impacts."

There are other points of interest inside NTS. Several artificial craters there were produced by atomic tests just under the surface. The most famous is the Sedan Crater, 1280 feet wide and 320 feet deep, created by the Plowshare Project, a program to see if nuclear explosions could cheaply excavate land for construction projects (don't laugh). Sedan Crater is on the National Register of Historic Places.

Other somewhat surreal areas of NTS are the so-called "Doom Towns," built to test the impact of nuclear explosions and fallout on civilian structures. One Doom Town was a replica of early 1950s American suburbia. In the 1950s these camera-rigged homes, many with cars parked in front, were filled with typical home furnishings (including bric-a-brac and fresh food) and populated by department store mannequins so the effects of nearby atomic explosions could be studied. (You may have seen the grainy black-and-white films of these tests, in one of which the blast wave from the explosion shatters living room windows and knocks "Dad" from his recliner, hurling him across the living room.) The other Doom Town was a startling sight: a Japanese village in the middle of the Nevada desert. This Doom Town was used to study the dispersion and spread of fallout, and used the data gathered from the explosions at Hiroshima and Nagasaki to study the fallout-producing capabilities of new bomb designs. Today only a few structures remain at these two Doom Towns.

Parts off the NTS are fenced off, and access roads are gated to prevent entry by those without the proper security clearance. The gates are numbered, and the most famous is Gate 700. It controls access to the road leading from the NTS into Area 51.

While contemporary NTS literature stresses safety efforts, there have been numerous serious safety failings there, including the inadvertent nuking of John Wayne.

"Harry" was the code name for a nuclear weapon tested at the NTS on May 19, 1953. The device, which used a novel hollow fissionable core, was tested on a tower three hundred feet above ground. The new core design and elevation produced unexpectedly heavy fallout; long before the Clint Eastwood movie, this test was referred to as "Dirty Harry."

The wind took the main fallout plume over St. George, a town in southwest Utah near the Arizona and Nevada borders. At least five residents of St. George developed radiation sickness, and the Atomic Energy Commission (AEC) had to order residents to stay indoors for several hours after the test. Hundreds of sheep in the area died after eating grass contaminated by the fallout, and for months afterwards livestock in the area had an exceptionally high number of stillbirths.

Shortly after the "Harry" test, *The Conqueror* was filmed around St. George. In addition to John Wayne, the movie starred Susan Hayward and Agnes Moorehead and was directed by Dick Powell. All four would die of cancer. A total of 220 people were in the cast and crew, and 91 of them had developed cancer by 1980. According to the AEC, this was a coincidence.

The NTS was the scene of the most serious nuclear accident in American history when the Baneberry underground test went awry on December 18, 1970. Although the bomb was located nine hundred feet below the surface, its yield was greater than expected and the explosion created fissures in the surface through which clouds of radioactive dust escaped. Expecting the explosion and all radioactivity to be contained underground, most workers in the area were caught without protective clothing and received large doses of radiation. The Department of Energy maintains that only eighty-six employees were exposed and that "none received exposure that exceeded the guideline for radiation workers." Over three hundred workers claimed to have been exposed, however, and at least that many showed clear symptoms of radiation poisoning, such as hair loss and passing of blood. Many who claimed exposure filed lawsuits against the DOE—most of them never settled, since the majority of the plaintiffs had died by the mid-1970s (most commonly of leukemia). The depositions taken for the suits repeatedly report that evidence of the exposure workers received, such as the radiation monitoring badges they were required to wear, had been destroyed after the test.

Even though the Baneberry accident is not so well known as 1979's Three Mile Island incident, the radiation released at Baneberry was several thousand times greater.

Is there still potentially dangerous, or even deadly, secret research going on at NTS? The probability seems high. The existence of the Community Environmental Monitoring Program (CEMP), a network of twenty monitoring stations in parts of Nevada and Utah downwind from NTS, supports this hypothesis. Sponsored by the Department of Energy, these stations are supposed to check for evidence of "manmade radioactivity," but the stations, in the DOE's own words, "collect a variety of environmental data." Why is checking for radioactivity necessary now, since the last underground test was several years ago? The obvious answer is that the CEMP stations monitor more than just radioactivity drifting from the NTS. Given the NTS' boasts of capabilities for testing hazardous materials spills and other simulated accidents, it seems likely that some sort of research on chemical or biological hazards is underway at NTS and that those are the sorts of hazards CEMP is designed to detect. The next real accident of Dirty Harry or Baneberry proportions could easily be chemical or biological instead of nuclear.

Further evidence in support of such speculations comes from a September 4, 2001 story in the *New York Times*. According to the report, a germ factory began operations during the late 1990s in the "Camp 12" (perhaps a misnomer for Area 12) section of the NTS. According to the *Times*, the Defense Threat Reduction Agency built it to assess the level of difficulty a rogue nation or terrorist group would face in constructing a germ weapons plant. (It turned out to be easy, as all components used in the plant came from hardware and construction supply stores). The simulation also tested whether such a factory would have telltale "signatures" (such as chemical or infrared emissions) detectable by surveillance planes or satellites. While the facility was fully capable of producing lethal organisms such as anthrax, officials say it only produced innocuous microbes and was strictly defensive in intent. The *Times* noted that the White House and Congress never learned of the project, supposedly because of its small scale and low cost.

Incredible as it might seem, the Nevada Test Site offered monthly guided tours before the September 11 attacks. Visitors shuttled to the site aboard buses departing from the Department of Energy Nevada Operations Office in Las Vegas. For security reasons, advance registration was required, and visitors had to provide a variety of personal data, including Social Security number, date and place of birth, employer's name, address, and telephone number, and official photo identification. Tour admission could be denied to anyone deemed a security risk. Visitors were not allowed to bring cameras, video recorders, binoculars, telescopes, or tape recorders, or make sketches, take any rock, soil, or plant samples, or remove any metal objects—they could only look. Visitors were also forbidden to wear shorts or sandals, and pregnant women were discouraged because, in the words of the NTS, "the long bus ride and uneven terrain" might pose health hazards.

So what did visitors get to see in exchange for being treated like a fourth-grader on a school trip? Quite a bit, actually. Tour stops included the HAZMAT Spill Center, Sedan Crater, the Low Level Radioactive Waste management Site, Control Point 1 (the command post used for above-ground atomic tests), Frenchman Flat (site of the first above-ground test at NTS), and the American "Doom Town." These tours may have resumed since this book was completed; the Department of Energy's web sites have details.

North of the NTS, near the town of Tonopah, is the Tonopah Test Range (TTR). This was home base of the first operational F-117 stealth fighter group when the project was still a SAP. The TTR was the perfect place to station the group, being almost as isolated as Area 51 and much further from Las Vegas and other densely populated areas. Its main entrance is via a paved road about fifteen miles east of Tonopah off Highway 6; a sign shaped like a rocket marks the road. The road goes about twenty miles south toward the TTR, leading to a guard gate that is always manned. Caution is required as you approach this gate, because the TTR boundary is before the gate and guardhouse; the boundary is poorly marked, and it is easy to stray into the TTR. The boundary area is highly developed, with numerous hangars, barracks, and support buildings visible from its perimeter.

The TTR occupies 625 square miles and was first opened in 1957 as an adjunct of the Nevada Test Site for research connected with the tests there. The Air Force first began using the TTR in 1979 and began major construction to house the F-117 stealth fighter being developed at Area 51. Later, facilities to support Air Force programs were added, but the Department of Energy still administers the TTR through Sandia Labs.

The TTR proved to be an ideal location for the first stealth fighters. The area north of it is the isolated Great Smokey Valley, a sparsely populated area well suited to the first nighttime training missions of the F-117. In addition to its isolation, the program benefited from the reticence of citizens of nearby Tonopah about the strange aircraft they saw cruising their nighttime skies. Although it was common knowledge in Tonopah during the early 1980s that something big and secret was going on at the TTR, the locals were tight-lipped about whatever they saw and heard.

The TTR was also a site during the 1980s for tests of Soviet aircraft, such as the MiG-21 and MiG-23, which the United States had obtained through clandestine means. (The fact that the United States had such aircraft is no longer classified, but the means of getting them still is.) Like the F-117, these were mainly tested at night; these tests continued at the TTR until the early 1990s.

When the F-117 was still secret, great efforts were made to keep the TTR as self-contained as possible so workers would not have to leave the base; thus, it had accommodations and recreational facilities superior to those found in Tonopah or other towns within reasonable driving distance. The barracks were hotel-like, far superior to housing on ordinary military bases. They included "blackout" curtains and soundproofing, since almost all stealth operations took place at night, requiring workers to sleep during the day.

In addition to its air bases, the TTR includes the Tonopah Electronic Combat Range (TECR), an extensive system of camera and radar systems to record data from aircraft and missiles tested there and to simulate threats (such as surface-to-air missiles) from enemy defenses. The TTR is known to have several Russian and Chinese radar systems obtained through various means (such as purchases via third countries and bribes paid to military and industrial officials connected to those nations); these test the radar "invisibility" of various weapons systems. It is believed that many projects under development at Area 51 are tested at the adjacent TTR's radar range.

The TECR is southeast of the base. While electronic warfare research is the stated purpose of this area, many other activities are believed to take place behind the screen provided by Tolicha Peak. Satellite photographs show several buildings there, including some that look like aircraft hangers, but no landing strip. The new Cedar Ranch entrance into the TTR leads to the TECR. This entrance is from the eastern side of the TTR, off Highway 375 just before the Queen City Summit marker. This road is marked on some maps as the Cedar Ranch Road. Formerly a dirt road leading to an unguarded gate, the road has recently been paved, and a manned guardhouse has been added a few hundred feet inside the secured perimeter. These enhancements strongly indicate new classified activity in this part of the range, where the TTR borders Area 51. Along Cedar Ranch Road one can also see, not surprisingly, Cedar Ranch, a small cattle ranch abandoned in the 1950s because of fallout from the Nevada Test Site. Several ranch buildings are still standing. Because water is available, cattle gather here to graze, and care must be taken on Cedar Ranch Road to avoid hitting them.

AREA 51

The most famous area controlled by the Shadow Government is Area 51, located in east-central Nevada, to the immediate east of the Nevada Test Site, along Highway 375 (named the "Extraterrestrial Highway" by the state of Nevada). Area 51 was born because the CIA needed a place to test its new U-2 spy plane; the area around Edwards Air Force Base had become too populated for daytime tests of top-secret aircraft. The tests required a new site with a large dry lakebed, a natural hard surface useful for take-offs and landings. In early 1955, several isolated lakebeds in the West were evaluated. Groom Lake met the CIA's requirements and had the further advantage of being adjacent to the Nevada Test Site (the CIA figured that fear of radioactive fallout would help keep adjacent areas lightly populated and discourage people from attempting to enter the area). In a matter of weeks, aircraft hangars, housing units, support buildings, tracking and navigation aids, and a paved runway had been added, and the U-2 was able to take its maiden test flight out of Groom Lake on August 4, 1955. Training of U-2 pilots began the next year at Groom Lake.

Originally, the facility at Groom Lake was known as "Paradise Ranch," a bitter commentary on its lack of amenities. A 1960 map of the Nellis Range Complex placed the Groom Lake site within "Area 51" on the map. While the facility was a closely guarded secret throughout the 1960s, military and civilian pilots knew something was going on there because its airspace was off-limits to all military and civilian traffic; military pilots training at Nellis or Tonopah quickly discovered that accidentally slipping only a few hundred feet inside the restricted airspace brought disciplinary action. The Groom Lake area became known as "Dreamland" among military pilots because that was the radio call sign used by its air traffic control center.

Paradise Ranch/Dreamland/Area 51 remains the premier test facility for highly advanced aircraft and, reportedly, other weapons systems. The U-2 was only the first in a long line of remarkable aircraft tested at Area 51, including the SR-71 spy plane and the F-117 stealth fighter. It is widely assumed that new secret aircraft, such as the next generation of stealth aircraft and unmanned aerial combat vehicles (UACVs), are being tested there. In addition, there is much speculation and some evidence that other advanced weapons systems, such as directed energy weapons, are being tested at Area 51.

But most visitors to Area 51 come hoping to see UFOs. The legend of Area 51 began in November 1989, when a man named Bob Lazar came forward claiming to be a physicist who had worked on UFOs being tested there. Lazar said the UFOs were being reverse-engineered from alien technology recovered from crashed UFOs; their power source was a mysterious "Element 115" used to power antimatter reactors. He said that he had seen golf balls bouncing off "gravity waves" emitted by the reactors, that he had read autopsy reports of aliens killed in UFO crashes, and that the government knew the UFOs came from a planet orbiting the star known as Zeta Reticuli. Lazar further said that he held advanced degrees from MIT and Cal Tech, was previously a staff scientist at Los Alamos National Laboratory, and had been hired at Area 51 as a result of a personal recommendation by Dr. Edward Teller, the developer of the hydrogen bomb.

Lazar claimed the best place to see these UFOs being tested at Area 51 was near a black mailbox along Highway 375 (known ever since as the Black Mailbox, even though it was later painted white). In fact, he said he had escorted people up to Area 51 and the Black Mailbox in the months before he went public, and these witnesses supported Lazar's claims that strange lights and disc-shaped objects could be seen in the night skies near Rachel, the closest "town" to Area 51.

Unfortunately for him and those who wanted to believe his story, Lazar's credibility soon crashed to Earth like the UFOs he described. The first big hit came in April 1990, when he was arrested in Las Vegas on charges of pandering for prostitution (he was later convicted). With that, some previously credulous reporters finally began looking into his past. It turned out he did not have degrees from MIT or Cal Tech, but instead had attended (but not graduated from) Pierce Community College in California. He had indeed lived near Los Alamos, but had been employed as a photofinishing technician, not as a scientist. His biggest claim to fame in Los Alamos was apparently his attempt to mount a jet engine on his Honda CRX (he had vanity license plates that read JETUBET). His record after he moved to Las Vegas raised more questions, showing that he had filed for bankruptcy in 1986 due to a failed photofinishing business and had married his second wife before divorcing his first.

One reason why the Groom Lake area was selected for what became Area 51 is that it is surrounded by high mountains and invisible from adjacent roads. Visitors to Area 51 will see only warning signs at the boundary and a guardhouse at one entrance. But while American citizens can get arrested for taking a photo of the entrance gate to Area 51, the Russians have released photos taken of the base by one of their spy satellites. The most recent released photo (from April 2000) shows a sprawling, busy facility. The centerpiece of Area 51 is a runway, reportedly built sometime in the early 1990s, that is 11,960 feet long and 140 feet wide. The length and width of this runway is far beyond what is required for normal military and civilian aviation; such a runway would be ideal for short-winged aircraft that require high speed for enough lift to become airborne. Tire skid marks on this runway show it is heavily used. There also shorter runways. A large building with a white roof adjacent to an airplane terminal is believed to be an engineering facility for employees who fly in on daily government flights from Las Vegas and other places. What is believed to be the base headquarters building is located near the original hangers built for the U-2 project. There are also housing units for workers who do not commute daily. Most of Area 51's layout is a neat grid; from space, it looks like a housing subdivision next to an airport. There are also several parking areas and a surprising number of cars, given that workers arrive by either plane or bus—as far as is known, workers are not allowed to drive their private cars into Area 51.

While those who lived inside Area 51 to work on previous projects (like the F-117 stealth fighter) are reluctant to talk about classified projects, they do talk about the living and recreational facilities. A baseball diamond and tennis courts are visible in the satellite photos, and an indoor swimming pool, bowling alley, and gymnasium are available. The dining hall (named Sam's Club, after the last CIA director of Area 51) reportedly offers fresh seafood such as shrimp and lobster along with a well-stocked bar. Duty at Area 51, however, is generally difficult. Since most tests happen at night, many must keep a vampire-like schedule. Workers are restricted to only those sections of Area 51 essential for their work and living; they may be ordered inside or told to look away when a secret aircraft or other project is scheduled to come into view.

One of the most closely guarded secrets of Area 51 during the Cold War involved not American airplanes but Soviet ones. Beginning in 1967, an Air Force program known as "Red Hat" tested captured, stolen, and otherwise surreptitiously obtained Soviet aircraft to determine their capabilities and weaknesses. Among the craft tested here were the MiG-17, MiG-21, MiG-23, Su-22, and Su-27. Efforts are still be made to obtain the latest military aircraft from both Russia and China (usually by bribing corrupt officials). In fact, Red Hat has never been officially acknowledged to exist, but numerous daytime photographs of Soviet aircraft in the air over Area 51 (and a photo of a MiG-21 on the Area 51 runway, taken from an area now closed to the public) have provided conclusive proof that such craft are there.

The boundary of Area 51 is patrolled by a legendary security force dubbed the "Cammo Dudes" because of the camouflage clothing they often wear (although they sometimes appear in khakis). At the time this book was written, the Cammo Dudes were employees of EG&G Corporation, but in the past they have been employees of Wackenhut. For years their vehicle of choice was a white Jeep Cherokee, although they switched recently to tan Ford pickups that blend in well with the desert. They are heavily armed, including automatic weapons, and they are authorized (just as the warning signs say) to use deadly force to stop trespassers. While the Cammo Dudes work inside Area 51, they are restricted to its perimeters and probably know nothing more about its inner workings than the average person.

When Area 51 first burst into national attention in the early 1990s, the Cammo Dudes were famous for their aggressive behavior toward visitors, even those on public land miles from the actual boundary. They would leave Area 51 to challenge any approaching visitors, such as those driving the gravel road from Highway 375 to the main gate. Such visitors would find their cars closely followed or the road ahead blocked by one of the Jeep Cherokees; the local sheriff was invariably called and a deputy would soon arrive. Even though nothing could be done to such visitors as long as they remained on public land and roads, such tactics discouraged all but the most determined. Those who hiked to then public areas from which one could view Area 51 were routinely followed by Cammo Dudes, and occasionally were buzzed by a low-flying helicopter. Campers on public land near the boundary could expect a middle-of-the-night visit from Cammo Dudes. Area 51 folklore was full of tales of Cammo Dudes brandishing firearms and even of tires of cars approaching the boundary being shot out. Now that Area 51 is a tourist attraction, the Cammo Dudes are likely to leave visitors alone who remain in plain sight on the main access roads, although they routinely photograph all cars and visitors near the gates.

There are two approaches to Area 51 from Highway 375. The closest entrance from Rachel is the north gate, the road to which begins approximately 1.4 miles south of Rachel near mile marker 11.4; on maps this may be identified as Valley Road or Groom Road (not to be confused with Groom Lake Road). While the road is generally well maintained, slow and careful driving is recommended, since large rocks can cause flat tires. Follow the road for a little over ten miles until the guardhouse comes into view. Watch carefully for the warning signs as you approach the guardhouse; you will need to stop well before the guardhouse to avoid entering Area 51. If you are speeding or fail to note the signs (which are easy to miss when approaching at night), you may cross the border without realizing it.

The main gate is south of Rachel and is the most visited place on the Area 51 boundary. The easiest way to reach it is via the Groom Lake Road, a graded gravel road similar to the one leading to the north gate and about 24.5 miles south of Rachel on Highway 375, a little over five miles south of the Black Mailbox. Groom Lake Road is unmistakable, a long, straight road leading toward the west and Area 51. Satellite photos indicate that this road continues through Area 51 into the Nevada Test Site and eventually to Highway 95. Groom Lake Road at the main gate boundary is not blocked by a security gate (unlike the north gate), and the guardhouse is not visible from the main gate border—it is around a bend in the road approximately a half-mile past the boundary. You must not go past the warning signs under any circumstances! Driving past them to the guardhouse invites arrest. Stop short of the border, turn around, and park well over to the side of Groom Lake Road so as not to block traffic.

Among the interesting sites outside of Nevada, the White Sands Missile Range in New Mexico is the historic cradle of the Shadow Government. It was home to the first SAP, the Manhattan Project. After World War II, captured German V-2 missiles were studied and the first American rocket weapons systems developed and tested here. Today, White Sands remains the primary test and development site for smaller rockets (typically air-launched missiles) and many other secret weapons systems. Rumors persist that operational but still-secret stealth aircraft are based here. White Sands is northeast of Las Cruces, New Mexico and is roughly rectangular in shape; it measures about forty miles wide and about one hundred miles from north to south. As with the Nellis Range, much of White Sands hides behind mountains.

At the northern end of the White Sands Missile Range is the Trinity Site, where the first atomic bomb was successfully tested on July 16, 1945. In recent years, the Trinity Site has been open twice a year for escorted tours from the main gate at White Sands. Visitors can walk inside the crater left by the Trinity test, inspect the remains of Jumbo (the 214-ton containment vessel built for the first bomb but never used), and walk through the McDonald Ranch house, where the bomb was assembled.

Before the creation of Area 51 and the Tonopah Test Range, Edwards Air Force Base in California was America's major secret aircraft test site. The growing population of southern California has greatly reduced its isolation and thus its usefulness for secret tests. To the northeast of Edwards is the China Lake Naval Weapons Station, main test site for the Navy's next generation of airborne weapons. Adjacent to China Lake is Fort Irwin, a Rhode Island-sized facility used by the Army for weapons development. Together these facilities occupy almost as much area as the Nellis Range Complex in Nevada. Like the NRC, they are mostly hidden by mountains, and most of the territory of China Lake and Fort Irwin is very isolated.

In Utah is Dugway Proving Ground, home of the military's chemical and biological warfare research. Dugway, under the command of the U.S. Army, occupies almost 800,000 acres about eighty miles west of Salt Lake City. While Dugway once served for development and testing of biological and chemical weapons, today it is used for development of defensive systems (such as protective clothing and decontamination systems) against biological and chemical attacks. All tests occur inside sealed buildings, but that was not always the case. In March 1968, over 6400 sheep were found dead outside Dugway's boundaries but downwind from it. Autopsies showed the sheep had been killed by a deadly nerve gas known as "VX." While the Army never admitted responsibility, it did pay ranchers over $1 million in compensation for the lost sheep. The Army did admit it had conducted open-air tests of various chemical and biological agents, and the resulting public outcry forced future tests indoors.

Exactly what was tested at Dugway and whether any of it managed to escape the boundaries of the site remain classified. Substantial evidence suggests that persons living near Dugway were indeed exposed to chemical or biological agents (mainly the prevalence among them of lingering nervous system disorders consistent with exposure to low levels of chemical weapons). Groups of those who lived near Dugway in the 1950s and 1960s and believe they were exposed have formed to seek information about the open-air tests conducted then.

Subcontractors of the Shadow Government

Until the mid-1970s, the CIA and other agencies engaged in classified activities (especially covert ones) created front companies to carry out those activities. These front companies presented themselves as independent, for-profit businesses with no connections to the U.S. government. They existed to hide the classified activities or to do something the agency or government was forbidden to do. Perhaps the most famous front company was Air America, the cargo airline established by the CIA to carry out paramilitary operations in Southeast Asia during the Vietnam era. The Church committee hearings on the CIA in the mid-1970s resulted in legislation prohibiting the CIA and other agencies from setting up front companies.

This did not stop classified activities from being carried out through nongovernmental entities, however. Legitimate, for-profit companies had worked closely with the government on classified projects for years. Over the past quarter-century, these companies have handled a steadily increasing number of tasks that government agencies either cannot legally perform or do not want to acknowledge publicly. In many of these companies, there is a revolving-door exchange of senior managers to and from government posts. While private and for-profit, these companies have a clearly symbiotic relationship with the Shadow Government.

The granddaddy of all such companies is Edgerton, Germeshausen & Grier (EG&G), born in the early days of the Shadow Government. Harold Edgerton, a professor at the Massachusetts Institute of Technology, developed the strobe technique of high-speed photography in 1931. He formed a consulting business with a former MIT student, Ken Germeshausen, to commercialize the process, and another former MIT student, Herbert Grier, joined them later. During the Manhattan Project, the nascent Shadow Government realized it needed a method to photograph the different stages of an atomic explosion. It turned to Edgerton, Germeshausen, and Grier, who designed the cameras that took the memorable sequence of photos of the first atomic bomb test in 1945. Soon the three incorporated as EG&G and were busy photographing atomic tests in Nevada and the Pacific. They won additional government contracts to develop instrumentation for monitoring atomic tests and provide support services for nuclear weapons testing and manufacturing. EG&G went public in 1959 and began to acquire additional companies, such as Reynolds Electrical and Engineering (REECo), which for years was the main contractor at the Nevada Test Site. Beginning in the 1960s, EG&G started providing security for various government sites, including the Nevada Test Site and what became known as Area 51.

In August 1999, EG&G underwent a metamorphosis. Its civilian engineering and research divisions were by then far larger in terms of revenue and employees than the government services division. That month, EG&G sold its government services division to the Carlyle Group, a private global equity firm based in Washington, DC. EG&G then renamed itself "Perkin Elmer" (after one of the companies it had acquired), and the now-privately owned government services division took the name "EG&G." No longer burdened with the detailed annual disclosures required of publicly held companies, the transformed EG&G can conceal its revenue sources.

The company, headquartered at 900 Clopper Road, Gaithersburg, Maryland, acknowledges contracts with NASA, the Defense Logistics Agency, and the Departments of Defense, Energy, and Treasury. It states that it has about 4200 employees and annual revenues of over $500 million.

The management of the Carlyle Group is well suited for business with the Shadow Government. Its current chairman is Frank Carlucci, secretary of defense during the Reagan Administration. Its senior counselor is James Baker, a former secretary of state. Many of its partners and managers have worked for various government agencies, especially the Department of Defense.

One of EG&G's most interesting operations is Janet Airlines, a commuter airline that transports over a thousand workers each day from Las Vegas to Area 51 and the Tonopah Test Range in Nevada. It is also reliably reported that some Janet flights go to White Sands Missile Range. Janet Airlines takes its name from the identifier used by its pilots when communicating with air-traffic controllers. The name does not appear on any of the aircraft, which are white with a single red stripe running down the length of the fuselage and identifying numbers that indicate they are registered to the Air Force. While the meaning of "Janet" is classified, it is rumored to stand for "Joint Air Network for Employee Transportation." Janet uses mainly Boeing 737s along with some smaller Beechcraft planes. Flights depart from a private, secure terminal near McCarran Airport on Haven Street in Las Vegas. Public records show that the terminal is leased to EG&G.

Flights follow normal work commuting hours, departing Las Vegas
in the morning and arriving from Area 51 in the late afternoon and early
evening. Flights operate on Monday through Friday; any weekend flights
are widely considered a good sign that something exceptional is happening
at one of the locations serviced by Janet. The little airline's terminal looks
ordinary, except for the high fence (topped with barbed wire) and security
guard patrols. Persons parked on Haven Street may be told to move by
Las Vegas police, but good view of the terminal, parking lot, and Janet
airplanes arriving and departing can be had from many high-rise hotels on
the strip. A room facing McCarran in the Mandalay Bay, Luxor, Excalibur,
Hacienda, MGM Grand, or Tropicana affords a view of activity at the
terminal, including arrivals and departures.

When the Shadow Government needs something built, it often calls
Bechtel Corporation of San Francisco. In Bechtel's promotional literature,
the company points with pride to some of the projects it has built: Hoover
Dam, the San Francisco-Oakland Bay Bridge, the "Chunnel" between
England and France, and the Bay Area Rapid Transit (BART) system. It
downplays its management of the Nevada Test Site, its offices in areas
(such as Oak Ridge, Tennessee) where the top-secret government is the
only game in town, and its history of serving as building contractor for
secret projects.

Bechtel, founded in 1898, has over 41,000 employees worldwide, with
revenues in recent years topping $14 billion. It is a private company mainly
owned and managed by the Bechtel family, although some prominent
outsiders with government connections (such as former secretary of state
George Shultz) have served as executives and board members.

Bechtel has special expertise in large-scale underground construction,
as demonstrated by the "Chunnel." The company even authored a report
for the National Science Foundation, *Research Report for Tomorrow's
Needs in Tunneling and Excavation*. Besides the usual tunneling methods
(water jets, various types of drills, borers, and hammers, etc.), the report
discussed such methods as lasers, plasmas, microwaves, electron beam
guns, and "electrical disintegration." Since Bechtel is a private company,
it does not have to publicize its income sources and projects in detail, but it
is likely that Bechtel has been involved in some large "black" construction
projects.

The most interesting part of Bechtel's operations is Bechtel Nevada,
which operates and manages the Nevada Test Site (and also has, despite

its name, operations outside of Nevada). As Bechtel's publicity materials explain, "Bechtel Nevada partners with the Lawrence Livermore National Laboratory, Los Alamos National Laboratory, and Sandia National Laboratories on many projects. Bechtel Nevada also works on projects for other federal agencies such as the Defense Threat Reduction Agency, NASA, the Nuclear Regulatory Commission, and the U.S. Air Force, Army, and Navy." Bechtel Nevada's operations are assisted by Lockheed Martin and Johnson Controls, Inc.

Two of Bechtel Nevada's other activities include, in their words, "stockpile stewardship" and "national security response." Stockpile stewardship involves "experimental capabilities necessary to maintain confidence in the safety and performance of weapons in the United States nuclear weapons stockpile," while national security response is described cryptically as "timely, worldwide support throughout the Emergency Response stages of pre-crisis, crisis, and consequence management."

Bechtel Nevada also maintains a special technologies laboratory in Santa Barbara, California, of which it says, "Scientists at the STL design and develop compact, rugged sensor systems for numerous projects including ground penetrating radar, thermo graphic phosphor techniques, associated particle imaging and laser-induced fluorescence imaging. Other activities include sensors for ultra-high magnetic fields, very high bandwidth optical data recording and radiation sensors." From this description, it seems likely that Bechtel Nevada is heavily involved with development of systems for the detection of clandestine nuclear facilities and stockpiles.

In Palmdale, California is the modestly named Plant 42, which is not a single plant, but several different installations inside a common restricted area encompassing 5800 acres. While most of the facilities are privately owned, they are operated under the control and direction of the Air Force. Lockheed Martin, Boeing, and Northup Grumman have operations at Plant 42; EG&G also operates inside Plant 42 and is believed to supply security guards and other support services. From the nearby Palmdale airport EG&G also operates some Janet Airlines flights believed to go to Area 51 and the Tonopah Test Range in Nevada.

There are eight main plants and numerous smaller buildings, each identified by a number. Buildings visible from public roads are enormous hangars clearly intended for aircraft construction, much like those used for building commercial jetliners. The airspace above Plant 42 is off-limits to all unauthorized civilian and military traffic. Under an agreement with the Air Force, the Palmdale Airport can accommodate a certain number of civilian flights each day. According to an Air Force press release, "Air Force Plant 42's production flight test installation is specifically tailored to the production, flight testing, modification and depot maintenance of the nation's most advanced aerospace systems built under government contract." Plant 42 employs about 8500 people.

Not everything at Plant 42 is military; the Space Shuttles were built there and undergo periodic refurbishing there. But Plant 42 is best known for building highly advanced, classified military aircraft and is the current home of Lockheed's famed Skunk Works (responsible for the U-2, SR-71, and F-117 stealth fighter). It is safe to assume that they are working on a new generation of similarly amazing aircraft inside Plant 10. As with most other high security installations, the most intriguing things happen late on weeknights. Air Force C-5 and C-141 transport planes sometimes depart here at such times, believed to be carrying disassembled aircraft to sites such as Area 51 and White Sands. Large covered flatbed trucks also leave Plant 42 in the wee hours and travel toward Edwards Air Force Base. Security is tight. Photography of the facilities is prohibited, and persons parked along public roads around the site have been told to move on by local sheriff's deputies.

Sometimes the Shadow Government needs a company to do its dirty work. In the past, one of those companies has been Wackenhut Corporation of Palm Beach Gardens, Florida, founded in 1954 by George Wackenhut. Wackenhut, a former FBI agent, was a close friend of Florida politicians, including Senator George Smathers (a close friend of President Kennedy) and Governor Claude Kirk, and he turned those connections into a contract for his company to provide security services at Cape Canaveral. Another contract quickly followed to provide security for Titan missile silos around the country. Soon Wackenhut Corporation was the largest supplier of security services to the federal government. It protected embassies in thirteen countries, including Chile, Greece, and El Salvador. It also protected the Alaskan oil pipeline, the Savannah River Plant and Hanford nuclear weapons facilities, the Strategic Petroleum Reserve, the Nevada Test Site, and Area 51.

Throughout its history, Wackenhut's board of directors has been a who's-who of the military-industrial complex, partly explaining its success in securing lucrative government contracts. Among the members have been Captain Eddie Rickenbacker, General Mark Clark, former FBI director Clarence Kelley, former secretary of defense Frank Carlucci, former Secret Service director James Rowley, and former CIA director Bobby Ray Inman.

Besides guarding government assets and secrets, Wackenhut also excelled at collecting data on Americans suspected of being Communist sympathizers or just leaning to the left. In 1965, the Wackenhut Corporation went public, and in its initial public offering documents filed with the Securities and Exchange Commission, the company boasted of maintaining files on 2.5 million Americans—that is, a file on one out of 46 Americans over the age of 18 then living. After Congress held hearings in 1975 on companies maintaining such files, Wackenhut donated its files to the Church League of America, a now-defunct anti-Communist group based in Wheaton, Illinois.

When the 1976 Congressional hearings chaired by Senator Frank Church of Idaho forced the CIA to abandon its practice of setting up front companies in the United States, the CIA began to contract with companies such as Wackenhut to do the same things. Wackenhut soon gained a reputation as one of the companies the CIA called when it wanted something done. "I don't have the slightest doubt that the CIA and Wackenhut overlap," said Philip Agee, a former CIA agent turned author. William Hinshaw, a retired FBI special agent, said, "It is known throughout the industry that if you want a dirty job done, call Wackenhut."

During much of the Reagan administration, those "dirty jobs" were in Central America. In 1981 Wackenhut formed a new Special Projects Division headed by George Berckmans, a former CIA agent assigned to the Mexico City CIA station (Berckmans left Wackenhut soon after the new division was formed). Wackenhut's expansion into Central America was rapid and large; in 1985, Wackenhut had over 1500 employees in El Salvador alone. Wackenhut employees kept company with such persons as Eden Pastora, military leader of the Nicaraguan Contras.

Wackenhut was also involved in some curious activities in the United States. The September 1992 issue of *Spy* magazine carried a report of some strange goings-on involving Wackenhut in the winter of 1990. David Ramirez and three other members of the company's special investigations division were sent to San Antonio from their headquarters in Miami. In San Antonio, they rented two Ford Tauruses and drove four hours to the Mexican border town of Eagle Pass. After night fell, they met two truck drivers and then went to a warehouse where an eighteen-wheel tractor-trailer waited. Ramirez's instructions were simple: to avoid looking inside the trailer, to secure it, and to make sure it got to Chicago. Armed with shotguns, the Wackenhut workers escorted the truck north. They drove for thirty hours, stopping only for food and fuel. They eventually drove the truck to an empty warehouse near Chicago, where others took possession of it and told them to fly home to Miami. Ramirez's superiors told him the truck contained $40 million in food stamps; other special investigations division employees told him they had made similar runs from the Mexican border.

Ramirez, however, found the "food stamps" story unbelievable because of the secrecy and high level of security, and he eventually talked to reporters after leaving Wackenhut. In its report, *Spy* queried the Department of Agriculture, who emphatically denied that any food stamps were ever shipped in such a way; nor was there any food stamp printing, distribution, or storage facility in the Eagle Pass area (moreover, food stamps are shipped from metropolitan areas to rural areas, not vice versa). *Spy* theorized the shipments were components of chemical weapons and were destined for Iraq. Whatever the truck's contents were, they were clearly of a clandestine or contraband nature.

After the election of President Clinton in 1992, Wackenhut began scaling back its government security operations and, it must be assumed, its other government services. It did not renew its contracts to provide security to the Nevada Test Site and Area 51, for example (these were taken over by EG&G). Instead, Wackenhut began expanding its "corrections" business, and is now the largest operator of privately run prisons in the United States. Reportedly, providing correction is more lucrative than providing security, although some believe that Wackenhut saw dim prospects for many of its previous contracts because of their dependence on the company's close ties to departed Republican administrations.

If the CIA were ever to be privatized, the result would probably be a company much like Veridian Corporation. Headquartered in Arlington, Virginia, Veridian is publicly traded on the New York Stock Exchange and employs over five thousand persons in more than fifty locations throughout the United States. Its business, according to its web site, is to be "a leading provider of information-based systems, integrated solutions and services to the U.S. government. We specialize in mission-critical national security programs, primarily for the national intelligence community, the Department of Defense, law enforcement and other U.S. government agencies."

Veridian lists among its offerings chemical, biological, and nuclear detection, intelligence, surveillance and reconnaissance, "knowledge discovery and decision support," counterintelligence, information protection, critical infrastructure protection, and network security. The company says it has over 1300 contracts with the government, but does not specify any of its clients or projects. There is obviously a need for its services, however; revenues for the fiscal year ending December 31, 2001 topped $690 million. Its managers and board members include many who have served at high levels of the military and federal government.

A recent advertisement by Veridian sought applicants for positions as "counterintelligence and antiterrorism analysts." Candidates would need "to have strong all-source and/or cyber-analytical experience in counterintelligence and antiterrorism" and the positions would be "in support of U.S. government contracts in fields of CI, antiterrorism/force protection, cyber CI, information operations and technology protection. . . [E]xperience may be in offensive or defensive mode." These are job descriptions and qualifications previously associated with the CIA, further indicating Veridian's role in government intelligence projects. The key question, however, is why the government works through a company such as Veridian instead of hiring the kinds of help it needs directly. The answer cannot be determined from publicly available information, but the most obvious reason would be that Veridian can do things the CIA is either prohibited from doing or does not wish to be associated with.

One of the front companies the CIA was forced to sell in the 1970s was Intermountain Aviation, which had provided charter services for a variety of CIA operations. Intermountain was purchased by Evergreen Aviation, a small helicopter services company based in McMinnville, Oregon. After the acquisition, one of Evergreen's directors was George Doole, the former head of all of the CIA's aviation front companies (including the legendary Air America). Doole steered much CIA-related business to Evergreen; for example, when the CIA needed to transport the recently deposed Shah of Iran from Panama to Egypt in 1980, Doole charted an Evergreen DC-8 for the trip. During the 1980s, Evergreen was described by the *New York Times* and CBS News as under contract to the CIA for transportation services in support of the Nicaraguan Contras.

Today Evergreen is privately held, so its revenues, and customers, are not publicly disclosed. In the mid-1990s, the company defaulted on $125 million in junk bonds issued to finance the acquisition of new aircraft (including 747s). It faced the possibility of having to declare bankruptcy, which would have opened up its financial records—including its creditors and customers. In December 1996, however, Evergreen announced that an unnamed financial institution had agreed to help it buy back all of the $125 million in defaulted junk bonds. Many have speculated that the unnamed financial institution was the U.S. government. Evergreen consistently denies any formal ties to the CIA or other elements of the U.S. intelligence community.

CHAPTER SIX

THE MILITARY AND CIVILIAN LAW ENFORCEMENT

IN LATE JULY OF 2002, proposals came from both Republicans and Democrats to give the U.S. military a larger and more active role in civilian law enforcement in order to battle terrorism. In an interview televised on Fox News Sunday, Senator Joseph Biden (D-Delaware) said that the Posse Comitatus Act of 1878, which prohibits the U.S. military from civilian law enforcement within the United States, "has to be amended." Senator Biden said, "We're not talking about general police power," but also said he was concerned about what the military could do if they found terrorists in the United States with chemical, biological, or nuclear weapons. "The military would not be able to shoot to kill if they were approaching the weapons," Biden said, nor could they arrest any of the terrorists. Tom Ridge, the homeland security director, echoed Biden's concerns later that day on CNN. "We need to be talking about military assets in anticipation of a crisis event," Ridge said. "And clearly if you're talking about using the military, then you should have a discussion about Posse Comitatus. It's not out of the question when, in support of civilian authorities, we would give the National Guard or troops arrest ability."

Some military leaders seemed anxious to assume new responsibilities within the United States. Air Force General Ralph Eberhardt, selected in June 2002 by President Bush to head the new Northern Command, told the *New York Times* that he personally favored new laws to give the U.S. military expanded domestic powers during national emergencies. "We should always be reviewing things like Posse Comitatus and other laws if we think it ties our hands in protecting the American people," General Eberhardt told the *Times*.

The reaction to these suggestions was strong and strangely bipartisan; both liberals and conservatives expressed alarm at the possibility of subjecting U.S. citizens to control by American armed forces. Supporters of Ridge's plan countered that soldiers, mostly from the National Guard, had long been involved in civilian law enforcement during emergencies, performing such duties as arresting looters after natural disasters. Further, supporters of the suggestion noted, National Guard troops had already been deployed at U.S. airports, after the September 11 attacks, to perform quasi-law enforcement tasks such as screening passengers and inspecting baggage. The proposed changes, they said, were only minor extensions of what the military was already doing in connection with civilian law enforcement.

Unfortunately, the role of the military in civilian law enforcement was not debated in time to help Ezequiel Hernandez, an eighteen-year-old high school student from Redford, Texas, a small town on the U.S.-Mexico border. On May 20, 1997, he was tending his family's herd of goats, carrying as usual a .22-caliber rifle to kill coyotes, rattlesnakes, javelinas, and other pests common there. Shortly before 6 p.m., Hernandez's sister and other locals heard a single shot. Investigation later revealed that Ezequiel had been killed by a shot fired from an M-16 rifle by a U.S. Marine.

The Marine was part of a patrol of four Marines, all in camouflage and full combat gear, assigned to the U.S.-Mexico border as part of Joint Task Force 6, a military-civilian anti-drug-smuggling effort based at Biggs Army Airfield near El Paso, Texas. No one in Redford knew that Marines would be on patrol near their town. The Marines claimed that Ezequiel had fired two shots at them, and two spent .22 shells were produced as evidence. But Ezequiel was described by the residents of Redford as someone with better sense than to open fire on armed soldiers. The Marines wore camouflage designed for the desert countryside around Redford, and locals speculated that Ezequiel may have seen some movement and opened fire thinking it was a coyote. Other locals, noting that no one was alerted about military patrols of the area, said Ezequiel may have thought the Marines were robbers or others out to harm him. Joint Task Force 6 issued few details about the incident (such as whether the Marines verbally warned Ezequiel before opening fire or did anything to provoke fire from him). And Ezequiel Hernandez could not tell his side of the story. A grand jury was convened to investigate but returned no charges against the Marines.

People in Redford angrily observed that the grand jury included many government employees, compromising its impartiality.

Surprisingly, the involvement of the U.S. military in civilian law enforcement was legal until 1878. After the Civil War, troops in the occupied South performed virtually all civilian law enforcement functions, and in 1876 President Grant used federal troops to supervise elections throughout the South. Worried that Grant was developing Bonapartist tendencies, Congress passed the Posse Comitatus Act of 1878, forbidding the use of the U.S. military for civilian law enforcement in the United States. The Act specified fines and imprisonment for anyone, general or president, who violated it.

As a result, American armed forces played a minor role in civilian law enforcement (most exceptions were during World War II) until the 1960s, when urban riots resulted in the development of contingency plans for using federal troops to restore order. In the 1970s, the "war on drugs" set precedents for the use of military hardware (such as helicopters, for surveillance of suspected drug smuggling and growing areas) in civilian law enforcement. The military also helped train paramilitary civilian law enforcement units such as the special weapons and tactics (SWAT) units that many big-city police departments seemed eager to have. This militarization increased steadily during the Reagan and first Bush administrations, but something curious started happening after the inauguration of Bill Clinton in 1993. Despite Clinton's reputation as a liberal with a distaste (if not a contempt) for the military, it was during his administration that military forces began conducting drills and simulated assaults in American urban areas. These drills had nothing whatsoever to do with the "war on drugs," but were instead obvious preparations for military actions against American civilians on U.S. soil. The Clinton administration sought and won Congressional approval for changes in the law that would allow the president or secretary of defense to use soldiers within the United States to respond to the threat of terrorist action. And what constitutes a "threat" of terrorist action? As with "national emergency," the definition is up to the president. A new command, the U.S. Joint Forces Command, was established on October 7, 1999 to coordinate the use of troops domestically if so ordered by the president or secretary of defense. Speaking at the ceremony inaugurating the new command, then secretary of defense William Cohen told his audience, "The American people should not be concerned about [the use of soldiers in domestic situations]. They should welcome it."

What Cohen did not mention—and may not have known—is that federal law had already permitted the president, when declaring a national emergency, also to declare a state of martial law and to use U.S. military forces to control, arrest, and, if necessary, use deadly force against the civilian population of the United States. In fact, if a local military commander feels the situation warrants the immediate imposition of martial law, he can do so in the absence of a presidential declaration.

Admittedly, this sounds like paranoid ravings from the political fringes. Unfortunately, it is also true.

THE POSSE COMITATUS ACT

"Posse comitatus" means, literally, the power of the county. The phrase originated in England, where the sheriff of a county would issue a declaration calling upon all able-bodied men to help him track down criminals or maintain public order. The posses formed by the local sheriff in so many Western movies were an example of the posse comitatus principle in action. While law enforcement in America today is usually the work of trained professionals, the principle of posse comitatus survives as part of common law, and there are some states where local sheriffs could, in theory, organize a posse of ordinary citizens to perform various law enforcement duties.

The British were not reluctant to use troops to enforce civilian laws, which was a major grievance of the American colonists. Indeed, the Declaration of Independence complains about such abuses; "He has affected to render the military independent of, and superior to, the civil power" and "quartering large bodies of armed troops among us" are two of its accusations against George III. The memory of such uses of military power partly explains the Constitution's naming of an elected civilian, the president, as commander in chief of all American military forces.

Despite this, presidents have often ordered American military forces to enforce federal laws. George Washington was the first to do so, sending in federal troops to put down Shay's Rebellion in 1787 and the Whiskey Rebellion in 1794. In 1807, Congress passed a law (later repealed) which named the U.S. Army as the enforcer of federal laws (this was aimed more at state governments that might try to ignore federal laws than at individuals). In 1846, federal troops were used in Philadelphia to suppress anti-Catholic riots, and in 1850 to restore calm during battle between pro-

and anti-slavery forces in Kansas. In 1854, Congress gave the U.S. Army the responsibility for enforcing fugitive slave laws, and in 1859 John Brown was captured and executed by federal troops for his attempts to start a slave rebellion.

Chapter two noted that Abraham Lincoln used executive orders freely during the Civil War, and used federal troops to enforce them. Besides sending them to arrest Clement Vallandigham, Lincoln also used Army soldiers to shut down newspapers opposed to the war and to round up draft resisters. In 1863, soldiers shot and killed several people opposed to the draft during "draft riots" (although we would call them "demonstrations" today) in New York City.

After the Civil War, the U.S. Army occupied the South and, in effect, governed it until 1877. By that time, there was widespread opposition to the use of federal troops for any sort of domestic law enforcement. The heavy-handed use of the Army in the northern states was still remembered, and in the South federal troops were keeping Republican state governments in power. Worried about the growing power of the Democrats, President Grant ordered federal troops to supervise the 1876 elections in the South. There were many reports of troops coercing voters to vote Republican; troops seized ballot boxes in areas known to favor the Democrats. The Republican presidential candidate, Rutherford B. Hayes, won in a disputed outcome (eventually decided by a commission composed of members of Congress and the Supreme Court) remarkably similar to the 2000 presidential election. But Democrats managed to win working control of Congress, and they were able to force withdrawal of federal troops from the South and to enact the Posse Comitatus Act in 1878.

The key portion of the Act reads, "Whosoever, except in cases and under circumstances expressly authorized by the Constitution or Act of Congress, willfully uses any part of the Army or a force as a posse comitatus or otherwise to execute the laws shall be fined under this title or imprisoned." Exceptions were later made for the National Guard, which was considered to be under the command of state governors, and for the Coast Guard, which, in its history, has been part of civilian agencies such as the Treasury and the Department of Transportation.

From 1878 to World War II, the military kept out of domestic law enforcement, except for President Wilson's use of Army troops in a mining labor dispute in Colorado. That changed after Pearl Harbor. For example, the forced relocation of Japanese Americans to detention centers was carried out by Army soldiers. On occasion, federal troops were used to close public highways to permit military traffic to pass or to close off public lands, normally open to everyone, where drills and exercises were being conducted. The degree of restraint shown in domestic use of military forces was remarkable, considering the tenor of the times and the threat facing the United States. After World War II, the domestic use of regular federal soldiers became extremely rare.

But that started to change in the 1960s with Operation Garden Plot, which is still the basic plan for using U.S. military forces domestically.

OPERATION GARDEN PLOT

The summer of 1967 was a violent one in cities such as Detroit, Newark, Cleveland, Seattle, Cincinnati, and Milwaukee, as angry blacks took to the streets and rioted. Over one hundred cities reported riots that summer, including small cities such as Augusta, Georgia. The riots were especially violent in Detroit and Newark, where civil government, for all intents and purposes, broke down for several days. Twenty-seven people died in Newark, and forty-three died in Detroit. The riots continued in both cities for six days before finally being brought under control. Their effect on the nation's psyche was shattering. In response to the riots President Lyndon Johnson issued Executive Order 11365 on July 29, 1967. This established the National Advisory Commission on Civil Disorders, chaired by Illinois governor Otto Kerner. The "Kerner Commission" was directed to investigate the causes of the riots and possible measures to prevent future ones.

On March 1, 1968, the Kerner Commission presented its report, which included the memorable observation that "we live in two increasingly separate Americas." The Kerner Commission recommended improved educational opportunities, social services, housing, and economic development in the areas hardest hit by the riots. Because of such recommendations, the Kerner Commission report today is remembered mainly as a statement of social conscience and government responsibility toward America's underclass. But a close reading of the full report reveals something else: the Kerner Commission also recommended an expanded role for the military in dealing with extraordinary events like the 1967 riots. In the section headed "Army Response to Civil Disorders," the report includes such statements as "the Department of the Army should participate fully in efforts to develop nonlethal weapons and personal protective equipment for use in civil disorders," and "the Army should investigate the possibility of using psychological techniques to ventilate hostility and lessen tension in riot control." The report recommended improved riot control training for National Guard troops and that the Army investigate the possibility of special riot training for its troops.

The Army liked the Kerner Commission's suggestions. Beside the threat of more riots in black urban areas, protests against the Vietnam War were growing larger and more militant. In June 1968 a "Directorate of Military Support" had been established at the Pentagon under the Department of the Army. According to James Button, author of *Black Violence: The Political Impact of the 1960s Riots*, the Directorate had 150 officers who monitored domestic civil disturbances around the clock, much as their colleagues at Cheyenne Mountain maintained a constant vigil for Soviet attack. Sophisticated computer systems were installed to store and analyze all public displays of political dissent. Over 20,000 troops were made available for riot control duty. And the Directorate developed policies and advice for handling domestic situations, much as other Army officers at the Pentagon developed plans for repelling a Warsaw Pact attack.

Somewhere along the line, the plans produced by the Directorate acquired the name "Operation Garden Plot," first publicly uttered in 1971 when Senator Sam Ervin (D-North Carolina), chair of the Senate Subcommittee on Constitutional Rights, held hearings about allegations of Army spying on U.S. civilians. The hearings revealed that the Army had indeed been keeping records on hundreds of thousands of American citizens connected with antiwar and radical politics, and that such activities were part of Operation Garden Plot. The Subcommittee also found that the Army had trained civilian law enforcement workers with simulated battles against rioters and large groups of protesters. It also found that Army units went on alert in May 1970 for possible response to campus demonstrations in the wake of the Kent State shootings.

There is a large gap from 1971 to 1984 in our knowledge of Operation Garden Plot. While it was apparently still operational in those years, information about it either remains classified or has yet to be uncovered through Freedom of Information Act (FOIA) requests. But Operation Garden Plot was active in 1984—an understatement. A document titled "United States Air Force Civil Disturbance Plan 55-1, Garden Plot" was obtained in 1990 by researchers under a FOIA request. Dated July 11, 1984, the document is over 200 pages (although the pages are not numbered) and was not classified. The opening of Plan 55-1 noted, however, "Although it is unclassified, it is for official use only as directed by AFR 12-30. This plan contains information that is of internal use to DOD and, through disclosure, would tend to allow persons to violate the law or hinder enforcement of the law." It also said, "operations orders and operating procedures must be designed to provide the highest degree of security possible" and "in the event of organized opposition some sort of advisory intelligence gathering capability should be assumed."

It can be safely assumed that the Army and Navy/Marine Corps have similar Operation Garden Plot planning documents, and that a master plan belongs to the Department of Defense. It is also safe to assume that FEMA and other civilian agencies have planning documents for their participation in Operation Garden Plot, although repeated FOIA requests to those agencies have produced no comparable documents to the Air Force's Plan 55-1. Many believe that the release of Plan 55-1 was inadvertent and the document should have been classified; the Operation Garden Plot documents at other agencies are believed classified and thus exempt from release under FOIA.

Plan 55-1 says the Air Force's role in Operation Garden Plot would include "aerial resupply, aerial reconnaissance, airborne psychological operations, command and control communications systems, aeromedical evacuation, helicopter and weather support." As an example of the Air Force's role, Plan 55-1 includes this remarkable statement: "In response to the US invasion of Cambodia, student unrest broke out. Under Operation Garden Plot, from April 30 through May 4, 1970 9th Air Force airlift units transported civil disturbance control forces from Ft. Bragg to various locations throughout the eastern US." This confirmed the findings of the 1971 Ervin Subcommittee.

Plan 55-1 specifies the targets of Operation Garden Plot as "disruptive elements, extremists or dissidents perpetrating civil disorder." "Civil disorder" is defined as "riot, acts of violence, insurrections, unlawful obstructions or assemblages, or other disorders prejudicial to public law and order." It also defines "civil disturbance" as "all domestic conditions requiring the use of federal forces pursuant to the provisions of Chapter 15, Title 10, United States Code." When will Operation Garden Plot be put into effect? When situations exist "that threaten to reach or have reached such proportions that civil authorities cannot or will not maintain public order." The authority for putting it into effect will be "the Presidential Proclamation and Executive Order in which the Secretary of Defense has been directed to restore law and order" with additional details "further defined by the Letter of Instruction issued to Task Force Commanders by the Chief of Staff, US Army."

Plan 55-1 states, under the heading "Force Requirements," that "US Army and Marine Corps units designated for civil disturbance operations will be trained, equipped and maintained in readiness for rapid deployment, ten brigades, prepared for rapid deployment anywhere in CONUS. A Quick Reaction Force (QRF) will be considered to be on a 24 hour alert status and capable of attaining a CIDCON 4 status in 12 hours." Under the heading "Summary of the Counterintelligence and Security Situation," it adds, "spontaneous civil disturbances which involve large numbers of persons and/or which continue for a considerable period of time, may exceed the capacity of local civil law enforcement agencies to suppress. Although this type of activity can arise without warning as a result of sudden, unanticipated popular unrest (past riots in such cities as Miami, Detroit and Los Angeles serve as examples) it may also result from more prolonged dissidence. . . if military forces are called upon to restore order, they must expect to have only limited information available regarding the perpetrators, their motives, capabilities, and intentions."

Another FOIA request turned up United States Army field manual 19-15, dated November 1985 and titled "Civil Disturbances." The introduction says that the purpose of the manual is to provide "guidance for the commander and his staff in preparing for and providing assistance to civil authorities in civil disturbance control operations" and notes, "the DA Civil Disturbance Plan, known as Garden Plot, provides guidance to all DOD components in planning civil disturbance missions."

Field manual 19-15 further states, "the president can employ armed federal troops to suppress insurrection, domestic violence, unlawful assemblies, and conspiracy if such acts deprive the people of their constitutional rights and a state's civil authorities cannot or will not provide adequate protection . . . federal intervention in civil disturbances begins with the issuance of a presidential proclamation to the citizens engaged in the disturbance."

Some of the most eye-opening sections of field manual 19-15 discuss actions the Army could take if ordered by the president to intervene in a civil disturbance. For example, "when at all possible, civil law enforcement agents are integrated with the military control force team making apprehensions," but "if police are not available, military personnel may search people incident to an apprehension." Further, "authorities must be prepared to detain large numbers of people. . . if there are more detainees than civil detention facilities can handle, civil authorities may ask the control forces to set up and operate temporary facilities. . . These temporary facilities are set up on the nearest military installation or on suitable property under federal control. . . supervised and controlled by MP officers and NCOs trained and experienced in Army correctional operations. Guards and support personnel under direct supervision and control of MP officers and NCOs need not be trained or experienced in Army correctional operations. But they must be specifically instructed and closely supervised in the proper use of force." The manual includes information on processing detainees and says, "release procedures must be coordinated with civil authorities and appropriate legal counsel." In an echo of Lincoln's suspension of the writ of habeas corpus during the Civil War, it further states that if a state court issues a writ of habeas corpus demanding a detainee be charged or released, the local Army commander should "respectfully reply that the prisoner is being held by authority of the United States." Concerning training for Operation Garden Plot, the manual says that the objective is to "develop personnel who are able to perform distasteful and dangerous duties with discipline and objectivity. . . every member of the control force must be trained to use his weapon and special equipment, riot batons, riot control agent dispersers and CS grenades, grenade launchers, shotguns, sniper rifles, cameras, portable videotape recorders, portable public address systems, night illumination devices, firefighting apparatus, grappling hooks, ladders, ropes, bulldozers, Army aircraft, armored personnel carriers, and roadblock and barricade materials."

Field manual 19-15 also touches on the uses of martial law. It says "martial rule is based on public necessity. Public necessity in this sense means public safety." The manual continues, "If the need for martial rule arises, the military commander at the scene must so inform the Army Chief of Staff and await instructions. If martial rule is imposed, the civilian population must be informed of the restrictions and rules of conduct that the military can enforce." What are these "restrictions and rules of conduct"? According to the manual, "during a civil disturbance, it may be advisable to prevent people from assembling. Civil law can make it unlawful for people to meet to plan an act of violence, rioting, or civil disturbance. Prohibitions on assembly may forbid gatherings at any place and time. . . making hostile or inflammatory speeches advocating the overthrow of the lawful government and threats against public officials, if it endangered public safety, could violate such law."

That section of field manual 19-15 raises the question of what exactly constitutes martial law. Interestingly, there appear to be no federal statutes defining "martial law," so presumably we are left with its common law definition as control of a civilian population by military forces and the suspension of civil law in favor of direct military orders. The clearest statement about martial law in federal law is in the Code of Federal Regulations, Title 32 (National Defense), Subtitle A (Department of Defense), Chapter V (Department of the Army), Subchapter A (Aid of Civil Authorities and Public Relations), Part 501 (Employment of Troops in Aid of Civil Authorities). The relevant section is 501.4, and here it is in its entirety:

§501.4 MARTIAL LAW

It is unlikely that situations requiring the commitment of Federal Armed Forces will necessitate the declaration of martial law. When Federal Armed Forces are committed in the event of civil disturbances, their proper role is to support, not supplant, civil authority. Martial law depends for its justification upon public necessity. Necessity gives rise to its creation; necessity justifies its exercise; and necessity limits its duration. The extent of military force used and the actual measures taken, consequently, will depend upon the actual threat to order and public safety which exists at the time. In most instances the decision to impose martial law is made by the President, who normally announces his decision by a proclamation, which usually contains his instructions concerning its exercise and limitations thereon. However, the decision to impose martial law may be made by the commander on the spot, if the circumstances demand immediate action, and time and available communications facilities do not permit obtaining prior approval from higher authority (§ 501.2). Whether or not a proclamation exists, it is incumbent upon commanders concerned to weigh every proposed action against the threat to public order and safety it is designed to meet, in order that the necessity therefore may be ascertained. When Federal Armed Forces have been committed in an objective area in a martial law situation, the population of the affected area will be informed of the rules of conduct and other restrictive measures the military is authorized to enforce. These will normally be announced by proclamation or order and will be given the widest possible publicity by all available media. Federal Armed Forces ordinarily will exercise police powers previously inoperative in the affected area, restore and maintain order, insure the essential mechanics of distribution, transportation, and communication, and initiate necessary relief measures.

From the wording of 501.4, it seems that "martial law," like "national emergency," can mean almost anything the president wants it to mean. That is to be expected, but it is surprising that 501.4 also lets "the commander on the spot" impose martial law. Perhaps this wording is supposed to address situations (such as nuclear attack) in which communications with the president or other civil authorities are disrupted, but its potential for abuse is clear.

How effective would such drastic measures be? The first large-scale activation of Operation Garden Plot was in response to the 1992 Los Angeles riots, and the plan proved far less impressive in practice. Over ten thousand troops of the National Guard were activated and placed under federal control in response to the riot, supported by two thousand regular Army soldiers from the 7th Infantry Division and 1500 Marines from Camp Pendleton. The troop deployments were slow and poorly coordinated, however, allowing the riots to continue unchecked (since the Los Angeles Police Department had, in effect, ceased even trying to control the riots shortly after they began on April 29). There were many other problems, including confusion over what the federal troops could or could not do, and the civilian leadership of Los Angeles—the mayor, the police chief, and the country sheriff—were divided and unable to come up with a unified, coherent response to the riots. Command and control of the troops on the streets of Los Angeles was difficult. The troops and civilian law enforcement did not even speak the same language. Writing in the Summer 1997 issue of *Parameters*, Christopher Schnaubelt related the story of Marines who accompanied Los Angeles police on the search of a building. Two shotgun rounds were fired behind a door to the building. A police officer called out, "Cover me!" To police officers, that meant to point weapons at the door and be prepared to open fire. But to the Marines, it meant to fire into the area where the shots came from, and they fired over two hundred rounds into the door and building before stopping. While troops did provide visible and respected (or feared?) authority once they were deployed, they were not deployed in large numbers until the riots had begun to subside on their own.

In the aftermath of the Los Angeles riots, it was clear that much work had to be done to use the military effectively in civilian situations. One result was the issuance of United States Army field manual 100-19, "Domestic Support Operations," in July 1993. This field manual attempted to resolve some of the ambiguities and uncertainties concerning the operations that federal troops could carry out in support of civilian law enforcement; chapters 1 and 8 of field manual 100-19 are reproduced in Appendix F. Another result of failures during the riots was Department of Defense Directive 3025.12, "Military Assistance for Civil Disturbances (MACDIS)," issued on February 4, 1994 by Secretary of Defense William Perry. It stated, "the President is authorized by the Constitution and laws of the United States to suppress insurrections, rebellions, and domestic violence under various conditions and circumstances. Planning and preparedness by the Federal Government and the Department of Defense for civil disturbances are important due to the potential severity of the consequences of such events for the Nation and population."

As noted before, the Clinton administration showed a surprising willingness to expand the role of the military in civilian law enforcement. For example, during the 1993 siege of the Branch Davidian complex in Waco, Texas, the Bureau of Alcohol, Tobacco, and Firearms (BATF) requested military support, including tanks and training sessions by Green Berets, basing their request on a single drug charge pending against one of the Davidians (the legal basis for using the military in anti-drug operations is discussed below). Military lawyers blocked the request on grounds that it would be a clear violation of the Posse Comitatus Act.

In 1998 several persons complained that the Columbus, New Mexico U.S.-Mexican border crossing was manned by Army troops assisting the Border Patrol guards, and that in many cases it was the troops, not the Border Patrol, who cleared persons for access into the United States. In 1999 the Clinton administration supported H.R. 628, which would have allowed the military to assist the Immigration and Naturalization Service and Customs Service if requested. The bill would have allowed military inspections of cargo, vehicles (including private cars), and aircraft at all points of entry into the U.S. This bill was actually an attempt to provide securer legal standing for the existing practice of using federal troops for anti-drug patrols at the borders (as was being done in the Ezequiel Hernandez case). 1999 also saw the establishment of the previously mentioned U.S. Joint Forces Command to respond to severe domestic incidents, including the use of chemical, nuclear, or biological weapons. In August 2000, a FEMA document obtained by Wired News revealed that the Army had plans to airlift thousands of troops into Philadelphia in case of a civil disturbance or terrorist incident during the Republican national convention.

It can be assumed that major revisions have been made to Operation Garden Plot since the September 11 attacks. In addition to the previous concerns about riots and other civil disturbances, there is now the possibility of military units being assigned to such duties as quarantines of areas affected by diseases such as smallpox, the forced evacuation of an area if a biological or chemical attack was feared or had actually occurred, removing certain persons (such as those from Middle Eastern nations) from an area and detaining them, or maintaining order in an urban area where civil authority had been rendered ineffective after a chemical, biological, or nuclear terrorist attack.

WOULD AMERICAN SOLDIERS REALLY SHOOT AMERICAN CITIZENS?

Those who see no problem with the increased use of the U.S. military in civilian law enforcement often make the point that American soldiers would never use deadly force against their fellow citizens unless forced to, such as to defend themselves against deadly force. Is this assumption justified?

In 1994, Lieutenant Commander Ernest Cunningham was working on a master's degree at the Naval Postgraduate School. His master's thesis, "Peacekeeping and U.N. Operational Control: Their Effect on Unit Cohesion," tested the hypothesis that operations other than war (including peacekeeping duties) eroded unit cohesion. As part of his research, Cunningham administered a survey to three hundred U.S. Marines to assess their attitudes and responses to various hypothetical situations. The final question on the survey, number 46, described the following scenario:

The U.S. government declares a ban on the possession, sale, transportation, and transfer of all non-sporting firearms. A thirty day (30) day amnesty period is permitted for these firearms to be turned over to local authorities. At the end of this period, a number of citizen groups refuse to turn over their firearms.

The Marines were then asked to answer the following question by selecting the most appropriate response:

I would fire upon U.S. citizens who refuse or resist confiscation of firearms banned by the U.S. government.

( ) No opinion

( ) Strongly disagree

( ) Disagree

( ) Agree

( ) Strongly agree

88% of the Marines answered this question. Of those, 42.33% strongly disagreed, 19.33% disagreed, 18.67% agreed, 7.67% strongly agreed, and 12% had no opinion.

On one hand, the results of this survey are comforting, for over 61.5% of those responding indicated they would not use force against U.S. citizens, and 42.33% said they strongly felt so. But, on the other hand, 26.34% indicated they would follow such an order. In a real-world scenario, it would not be difficult to separate out those willing to follow such orders (perhaps simply by asking for volunteers) and to organize them into special units willing to use deadly force against U.S. civilians.

Because of the small sample (only three hundred) of Marines surveyed, the accuracy of these findings is open to question. We have no data on how Army soldiers would answer a similar question, nor do we know the attitude of the officer corps in the various services or whether members of elite combat units (such as the Army Rangers) might have different attitudes than rank-and-file soldiers. But the results do suggest that a significant minority of the U.S. military would be willing to follow orders to shoot American citizens.

COMBAT EXERCISES IN AMERICAN CITIES

On March 4, 1997, a dozen U.S. Army Black Hawk helicopters descended from the night skies into downtown Charlotte, North Carolina. Windows in downtown restaurants and homes rattled as the helicopters swooped low overhead. The helicopters converged and hovered over an abandoned warehouse in the Third Ward, a predominantly black area of Charlotte. Residents of the Third Ward watched as troop transports rolled into their neighborhood. Troops sprang from the transports, and the area rang with the sound of "flash bang" grenades and automatic weapons fire. Roadblocks were set up on roads leading into and out of the area. Local 911 operators were overwhelmed by calls from terrified residents. Some Third Ward residents called Charlotte mayor Pat McCrory at his home. As McCrory later told the *Charlotte Observer*, "I could barely hear the callers because of the helicopter noise and gunfire in the background."

McCrory quickly realized what was going on, however. It was a Military Operations in Urban Terrain (MOUT) training exercise that he had discussed with Army representatives in December 1996. And McCrory was livid. "We were misled," McCrory told the press. He said that when he was approached by the Army about their holding a training exercise in downtown Charlotte, he was told it would be a "low key, in and out" operation that would use "possibly one helicopter" and that citizens would likely not even know the exercise was taking place. "The clear impression was that this was a very reasonable operation that would not interfere with our community," McCrory told the *Observer*. He agreed to sign a confidentiality agreement when told that disclosure of the planned exercise could compromise its training effectiveness. "Their personalities fit the type of work they did," McCrory said. "They were extremely serious, secretive, and to the point. I wanted to cooperate, knowing that terrorist activity is a very serious concern in our country."

McCrory heard nothing more from the Army and the March 4 effort took him, and other city officials, by surprise. "It was almost like a blitzkrieg operation," McCrory said. "People went and got their guns. I feel fortunate that no one was hurt." Charlotte police chief Dennis Nowicki said he was notified of the operation only hours before it started and even then was not informed of its scope and the weapons used. "When you're holding back information, you're deceiving," said Nowicki. "My advice to them was that they ought to rethink their policy."

In a potentially deadly decision, the Federal Aviation Administration and local airports were not notified, and the Black Hawk helicopters crossed flight paths used by civil aviation.

"The city got hoodooed," said Malachi Greene, the Charlotte city council member representing the Third Ward. "These guys were not truthful. They lied by omission. This is the Army. They've been known to put out disinformation. It's a deliberate thing on the part of these guys."

McCrory dispatched a scathing letter to President Clinton. "The exercise," McCrory wrote, "was misrepresented to all parties involved. Had we known the scope of the operation, we would have never allowed it to take place . . . It is also clear that had anything gone wrong, our citizens would have indeed been in danger, a fact that was never mentioned in the few and incomplete planning discussions for the exercise. . . I can only hope the Department of Defense learned from this experience and that they will not subject other cities to the fear and confusion they created in Charlotte. Rest assured, we learned a valuable lesson and will be on our guard should we receive any other requests to stage training exercises in this city."

Despite McCrory's hopes that other cities would not have to experience what Charlotte did, other cities were the "targets" of MOUT exercises in the late 1990s. Chicago, Atlanta, New Orleans, Detroit, Houston, Miami, Seattle, and Pittsburgh were among those selected, and often the results were similar to Charlotte. Nine helicopters and two hundred troops participated in the Pittsburgh operation, and citizens there called police in panic when they heard gunfire and explosions. In the Chicago suburbs of Des Plaines, Lamont, and Homer, homes were buzzed by helicopters and explosions rattled windows. As was the case with Charlotte, local elected officials and police bitterly complained of being misled and kept in the dark by the Army about the nature and scope of the exercises.

It was not just urban areas that were selected. The rural area around Anniston, Alabama came under "attack" around 8 p.m. of March 12, 1999. Residents near the Anniston municipal airport had their homes shaken by helicopters flying low over them. Even more ominously, the power went out to homes around the airport. Terrified residents huddled in the dark as they heard gunfire and saw explosions and paratroopers landing amid flashes of light at the airport. Callers to the Calhoun County sheriff's department were told, truthfully, that the sheriff's department had no idea what was going on. And, as in the bigger cities, local officials were angry afterwards. "I don't feel it's right," said Marshall Shaddix, a member of the Oxford, Alabama city council, "They should have let them know. If I lived over there, I'd sure like to be notified."

The Army was unrepentant about the fear and confusion it had caused. In the aftermath of the Charlotte incident, Walter Sokalski of the Army Special Operations Command told the *Charlotte Observer*, "We can appreciate people's fear, but we can't contact everybody that might hear the sound of the training. We do try to let as many know as possible, and I'd think, with people seeing the street blocked, they'd know something was going on."

Sokalski surfaced again in connection with exercises conducted in Houston. Explaining why they were conducted in such secrecy and with minimal notification to local officials, he told the *Houston Chronicle*, "It's like when the circus comes to town. Everybody wants to see the elephants."

What was surprising is that these exercises first began during the Clinton Administration and attracted little notice outside the affected areas; one has to wonder how the national press would have reacted if a Republican president had sent special operations troops at night into predominantly black urban areas. We may get a chance to find that out, however; such exercises continued under President George W. Bush but were greatly scaled back after the September 11 attacks to avoid widespread panic. They may be resumed at their former levels in the future.

MILITARIZING THE WAR ON DRUGS

The term "black helicopter" has become a way to label someone as a political paranoid, especially those on the extreme right or who put forth conspiracy theories. That is because a frequent theme in the literature of the extreme right or of government conspiracies is the surveillance of American citizens by unmarked black helicopters. But it happens that right-wing conspiracy theorists are right—unmarked black helicopters are buzzing isolated ranches in Idaho and following cars at night down lonely Nevada roads. But these helicopters are not operated by the United Nations or the New World Order; instead, they are operated by the U.S. military, and they are looking for drugs.

In 1982 Congress passed the Defense Authorization Act. While its title sounds innocuous, the Act was one of the most revolutionary pieces of legislation ever enacted by Congress, for it authorized—for the first time—the involvement of the U.S. military in enforcing civilian laws not related to military matters. The Act authorized America's military forces to provide equipment, intelligence, facilities, and "technical assistance" to civilian agencies in enforcing drug and immigration laws. In 1986, the Posse Comitatus Act was amended to resolve conflicts between it and the 1982 law. A national security decision directive (another form of executive order) swiftly followed declaring drugs to be a threat to national security and directing the military to give all permissible and appropriate aid to civilian agencies fighting drugs. The main thrust of the effort would be to stop drugs crossing into America, especially over the Mexican border.

This decision was opposed by Secretary of Defense Casper Weinberger. "Calling for the use of the government's full military resources to put a stop to the drug trade makes for hot, exciting rhetoric," he wrote after he left office. "But responding to those calls would make for terrible national security policy, poor politics, and guaranteed failure in the campaign against drugs." As expected, military officers publicly voiced support of the president's decision, and many privately supported it as well. But many others had misgivings. Some were worried that soldiers' combat training was incompatible with the demands of peacetime law enforcement. Others worried about the novel involvement of the military in what was, at its root, a domestic political issue on which many Americans disagreed with official government policy and existing law. (The military was never involved with enforcing Prohibition.) And others were worried about the possibility of corruption. Many police officers and even judges had been successfully bribed by drug money; would military involvement in anti-drug efforts lead to similar payoffs to soldiers and their officers?

Despite such misgivings, 1986 saw the creation of Operation Alliance, headed by Vice President George Bush and Attorney General Ed Meese. This brought together the FBI, CIA, Drug Enforcement Administration (DEA), Customs Service, Immigration and Naturalization Service, Bureau of Alcohol, Tobacco, and Firearms, U.S. Coast Guard, Department of Defense, and state and local law enforcement agencies. While soldiers could not arrest lawbreakers, they could patrol and report them to civilian law enforcement (often, the civilian officers rode along with the military patrols). And federal troops were allowed to carry their combat firearms and to shoot to kill if they or accompanying civilians were endangered (this was the reason given for the shooting of Ezequiel Hernandez).

The patrols that began in 1986 were not merely passive flyovers. Cars traveling along rural roads in the west near the Mexican border were often followed for several miles by the Army's black, unmarked helicopters (thus starting the "black helicopter" paranoia, understandably). Hikers near the border sometimes encountered military patrols that asked them to provide identification and say what they were doing. While the hikers were under no obligation to identify themselves or answer any questions, almost everyone complied (as would most who encountered a group of heavily armed men miles from the nearest road or assistance). While foot patrols could take place only on public lands, helicopters could fly over private property, and residents of rural areas near the border soon became familiar with the thup thup of helicopters hovering over their property while the crews looked for drugs.

Toward the end of the 1980s, military assistance to drug enforcement personnel spread beyond the U.S.-Mexico border. Residents of other areas where marijuana growing was common, such as northern California and the Big Island of Hawaii, soon found themselves under siege from low-flying helicopters and military patrols. As the 1980s ended, the patrols spread into isolated regions of such states as Montana, and the target list grew to include clandestine drug labs as well as marijuana plants. The patrols were more than merely annoying; for example, low-flying helicopters panicked farm animals (such as horses) and caused them to stampede or injure themselves. And there were the inevitable snafus. In one case, military helicopters spotted what appeared to be marijuana plants growing inside the greenhouse of Michigan farmer Joseph Astro. The helicopter landed, federal and county drug enforcement agents stormed the greenhouse, smashing through its plastic sides — and found tomato and green pepper plants instead of pot.

There were other types of assistance given by the military. For example, the Army Corps of Engineers created paved roads out of the dirt roads along the border, giving Border Patrol agents easier access. Military tools such as night vision scopes were given to civilian agencies, and their workers were trained to use them. By the end of the 1980s, over $800 million was being spent annually on military assistance in the war on drugs.

President George Bush came to office in 1989 determined to expand the military's role in drug enforcement. In a memorable 1989 press conference, he displayed bags of crack cocaine as he called for Congress to expand and formalize the military's involvement in the drug wars. The result, the Defense Authorization Act of 1989, assigned to the Pentagon the integration of command, control, and intelligence assets to monitor the flow of illegal drugs into the U.S., while expanding the National Guard's role in drug enforcement (for example, National Guard members may be deputized by local sheriffs and empowered to make arrests) and making the Department of Defense the lead agency in detecting and monitoring the transportation of illegal drugs into the United States. And in 1991, Congress voted to allow the military to establish anti-drug operations bases and to train members of federal, state, and local law enforcement agencies in anti-drug operations.

But the cornerstone of Bush's anti-drug strategy was the creation of Joint Task Force 6. Its stated mission is to be the planning, coordinating, and operating headquarters for all Department of Defense anti-drug operations under Operation Alliance. Joint Task Force 6 supports civilian law enforcement agencies in a variety of ways, and some units operate without civilian accompaniment (as did the one that shot Ezequiel Hernandez, for example). According to the Army, Joint Task Force 6 conducted 1260 anti-drug missions, most of them patrols, along the U.S.-Mexico border from 1990 to 1993. Joint Task Force 6 works closely with the El Paso Intelligence Center (EPIC), which is also based at Biggs Army Airfield. EPIC is managed by the Drug Enforcement Administration and supplies intelligence to fifteen federal agencies involved in anti-drug operations, including the Department of Defense. Part of EPIC is "NADDIS-X.21," a computer database holding criminal, financial, and political information on U.S. and foreign citizens believed to be connected with drug trafficking or smuggling illegal immigrants into the United States.

As noted earlier, Joint Task Force 6 came very close to involvement with the assault on the Branch Davidian compound in Waco, Texas. According to Colonel Sean Byrne of the U.S. Army, the Bureau of Alcohol, Tobacco, and Firearms requested helicopters, tanks, tear gas, and special training by Green Berets in preparation for the raid. The BATF rationale was that one member of the Davidians had a prior drug offense and BATF suspected there was a drug lab inside the compound. But military lawyers rejected the BATF request, finding insufficient evidence to justify it. "Had legal advisers assigned to Joint Task Force 6 which supported the BATF during the 1993 siege at the Branch Davidian Compound in Waco, Texas, not questioned that agency's requests for support, the Armed Forces would have been inappropriately and illegally involved in an operation that ultimately led to the deaths of U.S. citizens," wrote Byrne. "Military lawyers saved the day when they conducted a further legal review that resulted in the request not being acted upon. Had they not questioned what appeared to be a routine request, JTF 6 would have been involved in a clear violation of Posse Comitatus."

Joint Task Force 6's missions increased during the Clinton presidency. For example, it performed 1260 missions in the last two years of the first Bush presidency, but the number leapt to more than 4000 during 1995 alone. Patrols also became more aggressive during the late 1990s. In addition to the 1997 shooting of Ezequiel Hernandez, residents of the southwest encountered traffic stops manned by soldiers where local police would question drivers arbitrarily (stopping every third car, for example) and check identification of all adult passengers. Remote sensing and detection devices (such as motion sensors) have been installed along much of the border. And since the September 11 attacks, it is a given that security and monitoring along the Mexican border have increased in other ways too.

THE DANGER OF MILITARIZED LAW ENFORCEMENT

As noted earlier, there are career officers within the U.S. military who better recognize the dangers of getting the military involved in civilian law enforcement than do most politicians. The functions and purposes of civilian law enforcement and the military are critically different. Civilian law enforcement is part of a larger criminal justice system that presumes innocence and is based on due process, including a trial and other legal protections, for anyone accused of a crime. In that system, the main goals of the police are deterrence, prevention, and apprehension; deadly force is used as a last resort when all else fails. The military operates by the rules of the battlefield, however, with emphasis on using deadly and overwhelming force against an opponent presumed to be "guilty" and intent upon causing harm. The military and civilian law enforcement cultures are incompatible and in many ways polar opposites. To militarize civilian law enforcement is to deform it beyond recognition.

Perhaps the best statement of the danger of militarized law enforcement came from Marine Corps General Stephen Olmstead in his testimony before Congress in 1989: "One of the United States' greatest strengths is that the military is responsive to civilian authority and that we do not allow the Army, Navy, Marines, or the Air Force to be a police force. History is replete with countries that allowed that to happen. Disaster is the result."

EPILOGUE

AFTER THE WORLD TRADE CENTER was destroyed, the composer Karlheinz Stockhausen called the act "the greatest work of art of all time." This comment was justifiably greeted with outrage, but Stockhausen was on to something. Like art, people tended to see in the September 11 attacks what they wanted to see. And how people reacted often told more about themselves than attacks.

Ominously, the reaction of many in Washington was that the attacks were caused by inadequate internal security and in order to fight terrorism, Americans must give up some of their rights. "We are in a new world," said House Minority Leader Dick Gephardt (D-Missouri) in late 2001. "This event will change the balance between freedom and security."

Gephardt introduced legislation to create a national identification card for American citizens (even though none of the September 11 hijackers were using false identification or were American citizens). And, as noted earlier in the book, other politicians called to relax the Posse Comitatus Act and give the military an expanded role in civilian law enforcement.

A little over six weeks after the attacks, the "USA Patriot Act" was overwhelmingly approved by Congress. This massive bill (over 340 pages) greatly expanded government wiretap and surveillance powers (especially without warrant), created a vaguely defined new crime of "domestic terrorism," allowed the government to track e-mail and internet use without a warrant, greatly expanded the ability to conduct searches under a warrant without notifying the targets of the search and loosened the Constitution's fourth amendment "Probable Cause" restrictions. In many respects the USA Patriot Act seemed to have as its basic premise that the Bill of Rights was the true cause of the September 11 attacks instead of massive and well documented failures by such government agencies as the FBI and the INS. And some in the Bush administration even attempted to link the war on terrorism with the war on drugs through ads, aired during the 2002 Super Bowl, claiming that drug sales financed terrorism (although, as it later developed during 2002, a significant chunk of the funds for the September 11 attacks came from the Saudi royal family).

Most "anti-terrorism" proposals merely called for increased snooping on American citizens, even though no American citizens were among the September 11 plotters. One such effort was the Terrorism Information and Prevention System (TIPS). This would have enlisted mail carriers, utility meter readers, installation/service personnel, pizza delivery people and others with access to private residences (a group estimated to total over 11 million) to report any "suspicious" activity or people to the FBI and other branches of the Department of Justice. When TIPS was announced, the outcry from civil libertarians, much of the media and some members of Congress caused the plan to be quickly abandoned.

However, many TIPS critics were silent when a more ominous effort to "fight terrorism," the Total Information Awareness Program (TIAP) was announced in November, 2002. Edward Aldridge, the Pentagon's Undersecretary of Acquisitions and Technology, described it as a "prototype database to seek patterns indicative of terrorist activity." And how would it be able to seek such patterns? By collecting data on credit card and bank transactions (including loans, checking accounts and ATM withdrawals), travel (air, rail, rental car and hotel records), traffic and driver's license records, insurance records, telephone records, medical records (including prescription drug purchases), passport and visa applications, tax records, marriage and divorce records and what was described as "reports of suspicious activity given to law enforcement and intelligence agencies." In short, almost any transaction or activity for which some kind of record is produced, would eventually find its way into the TIAP database. All this data, some from private databases such as those used by telemarketers and credit reporting agencies, some from public records and some from government agencies, would then be analyzed to find those as yet undefined "patterns indicative of terrorist activity."

It's clear that many Americans could quickly find themselves flagged as potential terrorists under TIAP. One-way air travel booked on short notice is one factor supposedly indicative of terrorist activity. But anyone who travels often on business must sometimes book a flight on short notice (such as a few hours) and without a return trip, since they do not know how long they will need to be at their destination. Under TIAP, such business travelers might wind up on a terrorist watch list. The same thing could happen to those who have rented apartments near suspected terrorists, taken certain classes (like Arabic or Middle Eastern Studies) at college or who make frequent cash withdrawals from an ATM. "What this (TIAP) is talking about is making us a nation of suspects," said Chuck Pena, a senior analyst at the Cato Institute.

Some people were unconcerned about TIAP, noting that much of the data would come from private records that are already available for rent by telemarketers, insurance companies and other businesses. However, no private database is remotely as comprehensive as the proposed TIAP database for each American. The TIAP database would have access to government records that are not available to businesses and, most importantly, private businesses using a database don't have the power to arrest and imprison people.

Inevitably, substantial errors would creep in the TIAP database for some individuals (just as they do in credit bureau records, for example) and some people will be unfairly targeted as terror suspects and conversely, legitimate terror suspects will go undetected because of erroneous information. The potential for misuse of TIAP by a future Richard Nixon, Lyndon Johnson or J. Edgar Hoover staggers the mind. For example, one can easily envision the TIAP database being used to dig up dirt (such as history of renting DVDs of Sharon Stone films?) on political opponents or overly inquisitive journalists.

Adding to the anxiety over TIAP and its potential for misuse, was that its development was headed by Admiral John Poindexter, the former national security advisor to President Reagan. Before TIAP, Poindexter was best known for his role in the Iran-Contra scandal; he was found guilty on five counts of conspiracy, obstruction of Congress and false statements in 1990. Those convictions were overturned on appeal in 1991 on the grounds that his testimony before Congress, which was given under immunity, may have influenced witnesses against him during his trial. During his testimony before Congress, Poindexter admitted not informing President Reagan of the arms sales to Iran to fund the Contras because he "wanted the President to have some deniability so that he would be protected." Poindexter also said he "could not recall" certain events in response to 184 questions during his testimony to Congress. It was later discovered that Poindexter and Oliver North had deleted over 5000 e-mails pertaining to Iran-Contra from White House servers. Unfortunately for them, those e-mails were saved on backup and they revealed Poindexter had been intimately involved in the scandal from the beginning.

As if having a convicted (if overturned) felon heading TIAP wasn't scary enough, the TIAP logo looked like something designed by Orwell —an eye perched atop a Masonic pyramid, scanning the world with the slogan "scientia est potentia" (knowledge is power).

Encouragingly, the criticisms of TIAP resulted in the program's development being suspended by the Pentagon in January of 2003. The Pentagon announced that research into less intrusive, more narrowly focused methods of compiling data on potential terrorists would continue but without Poindexter in a key capacity. But the temporary defeat of TIAP was soon offset by efforts spearheaded by Senator Orrin Hatch (R-Utah) to expand the USA Patriot Act. These efforts included making permanent several provisions set to expire in 2005 and enhancing permissible internet monitoring without a court order (such as keeping track of web sites a person visits).

Some people even felt the U.S. legal system and Constitutional safeguards were not up to the task of fighting terrorism and must be discarded. The December 1, 2002 *Washington Post* reported the Bush administration was developing a parallel (shadow?) legal system under which all terrorism suspects, including U.S. citizens, could be investigated, detained, questioned, tried and punished without the full rights—like being represented by an attorney—normally available to civilians accused of a crime under U.S. law. According to the *Post*, several elements of the parallel system are already in place, such as indefinite military detention for those designated as "enemy combatants" and the liberal use of "material witness" warrants to detain those who have not been charged with any crime.

Sources who spoke to the *Post* pointed to the case of Jose Padillla, an American citizen arrested on May 8, 2002 when he flew into Chicago from Pakistan. Padilla had been linked to Abu Zubaydah, an Al Qaeda planner in Pakistan. Reportedly Padilla was returning to the United States to do reconnaissance and planning for a radioactive "dirty bomb" attack. Soon after his arrest, he was declared an enemy combatant by President Bush and transferred to the brig of a South Carolina naval base where he remains and could, in theory, be held until the President declares an end to the "war on terrorism." Padilla has been unable to communicate with anyone, including family or lawyers and Bush administration sources have indicated that if Padilla is ever brought to trial, it would be in a military tribunal instead of a civilian court.

TIAP and the Padilla case are just two examples of the message that has been conveyed in multiple ways to the American people since September 11, 2001:

> If you want to be protected from terrorism, you're going to have to sacrifice your privacy and liberty and accept a more intrusive, powerful government role in your life.

That's why some people will see a book like this as either treason or lunacy. Instead of less government secrecy and emergency powers, those people will demand more. They will be willing to give the government whatever it wants to fight terror. But there is a problem with such reasoning. The government was already spending billions on secret projects and planning prior to September 11, 2001. The government had supposedly created a worldwide eavesdropping program operated by the NSA. The military was already training to fight terrorism in the United States and was helping to patrol the country's borders. Contingency plans had been made for all manner of conceivable terrorist threats and attacks.

And it all failed on September 11, 2001. It all failed completely, wretchedly and catastrophically, leaving almost 3000 dead. And, except for some luck and bravery from the New York Fire and Police departments, the death toll could have been far greater. The response on the federal level was confusion bordering on panic. Instead of orderly and well-drilled evacuation and relocation of national leaders, there was initially confusion on where President Bush should go after leaving Florida. Congressional leaders and other government officials in Washington were not evacuated until hours after the attacks and could have been sitting ducks for other terrorist strikes. For all of the supposed planning and relocation facilities awaiting use, the result was near panic in Washington and a slow response to the crisis in New York. Where was FEMA when New York desperately needed medical supplies, construction equipment, communications facilities and similar items for rescue and recovery efforts at the World Trade Center site?

For all its bluster and superficial impressiveness, the Shadow Government failed at every vital task on September 11.

And has anything been learned from the experience? The possibility of another terrorist attack is high, yet the plans for coping with it (if any) have not yet been communicated to the public. Suppose you were to hear in the next hour that some sort of biological, chemical, or even radiological attack had been made in your city. What are you supposed to do, for example, if you hear a news bulletin that a large bomb hidden in a parked van had exploded and released large quantities of powdered Cobalt-60 — a lethal isotope used and available worldwide for food irradiation — into the air? What are you supposed to do if you hear that powdered "weaponized" smallpox had been detected in your city? Or if some form of nerve gas had been released? Would you know how to protect yourself? How to decontaminate yourself from a chemical or biological attack? What the symptoms are of exposure to chemical, biological, or radiological agents?

In many ways, we are just as unprepared as we were on the morning of September 11, 2001. Perhaps we have reduced the possibility of another terrorist incident involving an airliner hijacking (although none of the measures taken to date would stop, for example, the hijacking of an incoming 747 from an overseas origin point and the crashing of that plane into the Empire State Building, Space Needle, or Golden Gate Bridge). But there are numerous other possible terrorist scenarios that are highly plausible — like chemical, biological, and radiological attacks — for which the American government seems totally unprepared. While the possibility is almost too horrible to contemplate, an event like the release of weaponized smallpox or radioactive materials in New York City is clearly a real possibility. What would the citizens of the New York area do in such an event? They would have to be evacuated, but how? Where would they go? What would be done with the injured? The infected? The irradiated? The dead?

No one seems to know. Instead of concrete plans for such possibilities, the American people are just getting hot air about national identification cards and marijuana smoking leading to terrorism.

Before surrendering more freedom to the government and granting it more secret powers, maybe we should ask what we're getting in return.

Some secrecy is indeed necessary in any government, and especially when fighting an elusive, faceless enemy like terrorism. But it must be remembered that American citizens exercising their constitutional rights did not carry out the September 11 attacks. Instead, the attacks were made possible by the failure of FBI managers to properly heed warnings they were getting from the field about suspicious flight school students from the Middle East. The attacks were also made possible by an INS that had lost track of foreign citizens that had overstayed or violated their visas. Before giving the government new powers, maybe we should first demand they more professionally enforce the laws already on the books and more intelligently use the powers they have already been granted.

Maybe the term "Shadow Government" was more appropriate than anyone realized. A shadow, after all, has no substance.

What we need instead is a "Sunshine Government" with open, honest debate on how best to respond to new threats such as terrorism. For example, the issue on how, or even whether, to use military forces in civilian law enforcement can be openly debated without endangering national security—and if the American people decide they want more military involvement in civilian law enforcement, such military involvement will be more widely accepted and considered legitimate if it's the result of Congressional action instead of secret planning. During the Cold War years, information was readily available to the public on what to do in the event of a nuclear attack or warning of such an attack. Similar information needs to be distributed to the public for new terrorist threats such as chemical or biological attacks—and if there is nothing the government could reasonably do in the event of such attacks on a metropolitan area, that should be made clear to the public as well. The definition of "national emergency" needs to be clarified (such as a situation involving the actual or imminent threat of widespread death and destruction) instead of being left up to the whims of the current occupant of the Oval Office. Instead of relying on presidential executive orders, emergency plans and procedures can, and should be, developed through the process provided in the Constitution for creating new laws. Classification of information needs to be reformed so that it is used to protect matters of genuine national importance instead of as a shield to hide missing funds and a failure to perform.

Some may feel such matters are too important to be trusted to the public, or that the American people are incapable of responding adequately to legitimate national emergencies. But such people should reflect on the only effective action taken against terrorism on September 11. While the

Shadow Government—and its billion dollar budgets, thousands of people, and top-secret plans—failed miserably on that day, the ordinary Americans aboard United Flight 93 did not. When they learned what had happened in New York and Washington, they realized their hijacked flight was on a similar mission. They discussed the situation among themselves instead of making secret plans. They held a vote on what to do instead of blindly following an executive order. And then they fought back. In the process, they lost their lives but managed to save the Capitol, the White House, or some other landmark in Washington. In their final minutes, the passengers used the basic tools of democracy—adequate information, free discussion, and voting—and succeeded in stopping the last group of terrorists from achieving their goal. Their performance is a stark contrast to the failure and incompetence of the Shadow Government on that day.

If you tell the American people the truth and trust them, they will do the right thing. As the pressure builds to further restrict the rights and liberties of American citizens in the name of "national security," the lessons of United 93 need to be remembered.

EXECUTIVE ORDER 9066: AUTHORIZING THE SECRETARY OF WAR TO PRESCRIBE MILITARY AREAS

WHEREAS the successful prosecution of the war requires every possible protection against espionage and against sabotage to national-defense material, national-defense premises, and national-defense utilities as defined in section 4, Act of April 20, 1918, 40 Stat. 533, as amended by the act of November 30, 1940, 54 Stat. 1220, and the Act of August 21, 1941, 55 Stat. 655 (U.S.C., Title 50, Sec. 104):

NOW, THEREFORE, by virtue of the authority vested in me as President of the United States, and Commander in Chief of the Army and Navy, I hereby authorize and direct the Secretary of War, and the Military Commanders whom he may from time to time designate, whenever he or any designated Commander deems such actions necessary or desirable, to prescribe military areas in such places and of such extent as he or the appropriate Military Commanders may determine, from which any or all persons may be excluded, and with such respect to which, the right of any person to enter, remain in, or leave shall be subject to whatever restrictions the Secretary of War or the appropriate Military Commander may impose in his discretion. The Secretary of War is hereby authorized to provide for residents of any such area who are excluded therefrom, such transportation, food, shelter, and other accommodations as may be necessary, in the judgment of the Secretary of War or the said Military Commander, and until other arrangements are made, to accomplish the purpose of this order. The designation of military areas in any region or locality shall supersede designations of prohibited and restricted areas by the Attorney General under the Proclamations of December 7 and 8, 1941, and shall supersede the responsibility and authority of the Attorney General under the said Proclamations in respect of such prohibited and restricted areas.

I hereby further authorize and direct the Secretary of War and the said Military Commanders to take such other steps as he or the appropriate Military Commander may deem advisable to enforce compliance with the restrictions applicable to each Military area hereinabove authorized to be designated, including the use of Federal troops and other Federal Agencies, with authority to accept assistance of state and local agencies.

I hereby further authorize and direct all Executive Departments, independent establishments and other Federal Agencies, to assist the Secretary of War or the said Military Commanders in carrying out this Executive Order, including the furnishing of medical aid, hospitalization, food, clothing, transportation, use of land, shelter, and other supplies, equipment, utilities, facilities and services.

This order shall not be construed as modifying or limiting in any way the authority heretofore granted under Executive Order No. 8972, dated December 12, 1941, nor shall it be construed as limiting or modifying the duty and responsibility of the Federal Bureau of Investigation, with respect to the investigation of alleged acts of sabotage or the duty and responsibility of the Attorney General and the Department of Justice under the Proclamations of December 7 and 8, 1941, prescribing regulations for the conduct and control of alien enemies, except as such duty and responsibility is superseded by the designation of military areas hereunder.

FRANKLIN D. ROOSEVELT
February 19, 1942

EXECUTIVE ORDER 11490: ASSIGNING EMERGENCY PREPAREDNESS FUNCTIONS TO FEDERAL DEPARTMENTS AND AGENCIES

WHEREAS our national security is dependent upon our ability to assure continuity of government, at every level, in any national emergency type situation that might conceivably confront the nation; and

WHEREAS effective national preparedness planning to meet such an emergency, including a massive nuclear attack, is essential to our national survival; and

WHEREAS effective national preparedness planning requires the identification of functions that would have to be performed during such an emergency, the assignment of responsibility for developing plans for performing these functions, and the assignment of responsibility for developing the capability to implement those plans; and

WHEREAS the Congress has directed the development of such national emergency preparedness plans and has provided funds for the accomplishment thereof; and

WHEREAS this national emergency preparedness planning activity has been an established program of the United States Government for more than twenty years:

NOW, THEREFORE, by virtue of the authority vested in me as President of the United States, and pursuant to Reorganization Plan No. 1 of 1958 (72 Stat. 1799), the National Security Act of 1947, as amended, the Defense Production Act of 1950, as amended, and the Federal Civil Defense Act, as amended, it is hereby ordered as follows—
THE PRESIDENT

PART 1
PURPOSE AND SCOPE

SECTION 101 Purpose
This order consolidates the assignment of emergency preparedness functions to various departments and agencies heretofore contained in the 21 Executive orders and 2 Defense Mobilization orders listed in Section 3015 of this order. Assignments have been adjusted to conform to changes in organization which have occurred subsequent to the issuance of those Executive orders and Defense Mobilization orders.

SEC.102 Scope
(a) This order is concerned with the emergency national planning and preparedness functions of the several departments and agencies of the Federal Government which complement the military readiness planning responsibilities of the Department of Defense; together, these measures provide the basic foundation for our overall national preparedness posture, and are fundamental to our ability to survive.

(b) The departments and agencies of the Federal Government are hereby severally charged with the duty of assuring the continuity of the Federal Government in any national emergency type situation that might confront the nation. To this end, each department and agency with essential functions, whether expressly identified in this order or not, shall develop such plans and take such actions, including but not limited to those specified in this order, as may be necessary to assure that it will be able to perform its essential functions, and continue as a viable part of the Federal Government, during any emergency that might conceivably occur. These include plans for maintaining the continuity of essential functions of the department or agency at the seat of government and elsewhere, through programs concerned with:
   (1) succession to office;
   (2) predelegation of emergency authority;
   (3) safekeeping of essential records;
   (4) emergency relocation sites supported by communications and
       required services.
   (5) emergency action steps;
   (6) alternate headquarters or command facilities; and
   (7) protection of Government resources, facilities, and personnel. The
       continuity of Government activities undertaken by the departments
       and agencies shall be in accordance with guidance provided by,
       and subject to evaluation by, the Director of the Office of
       Emergency Preparedness.

(c) In addition to the activities indicated above, the heads of departments and agencies described in Parts 2 through 29 of this order shall:

(1) prepare national emergency plans, develop preparedness programs, and attain an appropriate state of readiness with respect to the functions assigned to them in this order for all conditions of national emergency;

(2) give appropriate consideration to emergency preparedness factors in the conduct of the regular functions of their agencies, particularly those functions considered essential in time of emergency, and

(3) be prepared to implement, in the event of an emergency, all appropriate plans developed under this order.

SEC. 103 Presidential Assistance.

The Director of the Office of Emergency Preparedness, in accordance with the provisions of Executive Order No. 11051 of September 27, 1962, shall advise and assist the President in determining national preparedness goals and policies for the performance of functions under this order and in coordinating the performance of such functions with the total national preparedness program.

SEC. 104 General and Specific Functions.

The functions assigned by Part 30, General Provisions, apply to all departments and agencies having emergency preparedness responsibilities. Specific functions are assigned to departments and agencies covered in Parts 2 through 29.

SEC. 105 Construction.

The purpose and legal effect of the assignments contained in this order do not constitute authority to implement the emergency plans prepared pursuant to this order. Plans so developed may be effectuated only in the event that authority for such effectuation is provided by a law enacted by the Congress or by an order or directive issued by the President pursuant to statutes or the Constitution of the United States.

PART 2
DEPARTMENT OF STATE

SECTION 201 Functions.

The Secretary of State shall prepare national emergency plans and develop preparedness programs to permit modification or expansion of the activities of the Department of State and agencies, boards, and commissions under his jurisdiction in order to meet all conditions of national emergency, including attack upon the United States. The Secretary of State shall provide to all other departments and agencies overall foreign policy direction, coordination, and supervision in the formulation and execution of those emergency preparedness activities which have foreign policy implications, affect foreign relations, or depend directly or indirectly, on the policies and capabilities of the Department of State. The Secretary of State shall develop policies, plans, and procedures for carrying out his responsibilities in the conduct of the foreign relations of the United States under conditions of national emergency, including, but not limited to:

(1) the formulation and implementation, in consultation with the Department of Defense and other appropriate agencies, and the negotiation of contingency and post-emergency plans with our allies and of the intergovernmental agreements and arrangements required by such plans;

(2) formulation, negotiation, and execution of policy affecting the relationships of the United States with neutral States;

(3) formulation and execution of political strategy toward hostile or enemy States, including the definition of war objectives and the political means for achieving those objectives;

(4) maintenance of diplomatic and consular representation abroad;

(5) reporting and advising on conditions overseas which bear upon the national emergency;

(6) carrying out or proposing economic measures with respect to other nations, including coordination with the export control functions of the Secretary of Commerce;

(7) mutual assistance activities such as ascertaining requirements of the civilian economies of other nations, making recommendations to domestic resource agencies for meeting such requirements, and determining the availability of and making arrangements for obtaining foreign resources required by the United States;

(8) providing foreign assistance, including continuous supervision and general direction of authorized economic and military assistance programs, and determination of the value thereof;

(9) protection or evacuation of American citizens and nationals abroad and safeguarding their property;

(10) protection and/or control of international organization and foreign diplomatic, consular, and other official personnel and property, or other assets, in the United States;

(11) documentary control of persons seeking to enter or leave the United States; and

(12) regulation and control of exports of items on the munitions list.

PART 3
DEPARTMENT OF THE TREASURY

SECTION 301 Functions.
The Secretary of the Treasury shall develop policies, plans and procedures for the performance of emergency functions with respect to

(1) stabilization aspects of the monetary, credit, and financial system;
(2) stabilization of the dollar in relation to foreign currencies;
(3) collection of revenue;
(4) regulation of financial institutions;
(5) supervision of the Federal depository system;
(6) direction of transactions in government securities;
(7) tax and debt policies;
(8) participation in bilateral and multilateral financial arrangements with foreign governments;
(9) regulation of foreign assets in the United States and of foreign financial dealings (in consultation with the Secretaries of State and Commerce);
(10) development of procedures for the manufacture and/or issuance and redemption of securities, stamps, coins, and currency;
(11) development of systems for the issuance and payment of Treasury checks;
(12) maintenance of the central government accounting and financial reporting system;
(13) administration of customs laws, tax laws, and laws on control of alcohol, alcoholic beverages, tobacco, and firearms;
(14) suppression of counterfeiting and forgery of government securities, stamps, coins, and currency;
(15) protection of the President and the Vice President and other designated persons;
(16) granting of loans (including participation in or guarantees of loans) for the expansion of capacity, the development of technological processes, or the production of essential material; and
(17) to the extent that such functions have not been transferred to the Secretary of Transportation, enforcement of marine inspection and navigation laws.

SEC. 302 Financial Coordination.

The Secretary shall assume the initiative in developing plans for implementation of national policy on sharing war losses and for the coordination of emergency monetary, credit, and Federal benefit payment programs of those departments and agencies which have responsibilities dependent on the policies or capabilities of the Department.

PART 4
DEPARTMENT OF DEFENSE

SECTION 401 Functions.

In addition to the civil defense functions assigned to the Secretary of Defense by Executive Order No. 10952, the Secretary of Defense shall perform the following emergency preparedness functions:

(1) Provide specific strategic guidance as required for emergency preparedness planning and programming, including, for example, guidance regarding such factors as accessibility of foreign sources of supply and estimated shipping loss discounts and aircraft losses in the event of war.

(2) Develop and furnish quantitative and time-phased military requirements for selected end-items, consistent with defined military concepts, and supporting requirements for materials, components, production facilities, production equipment, petroleum, natural gas, solid fuels, electric power, food, transportation, and other services needed to carry out specified Department of Defense current and mobilization procurement, construction, research and development, and production programs. The items and supporting resources to be included in such requirements, the periods to be covered, and the dates for their submission to the appropriate resource agency will be determined by mutual agreement between the Secretary of Defense and the head of the appropriate resource agency.

(3) Advise and assist the Office of Emergency Preparedness in developing a national system of production urgencies.

(4) Advise and assist the Office of Emergency Preparedness in developing a system, in conjunction with the Department of State, for the international allocation of critical materials and products among the United States and the various foreign claimants in the event of an emergency, including an attack on the United States.

(5) Plan for and administer priorities and allocations authority delegated to the Department of Defense. Authorize procurement and production schedules and make allotments of controlled materials pursuant to program determinations of the Office of Emergency Preparedness.

(6) Assist the Department of Commerce and other appropriate agencies in the development of the production and distribution controls plans for use in any period of emergency.

(7) Develop with industry, plans for the procurement and production of selected military equipment and supplies needed to fulfill emergency requirements, making maximum use of plants in dispersed locations, and, where essential and appropriate, providing for alternative sources of supply in order to minimize the effects of enemy attack.

(8) Develop with industry, plans and programs for minimizing the effect of attack damage to plants producing major items of military equipment and supply.

(9) Recommend to the Office of Emergency Preparedness measures for overcoming potential deficiencies in production capacity to produce selected military supplies and equipment needed to fulfill emergency requirements, when necessary measures cannot be effected by the Department of Defense.

(10) Furnish information and recommendations, when requested by the Office of Emergency Preparedness, for purposes of processing applications for defense loans under Title III of the Defense Production Act of 1950, as amended.

(11) Furnish advice and assistance on the utilization of strategic and critical materials in defense production, including changes that occur from time to time.

(12) Analyze problems that may arise in maintaining an adequate mobilization production base in military-product industries and take necessary actions to overcome these problems within the limits of the authority and funds available to the Department of Defense.

(13) Assist the Secretary of Commerce with respect to the identification and evaluation of facilities important to the national defense.

(14) Advise and assist the Office of Emergency Preparedness in the development and review of standards for the strategic location and physical security of industries, services, government, and other activities for which continuing operation is essential to national security, and

exercise physical security cognizance over the facilities
assigned to him for such purpose.

(15) Develop and operate damage assessment systems and assist
the Office of Emergency Preparedness and other
departments and agencies in their responsibilities as stated
in Section 3002 (2): participate with the Office of
Emergency Preparedness in the preparation of estimates of
potential damage from enemy attack.

(16) Advise and assist the Office of Emergency Preparedness in
the development of over-all manpower policies to be
instituted in the event of an emergency, including an attack
on the United States, including the provision of information
relating to the size and composition of the Armed Forces.

(17) Advise on existing communications facilities and furnish
military requirements for commercial communications
facilities and services in planning for and in event of an
emergency, including an attack on the United States.

(18) Furnish military requirements for all forms of transportation
and transportation facilities in planning for and in the event
of emergency, including an attack upon the United States.

(19) Assist the Office of Emergency Preparedness in preparation
of legislative programs and plans for coordinating
nonmilitary support of emergency preparedness programs.

(20) Develop plans and procedures for the Department of
Defense utilization of nonindustrial facilities in the event of an
emergency in order to reduce requirements for new construction
and to provide facilities in a minimum period of time.

(21) Advise and assist the Office of Emergency Preparedness in
(1) determining what key foreign facilities and operating
rights thereto are important to the security of the
United States, and
(2) obtaining through appropriate channels protection
against sabotage.

(22) Develop plans and procedure to carry out Department
of Defense responsibilities stated in the National Censorship
Agreement between the Department of Defense and the
Office of Emergency Preparedness.

(23) Advise and assist the Department of State in planning for
the evacuation of dependents from overseas areas, United
States teachers and administrators in the overseas
dependents schools, and such other United States citizens as
may be working in United States schools overseas.

(24) Develop plans for implementation of approved Department of State/Department of Defense policies and procedures for the protection and evacuation of United States citizens and certain designated aliens abroad.

(25) Develop plans and procedures for the provision of logistical support to members of foreign forces, their employees and dependents as may be present in the United States under the terms of bilateral or multilateral agreements which authorize such support in the event of a national emergency.

(26) Develop with the Department of Transportation and Federal Communications Commission plans and programs for the control of air traffic, civil and military, during an emergency.

(27) Develop with the Federal Communications Commission and the Office of Telecommunications Management (OEP) plans and programs for the emergency control of all devices capable of emitting electromagnetic radiation.

PART 5
DEPARTMENT OF JUSTICE

SECTION 501. Functions.
The Attorney General shall perform the following emergency preparedness functions:

(1) Emergency documents and measures. Provide advice, as appropriate, with respect to any emergency directive or procedure prepared by a department or agency as a part of its emergency preparedness function.

(2) Industry support. As appropriate, review the legal procedures developed by the Federal agencies concerned to be instituted if it becomes necessary for the Government to institute extraordinary measures with respect to vital production facilities, public facilities, communications systems, transportation systems, or other facility, system, or service essential to national survival.

(3) Judicial and legislative liaison. In cooperation with the Office of Emergency Preparedness, maintain liaison with Federal courts and with the Congress so there will be mutual understanding of Federal emergency plans involving law enforcement and the exercise of legal powers during emergencies of various magnitudes.

(4) Legal advice. Develop emergency plans for providing legal
advice to the President, the Cabinet, and the heads of
Executive departments and agencies wherever they may be
located in an emergency, and provide emergency
procedures for the review as to form and legality of
Presidential proclamations, Executive orders, directives,
regulations, and documents, and of other documents
requiring approval by the President or by the Attorney
General which may be issued by authorized officers after an
armed attack.

(5) Alien control and control of entry and departure. Develop
emergency plans for the control of alien enemies and other
aliens within the United States, and in consultation with the
Department of State and Department of the Treasury, develop
emergency plans for the control of persons attempting to
enter or leave the United States. These plans shall specifically
include provisions for the following:

  (a) The location, restraint, or custody of alien enemies.
  (b) Temporary detention of alien enemies and other
      persons attempting to enter the United States pending
      determination of their admissibility.
  (c) Apprehension of deserting alien crewmen and
      stowaways.
  (d) Investigation and control of aliens admitted as
      contract laborers.
  (e) Control of persons entering or departing from the
      United States at designated ports of entry.
  (f) Increased surveillance of the borders to preclude
      prohibited crossings by persons.

(6) Alien property. Develop emergency plans, in consultation
with the Department of State, for the seizure and
administration of property of alien enemies under provisions
of the Trading with the Enemy Act.

(7) Security standards. In consultation with the Department
of Defense and with other executive agencies, to the extent
appropriate, prepare plans for adjustment of security
standards governing the employment of Federal personnel
and Federal contractors in an emergency.

(8) Drug control. Develop emergency plans and procedures for
the administration of laws governing the import,
manufacture, and distribution of narcotics. Consult with and
render all possible aid and assistance to the Office of

Emergency Preparedness, the Department of Health, Education, and Welfare, and the General Services Administration in the allocation, distribution, and, if necessary, the replenishment of Government stockpiles of narcotic drugs.

SEC. 502 Civil Defense Functions.

In consonance with national civil defense programs developed by the Department of Defense, the Attorney General shall:

(1) Local law enforcement. Upon request, consult with and assist the Department of Defense to plan, develop, and distribute materials for use in the instruction and training of law enforcement personnel for civil defense emergency operations; develop and carry out a national plan for civil defense instruction and training for enforcement officers, designed to utilize to the maximum extent practicable the resources and facilities of existing Federal, State, and local public schools. academies, and other appropriate institutions of learning; and assist the States in preparing for the conduct of intrastate and interstate law enforcement operations to meet the extra- ordinary needs that would exist for emergency police services under conditions of attack or imminent attack.

(2) Penal and correctional institutions. Develop emergency plans and procedures for the custody and protection of prisoners and the use of Federal penal and correctional institutional resources, when available, for cooperation with local authorities in connection with mass feeding and housing, for the storage of standby emergency equipment, for the emergency use of prison hospitals and laboratory facilities, for the continued availability of prison-industry products, and, in coordination with the Department of Labor, for the development of Federal prisoner skills to appropriately augment the total supply of manpower, advise States and their political subdivisions regarding the use of State and local prisons, jails, and prisoners for the purpose of relieving local situations and conditions arising from a state of emergency.

(3) Identification and location of persons. Develop emergency plans and procedures for the use of the facilities and personnel of the Department of Justice in assisting the Department of Health, Education, and Welfare with the development of plans and procedures for the identification of the dead and the reuniting of families during a civil defense emergency.

PART 6
POST OFFICE DEPARTMENT

SECTION 601 Functions.
The Postmaster General shall prepare plans and programs for emergency mail service and shall cooperate with indicated Federal agencies, in accordance with existing agreements or directives, in the following national emergency programs:

    (1) Registering of persons. Assist the Department of Health,
      Education, and Welfare in planning a national program
      and developing technical guidance for States, and directing
      Post Office activities concerned with registering persons
      and families for the purpose of receiving and answering
      welfare inquiries and reuniting families in civil defense
      emergencies. The program shall include procurement,
      transportation, storage, and distribution of safety notification
      and emergency change of address cards in quantities and
      localities jointly determined by the Department of Defense
      and the Post Office Department.

    (2) Other emergency programs.

        (a) Censorship of international mails. (Department of
            Defense; Department of the Treasury; Office of
            Emergency Preparedness)

        (b) Provision for emergency mail service to
            Federal agencies at both regular
            and emergency sites. (General Services
            Administration)

        (c) Emergency registration of Federal
            employees. (Civil Service Commission)

        (d) Emergency leasing of space for Federal
            agencies. (General Services Administration)

    (3) Registration of enemy aliens. (Department of Justice)

PART 7
DEPARTMENT OF THE INTERIOR

SECTION 701 Resume of Responsibilities.
The Secretary of the Interior shall prepare national emergency plans and develop preparedness programs covering

    (1) electric power;
    (2) petroleum and gas;
    (3) solid fuels;

(4) minerals; and

(5) water, as defined in Section 702 of this part.

SEC. 702 Definitions. As used in this part:

   (1) "Electric power" means all forms of electric power and energy, including the generation, transmission, distribution, and utilization thereof.

   (2) "Petroleum" means crude oil and synthetic liquid fuel, their products, and associated hydrocarbons, including pipelines for their movement and facilities specially designed for their storage.

   (3) "Gas" means natural gas (including helium) and manufactured gas, including pipelines for their movement and facilities specially designed for their storage.

   (4) "Solid fuels" means all forms of anthracite, bituminous, sub-bituminous, and lignitic coals, coke, and coal chemicals produced in the coke-making process.

   (5) "Minerals" means all raw materials of mineral origin (except petroleum, gas, solid fuels, and source materials as defined in the Atomic Energy Act of 1954, as amended) obtained by mining and like operations and processed through the stages specified and at the facilities designated in an agreement between the Secretary of the Interior and the Secretary of Commerce as being within the emergency preparedness responsibilities of the Secretary of the Interior.

   (6) "Water" means water from all sources except water after its withdrawal into a community system, or an emergency system for treatment, storage, and distribution for public use.

SEC. 703 Resource functions.

With respect to the resources defined in Section 702, the Secretary of the Interior shall:

   (1) Minerals development. Develop programs and encourage the exploration, development, and mining of strategic and critical minerals for emergency purposes.

   (2) Production. Provide guidance and leadership to assigned industries in the development of plans and programs to insure the continuity of production in the event of an attack, and cooperate with the Department of Commerce in the identification and evaluation of essential facilities.

   (3) Water. Develop plans with respect to water, including plans for the treatment and disposal, after use, of water after its

withdrawal into a community system or an emergency
system for treatment, storage, and distribution for public use.
In developing any plans relating to water for use on farms
and in food facilities, assure that those plans are in consonance with
plans and programs of the Department of Agriculture.
(4) Electric power and natural gas. In preparedness planning for
electric power and natural gas, the Federal Power
Commission shall assist the Secretary of the Interior as set
forth in Section 1901 of this order.

PART 8
DEPARTMENT OF AGRICULTURE

SECTION 801 Resume of Responsibilities.
The Secretary of Agriculture shall prepare national emergency plans and develop
preparedness programs covering:
(1) food resources, farm equipment, fertilizer, and food resource
facilities as defined below;
(2) lands under the jurisdiction of the Secretary of Agriculture;
(3) rural fire control;
(4) defense against biological and chemical warfare and
radiological fallout pertaining to agricultural activities; and
(5) rural defense information and education.

SEC. 802 Definitions. As used in this part:
(1) "Food resources" means all commodities and products,
simple, mixed, or compound, or complements to such
commodities or products, that are capable of being eaten or
drunk, by either human beings or animals, irrespective of
other uses to which such commodities or products may
be put, at all stages of processing from the raw commodity
to the products thereof in vendible form for human or animal
consumption. For the purposes of this order, the term "food
resources" shall also include all starches, sugars, vegetable
and animal fats and oils, cotton, tobacco, wool, mohair,
hemp, flax fiber, and naval stores, but shall not include
any such material after it loses its identity as an agricultural
commodity or agricultural product.
(2) "Farm equipment" means machinery, equipment, and repair
parts manufactured primarily for use on farms in connection
with the production or preparation for market or use of "food
resources."

(3) "Fertilizer" means any product or combination of products for plant nutrition in form for distribution to the users thereof.

(4) "Food resource facilities" means plants, machinery, vehicles (including on farm), and other facilities (including farm housing) for the production, processing, distribution, and storage (including cold storage) of food resources, and for domestic distribution of farm equipment and fertilizer.

SEC. 803 Functions.

With respect to food resources, food resource facilities, lands under the jurisdiction of the Secretary, farm equipment, and fertilizer, the Secretary of Agriculture shall:

(1) Production, processing, storage, and distribution. Develop plans for priorities, allocations, and distribution control systems and related plans, including control of use of facilities designed to provide adequate and continuing production, processing, storage, and distribution of essential food resources in an emergency, and to provide for the domestic distribution of farm equipment and fertilizer.

(2) Stockpiles. In addition to the food stockpile functions identified in Executive Order No. 10958, take all possible measures in the administration of Commodity Credit Corporation inventories of food resources to assure the availability of such inventories when and where needed in an emergency. The Secretary shall also develop plans and procedures for the proper utilization of agricultural items stockpiled for survival purposes.

(3) Land management. Develop plans and direct activities for the emergency protection, management, and utilization of the lands, resources, and installations under the jurisdiction of theSecretary of Agriculture and assist in the development of plans for the emergency operation, production, and processing of forest products in cooperation with other Federal, State, and private agencies.

SEC. 804 Civil Defense Functions.

In consonance with national civil defense programs developed by the Department of Defense, the Secretary of Agriculture shall:

(1) Rural fire defense. In cooperation with Federal, State, and local agencies, develop plans for a national program and direct activities relating to the prevention and control of fires in the rural areas of the United States caused by the effects of enemy attack.

(2) Biological, chemical, and radiological warfare defense. Develop plans for a national program, direct Federal activities, and furnish technical guidance to State and local authorities concerning

  (a) diagnosis and strengthening of defensive barriers and control or eradication of diseases, pests, or chemicals introduced as agents of biological or chemical warfare against animals, crops, or products thereof;

  (b) protective measures, treatment, and handling of livestock, including poultry, agricultural commodities on farms or ranches, agricultural lands, forest lands, and water for agricultural purposes, any of which have been exposed to or affected by radiation. Plans shall be developed for a national program and direction of Federal activities to assure the safety and wholesomeness and to minimize losses from biological and chemical warfare, radiological effects, and other emergency hazards of livestock, meat and meat products, poultry and poultry products in establishments under the continuous inspection of the Department of Agriculture, and agricultural commodities and products owned by the Commodity Credit Corporation or by the Department of Agriculture.

(3) Defense information and education. Conduct a defense information and education program in support of the Department's emergency responsibilities.

PART 9
DEPARTMENT OF COMMERCE

SECTION 901 Resume of Responsibilities.
The Secretary of Commerce shall prepare national emergency plans and develop preparedness programs covering:

(1) The production and distribution of all materials, the use of all production facilities (except those owned by, controlled by, or under the jurisdiction of the Department of Defense or the Atomic Energy Commission), the control of all construction materials, and the furnishing of basic industrial services except those involving the following:

  (a) Production and distribution of and use of facilities for petroleum, solid fuels, gas, electric power, and water;

(b) Production, processing, distribution, and storage of food resources and the use of food resource facilities for such production, processing, distribution, and storage;

(c) Domestic distribution of farm equipment and fertilizer;

(d) Use of communications services and facilities, housing and lodging facilities, and health, education, and welfare facilities;

(e) Production, and related distribution, of minerals as defined in Subsection 702 (5), and source materials as defined in the Atomic Energy Act of 1954, as amended; and the construction and use of facilities designated as within the responsibilities of the Secretary of the Interior;

(f) Distribution of items in the supply systems of, or controlled by, the Department of Defense and the Atomic Energy Commission;

(g) Construction, use, and management of civil aviation facilities; and

(h) Construction and use of highways, streets, and appurtenant structures.

(2) Federal emergency operational control responsibilities with respect to ocean shipping, ports, and port facilities, except those owned by, controlled by, or under the jurisdiction of the Department of Defense, and except those responsibilities of the Department of the Treasury with respect to the entrance and clearance of vessels. The following definitions apply to this part:

(a) Ocean shipping includes all overseas, coastwise, intercoastal, and Great Lakes shipping except that solely engaged in the transportation of passengers and cargo between United States ports on the Great Lakes.

(b) Port or port area includes any zone contiguous to or associated in the traffic network of an ocean or Great Lakes port, or outport location, including beach loading sites, within which facilities exist for transshipment of persons and property between domestic carriers and carriers engaged in coastal, intercoastal, and overseas transportation.

(c) Port facilities includes all port facilities, port

equipment including harbor craft, and port services
normally used in accomplishing the transfer or
interchange of cargo and passengers between ocean-
going vessels and other media of transportation, or in
connection therewith (including the Great Lakes).

(3) Scientific and technological services and functions, essential
to emergency preparedness plans, programs, and operations
of the Federal departments and agencies, in which the
Department of Commerce has the capability, including, but
not limited to:

  (a) Meteorological and related services;
  (b) Preparation, reproduction, and distribution of nautical
      and aeronautical charts, geodetic, hydrographic, and
      oceanographic data, and allied services for
      nonmilitary purposes;
  (c) Standards of measurement and supporting services;
      and
  (d) Research, development, testing, evaluation,
      application, and associated services and activities
      in the various fields and disciplines of science and
      technology in which the Department has special
      competence.

(4) Collection, compilation, and reporting of census information
and the provision of statistical and related services, as
required, for emergency planning and operations.

(5) Regulation and control of exports and imports, under the
jurisdiction of the Department of Commerce, in support of
national security, foreign policy, and economic stabilization
objectives.

(6) Regulation and control of transfers of capital to, and
reinvestment of earnings of, affiliated foreign nationals
pursuant to authority conferred by Executive Order No.
11387 of January 1, 1968.

SEC. 902 Production Functions.
Within the areas designated in section 901 (1) hereof, the Secretary of
Commerce shall:

(1) Priorities and allocations. Develop control systems for
priorities, allocation, production, and distribution, including
provisions for other Federal departments and agencies, as
appropriate, to serve as allotting agents for materials and
other resources made available under such systems for

designated programs and the construction and operation of
facilities assigned to them.
(2) New construction. Develop procedures by which new
production facility construction proposals will be reviewed
for appropriate location in light of such area factors as
locational security, availability of labor, water, power,
housing, and other support requirements.
(3) Industry evaluation. Identify and evaluate the national
security essentiality of those products and services, and their
producing or supporting facilities, which are of exceptional
importance to mobilization readiness, national defense, or
post-attack survival and recovery.
(4) Production capability. Analyze potential effects of attack
on actual production capability, taking into account the
entire production complex, including shortages of resources,
and conduct studies as a basis for recommending pre-attack
measures that would strengthen capabilities for post-attack
production.
(5) Loans for plant modernization. Develop plans, in
coordination with the Small Business Administration, for
providing emergency assistance to essential small business
establishments through direct loans or participation loans for
the financing of production facilities and equipment.

SEC. 903 Maritime Functions.
Within the areas designated in section 901(2) of this part, the Secretary of
Commerce shall develop plans and procedures in consonance with international
treaties, under coordinating authority of the Secretary of Transportation and in
cooperation with other appropriate Federal agencies and the States and their
political subdivisions, to provide for Federal operational control of ocean ports
and shipping, including:
(1) Shipping allocation. Allocation of specific ocean shipping
to meet the national requirements, including those for
military, foreign assistance, emergency procurement
programs, and those essential to the civilian economy.
(2) Ship acquisition. Provision of ships for ocean shipping by
purchase, charter, or requisition, by breakout from the
national defense reserve fleet, and by construction.
(3) Operations. Operation of ocean shipping, directly or indirectly.
(4) Traffic control. Provisions for the control of passengers and
cargo through port areas to assure an orderly and continuous
flow of such traffic.

(5) Traffic priority. Administration of priorities for the movement of passengers and cargo through port areas.

(6) Port allocation. Allocation of specific ports and port facilities to meet the needs of the Nation and our allies.

(7) Support activities. Performance of supporting activities needed to carry out the above-described functions, such as: ascertaining national support requirements for ocean shipping, including those for support of military and other Federal programs and those essential to the civil economy; maintenance, repair, and arming of ships; recruiting, training, and assigning of officers and seamen; procurement, warehousing, and issuance of ships' stores, supplies, equipment, and spare parts; supervision of stevedoring and bunkering; management of terminals, shipyards, repair, and other facilities; and provision, maintenance, and restoration of port facilities.

SEC. 904 Census Functions.

Within the area designated in section 901(4) hereof, the Secretary of Commerce shall:

(1) Provide for the collection and reporting of census information on the status of human and economic resources, including population, housing, agriculture, manufacture, mineral industries, business, transportation, foreign trade, construction, and governments, as required for emergency planning purposes.

(2) Plan, create, and maintain a capability for the conduct of post-attack surveys to provide information on the status of surviving populations and resources as required for the programs of the Office of Emergency Preparedness.

(3) Provide for and maintain the ability to make estimates of attack effects on industry, population, and other resources for use within the Department of Commerce.

SEC. 905 Civil Defense Functions.

In consonance with national civil defense programs developed by the Department of Defense, the Secretary of Commerce shall:

(1) Weather functions. Prepare and issue currently, as well as in an emergency, forecasts and estimates of areas likely to be covered by radiological fallout in event of attack and make this information available to Federal, State, and local authorities for public dissemination.

(2) Geodetic, hydrographic, and oceanographic data. Provide geodetic, hydrographic, and oceanographic data and services to the Department of Defense and other governmental agencies, as appropriate.

PART 10
DEPARTMENT OF LABOR

SECTION 1001 Resume of Responsibilities.
The Secretary of Labor shall have primary responsibility for preparing national emergency plans and developing preparedness programs covering civilian manpower mobilization, more effective utilization of limited manpower resources, including specialized personnel, wage and salary stabilization, worker incentives and protection, manpower resources and requirements, skill development and training, research, labor-management relations, and critical occupations.

SEC. 1002 Functions.
The Secretary of Labor shall:
(1) Civilian manpower mobilization. Develop plans and issue guidance designed to utilize to the maximum extent civilian manpower resources, such plans and guidance to be developed with the active participation and assistance of the States and local political subdivisions thereof, and of other organizations and agencies concerned with the mobilization of the people of the United States. Such plans shall include, but not necessarily be limited to:
    (a) Manpower management. Recruitment, selection and referral, training, employment stabilization (including appeals procedures), proper utilization, and determination of the skill categories critical to meeting the labor requirements of defense and essential civilian activities;
    (b) Priorities. Procedures for translating survival and production urgencies into manpower priorities to be used as guides for allocating available workers; and
    (c) Improving mobilization base. Programs for more effective utilization of limited manpower resources, and, in cooperation with other appropriate agencies, programs for recruitment, training, allocation, and utilization of persons possessing specialized competence or aptitude in acquiring such competence.

(2) Wage and salary stabilization. Develop plans and procedures for wage and salary stabilization and for the national and field organization necessary for the administration of such a program in an emergency, including investigation, compliance, and appeals procedures; statistical studies of wages, salaries, and prices for policy decisions and to assist operating stabilization agencies to carry out their functions.

(3) Worker incentives and protection. Develop plans and procedures for wage and salary compensation and death and disability compensation for authorized civil defense workers and, as appropriate, measures for unemployment payments, reemployment rights, and occupational safety, and other protection and incentives for the civilian labor force during an emergency.

(4) Skill development and training. Initiate current action programs to overcome or offset present or anticipated manpower deficiencies, including those identified as a result of resource and requirements studies.

(5) Labor-management relations. Develop, after consultation with the Department of Commerce, the Department of Transportation, the Department of Defense, the National Labor Relations Board, the Federal Mediation and Conciliation Service, the National Mediation Board, and other appropriate agencies and groups, including representatives of labor and management, plans and procedures, including organization plans, for the maintenance of effective labor-management relations during a national emergency.

PART 11
DEPARTMENT OF HEALTH, EDUCATION, AND WELFARE

SECTION 1101 Resume of Responsibilities.
In addition to the medical stockpile functions identified in Executive Order No. 10958, the Secretary of Health, Education, and Welfare shall prepare national emergency plans and develop preparedness programs covering health services, civilian health manpower, health resources, welfare services, social security benefits, credit union operations, and educational programs as defined below.

SEC. 1102 Definitions.
As used in this part:
(1) "Emergency health services" means medical and dental care for the civilian population in all of their specialties

and adjunct therapeutic fields, and the planning, provision, and operation of first aid stations, hospitals, and clinics; preventive health services, including detection, identification and control of communicable diseases, their vectors, and other public health hazards, inspection and control of purity and safety of food, drugs, and biologicals; vital statistics services; rehabilitation and related services for disabled survivors; preventive and curative care related to human exposure to radiological, chemical, and biological warfare agents; sanitary aspects of disposal of the dead; food and milk sanitation; community solid waste disposal; emergency public water supply; and the determination of the health significance of water pollution and the provision of other services pertaining to health aspects of water use and water-borne wastes as set forth in an agreement between the Secretary of Health, Education, and Welfare and the Secretary of the Interior, approved by the President, pursuant to Reorganization Plan No. 2 of 1966, which plan placed upon the Secretary of the Interior responsibilities for the prevention and control of water pollution. It shall be understood that health services for the purposes of this order, however, do not encompass the following areas for which the Department of Agriculture has responsibility: plant and animal diseases and pest prevention, control, and eradication, wholesomeness of meat and meat products, and poultry and poultry products in establishments under continuous inspection service by the Department of Agriculture, veterinary biologicals, agricultural commodities and products owned by the Commodity Credit Corporation o the Secretary of Agriculture, livestock, agricultural commodities stored or harvestable on farms and ranches, agricultural land and water, and registration of pesticides.

(2) "Health manpower" means physicians (including osteopaths); dentists; sanitary engineers; registered professional nurses; and such other occupations as may be included in the List of Health Manpower Occupations issued for the purposes of this part by the Director of the Office of Emergency Preparedness after agreement by the Secretary of Labor and the Secretary of Health, Education, and Welfare.

(3) "Health resources" means manpower, material, and facilities required to prevent the impairment of, improve, and restore the physical and mental health conditions of the civilian population.

(4) "Emergency welfare services" means feeding; clothing;
lodging in private and congregate facilities; registration;
locating and reuniting families; care of unaccompanied
children, the aged, the handicapped, and other groups
needing specialized care or services; necessary financial or
other assistance; counseling and referral services to families
and individuals; aid to welfare institutions under national
emergency or post-attack conditions; and all other feasible
welfare aid and services to people in need during a civil
defense emergency. Such measures include organization,
direction, and provision of services to be instituted before
attack, in the event of strategic or tactical evacuation, and
after attack in the event of evacuation or of refuge in shelters.

(5) "Social security benefits" means the determination of
entitlement and the payment of monthly insurance benefits
to those eligible, such as workers who have retired because
of age or disability and to their dependent wives and
children, and to the eligible survivors of deceased workers.
It also includes determinations of eligibility and payments
made on behalf of eligible individuals to hospitals, home
health agencies, extended care facilities, physicians, and
other providers of medical services.

(6) "Credit union operations" means the functions of any credit
union, chartered either by a State or the Federal
Government, in stimulating systematic savings by members,
the investment and protection of those savings, providing
loans for credit union members at reasonable rates, and
encouraging sound credit and thrift practices among credit
union members.

(7) "Education" or "training" means the organized process of
learning by study and instruction primarily through public
and private systems.

SEC. 1103 Health Functions.

With respect to emergency health services, as defined above, and in consonance
with national civil defense plans, programs, and operation of the Department of
Defense under Executive Order No. 10952, the Secretary of Health, Education,
and Welfare shall:

(1) Professional training. Develop and direct a nationwide
program to train health manpower both in professional and
technical occupational content and in civil defense
knowledge and skills. Develop and distribute health

education material for inclusion in the curricula of schools, colleges, professional schools, government schools, and other educational facilities throughout the United States. Develop and distribute civil defense information relative to health services to States, voluntary agencies, and professional groups.

(2) Emergency public water supply. Prepare plans to assure the provision of usable water supplies for human consumption and other essential community uses in an emergency. This shall include inventorying existing community water supplies, planning for other alternative sources of water for emergency uses, setting standards relating to human consumption, and planning community distribution. In carrying on these activities, the Department shall have primary responsibility but will make maximum use of the resources and competence of State and local authorities, the Department of the Interior, and other Federal agencies.

(3) Radiation. Develop and coordinate programs of radiation measurement and assessment as may be necessary to carry out the responsibilities involved in the provision of emergency health services.

(4) Biological and chemical warfare. Develop and coordinate programs for the prevention, detection, and identification of human exposure to chemical and biological warfare agents as may be necessary to carry out the responsibilities involved in the provision of emergency health services, including the provision of guidance and consultation to Federal, State, and local authorities on measures for minimizing the effects of biological or chemical warfare.

(5) Food, drugs, and biologicals. Plan and direct national programs for the maintenance of purity and safety in the manufacture and distribution of food, drugs, and biologicals in an emergency.

(6) Disabled survivors. Prepare national plans for emergency operations of vocational rehabilitation and related agencies, and for measures and resources necessary to rehabilitate and make available for employment those disabled persons among the surviving population.

SEC. 1104 Welfare Functions.

With respect to emergency welfare services as defined above, and in consonance with national civil defense plans, programs, and operations of the Department of

Defense under Executive Order No. 10952, the Secretary of Health, Education, and Welfare shall:

(1) Federal support. Cooperate in the development of Federal support procedures, through joint planning with other Departments and agencies, including but not limited to the Post Office Department, the Department of Labor, and the Selective Service System, the Department of Housing and Urban Development, and resource agencies, including the Department of Agriculture, the Department of the Interior, and the Department of Commerce, for logistic support of State and community welfare services in an emergency.

(2) Emergency welfare training. Develop and direct a nationwide program to train emergency welfare manpower for the execution of the functions set forth in this part, develop welfare educational materials, including self-help program materials for use with welfare organizations and professional schools, and develop and distribute civil defense information relative to emergency welfare services to States, voluntary agencies, and professional groups.

(3) Financial aid. Develop plans and procedures for financial assistance to individuals injured or in want as a result of enemy attack and for welfare institutions in need of such assistance in an emergency.

(4) Non-combatant evacuees to the Continental United States. Develop plans and procedures for assistance, at ports of entry to U.S. personnel evacuated from overseas areas, their onward movement to final destination, and follow-up assistance after arrival at final destination.

SEC. 1105 Social Security Functions.

With respect to social security, the Secretary of Health, Education, and Welfare shall:

(1) Social security benefits. Develop plans for the continuation or restoration of benefit payments to those on the insurance rolls as soon as possible after a direct attack upon the United States, and prepare plans for the acceptance and disposition of current claims for social security benefits.

(2) Health insurance. Develop plans for the payment of health insurance claims for reimbursement for items or services provided by hospitals, physicians, and other providers of medical services submitted by or on behalf of individuals who are eligible under the Medicare program.

SEC. 1106 Credit Union Functions.

With respect to credit union functions, the Secretary of Health, Education, and Welfare shall:

(1) Credit union operations. Provide instructions to all State and Federally chartered credit unions for the development of emergency plans to be put into effect as soon as possible after an attack upon the United States in order to guarantee continuity of credit union operations.

(2) Economic stabilization. Provide guidance to credit unions that will contribute to stabilization of the Nation's economy by helping to establish and maintain a sound economic base for combating inflation, maintaining confidence in public and private financial institutions, and promoting thrift.

SEC. 1107 Education Functions.

With respect to education, the Secretary of Health, Education, and Welfare shall:

(1) Program guidance. Develop plans and issue guidance for the continued function of educational systems under all conditions of national emergency. Although extraordinary circumstances may require the temporary suspension of education, plans should provide for its earliest possible resumption.

(2) Educational adjustment. Plan to assist civilian educational institutions, both public and private, to adjust to demands laid upon them by a large expansion of government activities during any type of emergency. This includes advice and assistance to schools, colleges, universities, and other educational institutions whose facilities may be temporarily needed for Federal, State, or local government programs in an emergency or whose faculties and student bodies may be affected by the demands of a sudden or long-standing emergency.

(3) Post-attack recovery. Develop plans for the rapid restoration and resumption of education at all levels after an attack. This includes assistance to educators and educational institutions to locate and use surviving facilities, equipment, supplies, books, and educational personnel. Particular emphasis shall be given to the role of educational institutions and educational leadership in reviving education and training in skills needed for post-attack recovery.

(4) Civil defense education. In consonance with national civil defense plans, programs, and operations of the Department of

Defense, develop and issue instructional materials to
assist schools, colleges, and other educational institutions
to incorporate emergency protective measures and civil
defense concepts into their programs. This includes
assistance to various levels of education to develop
an understanding of the role of the individual, family, and
community for civil defense in the nuclear age.

PART 12
DEPARTMENT OF HOUSING AND URBAN DEVELOPMENT

SECTION 1201 Resume of Responsibilities.
The Secretary of Housing and Urban Development shall prepare national
emergency plans and develop preparedness programs covering all aspects of
housing, community facilities related to housing, and urban development (except
that housing assets under the jurisdiction and control of the Department of
Defense, other than those leased for terms not in excess of one year, shall be and
remain the responsibility of the Department of Defense).

SEC. 1202 Definition. As used in this part:
  (1) "Emergency housing" means any and all types of
      accommodations used as dwellings in an emergency.
  (2) "Community facilities related to housing" means installations
      necessary to furnish water, sewer, electric, and gas services
      between the housing unit or project and the nearest practical
      source or servicing point.
  (3) "Urban development" means the building or restoration of
      urban community, suburban, and metropolitan areas (except
      transportation facilities).

SEC. 1203 Housing and Community Facilities Functions.
The Secretary of Housing and Urban Development shall:
  (1) New housing. Develop plans for the emergency construction
      and management of new housing and the community
      facilities related thereto to the extent that it is determined
      that it may be necessary to provide for such construction and
      management with public funds and through direct Federal
      action, and to the extent that such construction of new
      housing may have to be provided through Federal financial or
      credit assistance.
  (2) Community facilities. Develop plans to restore community

facilities related to housing affected by an emergency
through the repair of damage, the construction of new
facilities, and the use of alternate or back-up facilities.

SEC. 1204 Urban Development Functions.

The Secretary of Housing and Urban Development shall:

(1) Regional cooperation. Encourage regional emergency
planning and cooperation among State and local governments
with respect to problems of housing and metropolitan development.

(2) Vulnerability and redevelopment. In cooperation with the
Office of Emergency Preparedness, develop criteria and
provide guidance for the design and location of housing and
community facilities related to housing to minimize the risk
of loss under various emergency situations. Develop criteria
for determining which areas should be redeveloped in the
event of loss or severe damage resulting from emergencies.

SEC. 1205 Civil Defense Functions.

In consonance with national civil defense plans, programs, and operations of
the Department of Defense under Executive Order No. 10952, the Secretary of
Housing and Urban Development shall:

(1) Transitional activities. Develop plans for the orderly transfer
of people from fallout shelters and from billets to temporary
or permanent housing, including advice and guidance for
State and local government agencies in the administration
thereof. These plans shall be coordinated with national plans
and guidance for emergency welfare services of the
Department of Health, Education, and Welfare.

(2) Temporary housing. Develop plans for the emergency repair
and restoration for use of damaged housing, for the
construction and management of emergency housing units
and the community facilities related thereto, for the
emergency use of tents and trailers, and for the emergency
conversion for dwelling use of non-residential structures,
such activities to be financed with public funds through direct
Federal action or through financial or credit assistance.

(3) Shelter. In conformity with national shelter policy assist
in the development of plans to encourage the construction
of shelters for both old and new housing, and develop
administrative procedures to encourage the use of low-cost
design and construction techniques to maximize protection in
connection with national programs.

Part 13
Department of Transportation

SECTION 1301 Resume of Responsibilities.
The Secretary of Transportation, in carrying out his responsibilities to exercise leadership in transportation matters affecting the national defense and those involving national or regional transportation emergencies, shall prepare emergency plans and develop preparedness programs covering:

(1) Preparation and promulgation of over-all national policies, plans, and procedures related to providing civil transportation of all forms — air, ground, water, and pipelines, including public storage and warehousing (except storage of petroleum and gas and agricultural food resources including cold storage): Provided that plans for the movement of petroleum and natural gas through pipelines shall be the responsibility of the Secretary of the Interior except to the extent that such plans are a part of functions vested in the Secretary of Transportation by law;

(2) Movement of passengers and materials of all types by all forms of civil transportation;

(3) Determination of the proper apportionment and allocation for control of the total civil transportation capacity, or any portion thereof, to meet over-all essential civil and military needs;

(4) Determination and identification of the transportation resources available and required to meet all degrees of national emergencies and regional transportation emergencies;

(5) Assistance to the various States, the local political subdivisions thereof, and non-governmental organizations and systems engaged in transportation activities in the preparation of emergency plans;

(6) Rehabilitation and recovery of the Nation's transportation systems; and

(7) Provisions for port security and safety, for aids to maritime navigation, and for search and rescue and law enforcement over, upon, and under the navigable waters of the United States and the high seas.

SEC. 1302 Transportation Planning and Coordination
Functions. In carrying out the provisions of Section 1301, the Secretary of Transportation, with assistance and support of other Federal, State and local governmental agencies, and the transport industries, as appropriate, shall:

(1) Obtain, assemble, analyze, and evaluate data on current and projected emergency requirements of all claimants for all forms of civil transportation to meet the needs of the military and of the civil economy, and on current and projected civil transportation resources — of all forms available to the United States to move passengers or materials in an emergency.

(2) Develop plans and procedures to provide— under emergency conditions — for the collection and analysis of passenger and cargo movement demands as they relate to the capabilities of the various forms of transport, including the periodic assessment of over-all transport resources available to meet emergency requirements.

(3) Conduct a continuing analysis of transportation requirements and capabilities in relation to economic projections for the purpose of initiating actions and/or recommending incentive and/or regulatory programs designed to stimulate government and industry improvement of the structure of the transportation system for use in an emergency.

(4) Develop systems for the control of the movement of passengers and cargo by all forms of transportation, except for those resources owned by, controlled by, or under the jurisdiction of the Department of Defense, including allocation of resources and assignment of priorities, and develop policies, standards, and procedures for emergency enforcement of these controls.

SEC. 1303 Departmental Emergency Transportation Preparedness. Except for those resources owned by, controlled by, or under the jurisdiction of the Department of Defense, the Secretary of Transportation shall prepare emergency operational plans and programs for, and develop a capability to carry out, the transportation operating responsibilities assigned to the Department, including but not limited to:

(1) Allocating air carrier civil air transportation capacity and equipment to meet civil and military requirements.

(2) Emergency management, including construction, reconstruction, and maintenance of the Nation's civil airports, civil aviation operating facilities, civil aviation services, and civil aircraft (other than air carrier aircraft), except manufacturing facilities.

(3) Emergency management of all Federal, State, city, local, and other highways, roads, streets, bridges, tunnels, and appurtenant structures, including:

(a) The adaptation, development, construction, reconstruction, and maintenance of the Nation's highway and street systems to meet emergency requirements;

(b) The protection of the traveling public by assisting State and local authorities in informing them of the dangers of travel through hazardous areas; and

(c) The regulation of highway traffic in an emergency through a national program in cooperation with all Federal, State, and local governmental units or other agencies concerned.

(4) Emergency plans for urban mass transportation, including:

(a) Providing guidance to urban communities in their emergency mass transportation planning efforts, either directly or through State, regional, or metropolitan agencies;

(b) Coordinating all such emergency planning with the Department of Housing and Urban Development to assure compatibility with emergency plans for all other aspects of urban development;

(c) Maintaining an inventory of urban mass transportation systems.

(5) Maritime safety and law enforcement over, upon, and under the high seas and waters, subject to the jurisdiction of the United States, in the following specific programs:

(a) Safeguarding vessels, harbors, ports, and waterfront facilities from destruction, loss or injury, accidents, or other causes of a similar nature.

(b) Safe passage over, upon, and under the high seas and United States waters through effective and reliable systems of aids to navigation and ocean stations.

(c) Waterborne access to ice-bound locations in furtherance of national economic, scientific, defense, and consumer needs.

(d) Protection of lives, property, natural resources, and national interests through enforcement of Federal law and timely assistance.

(e) Safety of life and property through regulation of commercial vessels, their officers and crew, and administration of maritime safety law.

(f) Knowledge of the sea, its boundaries, and its resources through collection and analysis of data in support of the national interest.

(g) Operational readiness for essential wartime
functions.

(6) Planning for the emergency management and operation of the
Alaska Railroad, and for the continuity of railroad and
petroleum pipeline safety programs.

(7) Planning for the emergency operation and maintenance of the
United States-controlled sections of the Saint Lawrence
Seaway.

PART 14
ATOMIC ENERGY COMMISSION

SECTION 1401 Functions.
The Atomic Energy Commission shall prepare national emergency plans
and develop preparedness programs for the continuing conduct of atomic
energy activities of the Federal Government. These plans and programs shall
be designed to develop a state of readiness in these areas with respect to all
conditions of national emergency, including attack upon the United States and,
consistent with applicable provisions of the Atomic Energy Act of 1954, as
amended, shall be closely coordinated with the Department of Defense and the
Office of Emergency Preparedness. The Atomic Energy Commission shall:

(1) Production. Continue or resume in an emergency, essential
    (a) manufacture, development, and control of nuclear
      weapons and equipment, except to the extent that the
      control over such weapons and equipment shall have
      been transferred to the Department of Defense;
    (b) development and technology related to reactors;
    (c) process development and production of feed material,
      special nuclear materials, and other special products;
    (d) related raw materials procurement, processing, and
      development; and
    (e) repair, maintenance, and construction related to the
      above.

(2) Regulation. Continue or resume in an emergency
    (a) controlling the possession, use, transfer, import, and
      export of atomic materials and facilities; and
    (b) ordering the operation or suspension of licensed
      facilities, and recapturing from licensees, where
      necessary, special nuclear materials whether related
      to military support or civilian activities.

(3) Public health and safety. Shut down, where required, in
anticipation of an imminent enemy attack on the United

States, and maintain under surveillance, all Commission-owned facilities which could otherwise constitute a significant hazard to public health and safety, and insure the development of appropriate emergency plans for nuclear reactors and other nuclear activities licensed by the Commission whether privately-owned or Government-owned.

(4) Scientific, technical, and public atomic energy information. Organize, reproduce, and disseminate appropriate public atomic energy information and scientific and technical reports and data relating to nuclear science research, development, engineering, applications, and effects to interested Government agencies, the scientific and technical communities, and approved, friendly, and cooperating foreign nations.

(5) International atomic energy affairs. Maintain, in consultation with the Department of State, essential liaison with foreign nations with respect to activities of mutual interest involving atomic energy.

(6) Health services. Assist the Department of Health, Education, and Welfare, consistent with the above requirements, in integrating into civilian health programs in an emergency the Commission's remaining health manpower and facilities not required for the performance of the Commission's essential emergency functions.

(7) Priorities and allocations. Plan for the administration of any priorities and allocations authority delegated to the Atomic Energy Commission. Authorize procurement and production schedules and make allotments of controlled materials pursuant to program determinations of the Office of Emergency Preparedness.

PART 15
CIVIL AERONAUTICS BOARD

SECTION 1501 Definitions.
As used in this part:

(1) "War Air Service Program" (hereinafter referred to as WASP) means the program designed to provide for the maintenance of essential civil air routes and services, and to provide for the distribution and redistribution of air carrier aircraft among civil air transport carriers after withdrawal of aircraft allocated to the Civil Reserve Air Fleet.

(2) "Civil Reserve Air Fleet" (hereinafter referred to as CRAF)
means those air carrier aircraft allocated by the Secretary of
Transportation to the Department of Defense to meet
essential military needs in the event of an emergency.

SEC. 1502 Functions.
The Civil Aeronautics Board, under the coordinating authority of the Secretary
of Transportation, shall:
(1) Distribution of aircraft. Develop plans and be prepared to
carry out such distribution and redistribution of all air carrier
civil aircraft allocated by the Secretary of Transportation
among the civil air transport carriers as may be necessary
to assure the maintenance of essential civil routes and
services under WASP operations after the CRAF
requirements have been met.
(2) Economic regulations. Develop plans covering route
authorizations and operations, tariffs, rates, and fares charged
the public, mail rates, government compensation and subsidy,
and accounting and contracting procedures essential to
WASP operations.
(3) Operational controls and priorities. Develop plans and
procedures for the administration of operational controls and
priorities of passenger and cargo movements in connection
with the utilization of air carrier aircraft for WASP purposes
in an emergency.
(4) Investigation. Maintain the capability to investigate
violations of emergency economic regulations affecting air
carrier operations.
(5) Contracting. Prepare to perform as a contracting agency, if
such an agency is necessary, in connection with distribution
and redistribution of aircraft for WASP.

Part 16
Export-Import Bank of the United States

SECTION 1601 Functions.
(a) Under guidance of the Secretary of the Treasury, the Export-
Import Bank shall develop plans for the utilization of the
resources of the Bank, or other resources made available
to the Bank, in expansion of productive capacity abroad for
essential materials, foreign barter arrangements, acquisition
of emergency imports, and in support of the domestic

economy, or any other plans designed to strengthen the
relative position of the Nation and its allies.
(b) In carrying out the guidance functions described above, the
Secretary of the Treasury shall consult with the Secretary of
State and the Secretary of Commerce as appropriate.

PART 17
FEDERAL BANK SUPERVISORY AGENCIES

SECTION 1701 Financial Plans and Programs.
The Board of Governors of the Federal Reserve System, the Comptroller of the
Currency, the Federal Home Loan Bank Board, the Farm Credit Administration,
and the Federal Deposit Insurance Corporation shall participate with the Office
of Emergency Preparedness, the Department of the Treasury, and other agencies
in the formulation of emergency financial and stabilization policies. The heads
of such agencies shall, as appropriate, develop emergency plans, programs, and
regulations, in consonance with national emergency financial and stabilization
plans and policies, to cope with potential economic effects of mobilization or an
attack, including, but not limited to, the following:
(1) Money and credit. Provision and regulation of money and
credit in accordance with the needs of the economy,
including the acquisition, decentralization, and distribution of
emergency supplies of currency; the collection of cash items
and non-cash items; and the conduct of fiscal agency and
foreign operations.
(2) Financial institutions. Provision for the continued or
resumed operation of banking, savings and loan, and farm
credit institutions, including measures for the re-creation of
evidence of assets or liabilities destroyed or inaccessible.
(3) Liquidity. Provision of liquidity necessary to the continued
or resumed operation of banking, savings and loan, credit
unions, and farm credit institutions, including those damaged
or destroyed by enemy action.
(4) Cash withdrawals and credit transfers. Regulation of the
withdrawal of currency and the transfer of credits including
deposit and share account balances.
(5) Insurance. Provision for the assumption and discharge of
liability pertaining to insured deposits and insured savings
accounts or withdrawable shares in banking and savings and
loan institutions destroyed or made insolvent.

SEC. 1702 Sharing of war losses.

Heads of agencies shall, as appropriate, participate with the Office of Emergency Preparedness and the Department of the Treasury in the development of policies, plans, and procedures for implementation of national policy on sharing war losses.

PART 18
FEDERAL COMMUNICATIONS COMMISSION

SECTION 1801 Definitions.

As used in this part:

(1) "Common carrier" means any person subject to Commission regulation engaged in providing for use by the public, for hire, interstate or foreign communications facilities or services by wire or radio; but a person engaged in radio broadcasting shall not, insofar as such person is so engaged, be deemed a common carrier.

(2) "Broadcast facilities" means those stations licensed by the Commission for the dissemination of radio communications intended to be received by the public directly or by the intermediary of relay stations.

(3) "Safety and special radio services" includes those non-broadcast and non-common carrier services which are licensed by the Commission under the generic designation "safety and special radio services" pursuant to the Commission's Rules and Regulations.

SEC. 1802 Functions.

The Federal Communications Commission shall develop policies, plans, and procedures, in consonance with national telecommunications plans and policies developed pursuant to Executive Order No. 10705, Executive Order No. 10995, Executive Order No. 11051, the Presidential Memorandum of August 21, 1963, "Establishment of the National Communications System," and other appropriate authority, covering:

(1) Common carrier service.

(a) Extension, discontinuance, or reduction of common carrier facilities or services, and issuance of appropriate authorizations for such facilities, services, and personnel in an emergency; and control of all rates, charges, practices, classifications, and regulations for service to Government and non-Government users during an emergency, in

consonance with overall national economic
stabilization policies.
(b) Development and administration of priority
systems for public correspondence and for the use
and resumption of leased inter-city private line
service in an emergency.
(c) Use of common carrier facilities and services to
overseas points to meet vital needs in an emergency.
(2) Broadcasting service. Construction, activation, or
deactivation of broadcasting facilities and services, the
continuation or suspension of broadcasting services and
facilities, and issuance of appropriate authorizations for such
facilities, services, and personnel in an emergency.
(3) Safety and special radio services. Authorization, operation,
and use of safety and special radio services, facilities, and
personnel in the national interest in an emergency.
(4) Radio frequency assignment. Assignment of radio
frequencies to, and their use by, Commission licensees in an
emergency.
(5) Electromagnetic radiation. Closing of any radio station or
any device capable of emitting electro-magnetic radiation
or suspension or amending any rules or regulations
applicable thereto, in any emergency, except for those
belonging to, or operated by, any department or agency of the
United States Government.
(6) Investigation and enforcement. Investigation of violations of
pertinent law and regulations in an emergency, and
development of procedures designated to initiate,
recommend, or otherwise bring about appropriate
enforcement actions required in the interest of national
security.

PART 19
FEDERAL POWER COMMISSION

SECTION 1901 Functions.
The Federal Power Commission shall assist the Department of the Interior, in
conformity with Part 7, in the preparation of national emergency plans and the
development of preparedness programs for electric power and natural gas in
the areas as set forth in the Memorandum of Agreement dated August 9, 1962,
between the Secretary of the Interior and the Chairman of the Federal Power
Commission.

Part 20
General Services Administration

SECTION 2001 Resume of Responsibilities.
The Administrator of General Services shall prepare national emergency
plans and develop preparedness programs designed to permit modification or
expansion of the activities of the General Services Administration under the
Federal Property and Administrative Services Act of 1949, as amended and other
statutes prescribing the duties and responsibilities of the Administrator. These
plans and programs shall include, but not be limited to:

    (1) operation, maintenance, and protection of Federal buildings
        and their sites; construction, alteration, and repair of public
        buildings; and acquisition; utilization, and disposal of real
        and personal properties;

    (2) public utilities service management for Federal agencies;

    (3) telecommunications to meet the essential requirements of
        civilian activities of executive departments and agencies;

    (4) transportation management to meet the traffic service
        requirements of civilian activities of Federal agencies;

    (5) records management;

    (6) Emergency Federal Register;

    (7) Government-wide supply support;

    (8) service to survival items stockpiles;

    (9) national industrial reserve;

    (10) guidance and consultation to Government agencies
        regarding facilities protection measures;

    (11) administration of assigned functions under the Defense
        Production Act; and

    (12) administration and operation of the stockpile of strategic
        and critical materials in accordance with policies and
        guidance furnished by the Office of Emergency
        Preparedness.

SEC. 2002 Functions.
The Administrator of General Services shall:

    (1) Public buildings. Develop emergency plans and procedures
        for the operation, maintenance, and protection of both
        existing and new Federally-owned and Federally-occupied
        buildings, and construction, alteration, and repair of public
        buildings. Develop emergency operating procedures for the
        control, acquisition, assignment, and priority of occupancy of

real property by the Federal Government and by State and local governments to the extent they may be performing functions as agents of the Federal Government.

(2) Public utility service management. Develop emergency operational plans and procedures for the claimancy, procurement, and use of public utility services for emergency activities of executive agencies of the Government.

(3) Communications. Plan for and provide, operate, and maintain appropriate telecommunications facilities designed to meet the essential requirements of Federal civilian departments and agencies during an emergency within the framework of the National Communications System. Plans and programs of the Administrator shall be in consonance with national telecommunications policies, plans, and programs developed pursuant to Executive Order No. 10705, Executive Order No. 10995, Executive Order No. 11051, and the Presidential Memorandum of August 21, 1963, "Establishment of the National Communications System," or other appropriate authority.

(4) Transportation. Develop plans and procedures for providing:

    (a) general transportation and traffic management services to civilian activities of Federal agencies in connection with movement of property and supplies, including the claimancy, contracting, routing, and accounting of Government shipments by commercial transportation in time of emergency; and

    (b) motor vehicle service to meet the administrative needs of Federal agencies, including dispatch and scheduled Government motor service at and between headquarters, field offices, relocation sites, and other installations of the Federal and State governments.

(5) Records. Provide instructions and advice on appraisal, selection, preservation, arrangement, reference, reproduction, storage, and salvage of essential records needed for the operation of the Federal Government after attack, on an emergency basis, including a decentralized system.

(6) Federal Register. Develop emergency procedures for providing and making available, on a decentralized basis, a Federal Register of Presidential Proclamations and Executive Orders, Federal administrative regulations, Federal emergency notices and actions, and Acts of Congress during a national emergency.

(7) Government-wide procurement and supply. Prepare plans and procedures for the coordination and/or operation of Government-wide supply programs to meet the requirements of Federal agencies under emergency conditions, including the development of policies, methods, and procedures for emergency procurement and for emergency requisitioning of private property when authorized by law and competent authority; identification of essential civil agency supply items under the Federal catalog system; development of emergency Federal specifications and standards; determination of sources of supply; procurement of personal property and non personal services; furnishing appropriate inspection and contract administration services; and establishment, coordination, and/or operation of emergency storage and distribution facilities.

(8) Survival item stockpiles. Assist the Department of Health, Education, and Welfare, insofar as civil defense medical stockpile items under its jurisdiction are concerned, and the Department of Defense, insofar as survival items under its jurisdiction are concerned, in formulating plans and programs for service activity support relating to stockpiling of such supplies and equipment. The Administrator shall arrange for the procurement, storage, maintenance, inspection, survey, withdrawal, and disposal of supplies and equipment in accordance with the provisions of interagency agreements with the departments concerned.

(9) National industrial reserve and machine tool program. Develop plans for the custody of the industrial plants and production equipment in the national industrial reserve and assist the Department of Defense, in collaboration with the Department of Commerce, in the development of plans and procedures for the disposition, emergency reactivation, and utilization of the plants and equipment of this reserve in the custody of the Administrator.

(10) Excess and surplus real and personal property. Develop plans and emergency operating procedures for the utilization of excess and surplus real and personal property by Federal Government agencies with emergency assignments or by State and local governmental units as directed, including review of the property holdings of Federal agencies which do not possess emergency functions to determine the availability of property for emergency use,

and including the disposal of real and personal property and
the rehabilitation of personal property.
(11) Facilities protection and building and shelter manager
service. In accordance with the guidance from the
Department of Defense, promote, with respect to Federal
buildings and installations, a Government-wide program
(a) to stimulate protection, preparedness, and control in
emergencies in order to minimize the effects of overt
or covert attack, including dispersal of facilities; and
(b) to establish shelter manager organizations, including
safety and service personnel, shelter manager
service, first aid, police, and evacuation service.

SEC. 2003 Defense Production.

Tile Administrator of General Services shall assist the Office of Emergency
Preparedness in the formulation of plans and programs relating to the certification
of procurement programs, subsidy payments, and plant improvement programs
provided for by the Defense Production Act of 1950, as amended.

SEC. 2004 Strategic and Critical Materials Stockpiles.

The Administrator of General Services shall assist the Office of Emergency
Preparedness in formulating plans, programs, and reports relating to the
stockpiling of strategic and critical materials. Within these plans and programs,
the Administrator shall provide for the procurement (for this purpose,
procurement includes upgrading, rotation, and beneficiation), storage, security,
maintenance, inspection, withdrawal, and disposal of materials, supplies, and
equipment.

PART 21
INTERSTATE COMMERCE COMMISSION

SECTION 2101 Resume of Responsibilities.

The Chairman of the Interstate Commerce Commission, under the coordinating
authority of the Secretary of Transportation, shall prepare national emergency
plans and develop preparedness programs covering railroad utilization, reduction
of vulnerability, maintenance, restoration, and operation in an emergency (other
than for the Alaska Railroad — see Section 1303(6)); motor carrier utilization,
reduction of vulnerability, and operation in an emergency; inland waterway
utilization of equipment and shipping, reduction of vulnerability, and operation
in an emergency; and also provide guidance and consultation to domestic
surface transportation and storage industries, as defined below, regarding

emergency preparedness measures, and to States regarding development of their transportation plans in assigned areas.

SEC. 2102 Definitions.
As used in this part:

(1) "Domestic surface transportation and storage" means rail, motor, and inland water transportation facilities and services and public storage;

(2) "Public storage" includes warehouses and other places which are used for the storage of property belonging to persons other than the persons having the ownership or control of such premises;

(3) "Inland water transportation" includes shipping on all inland waterways and Great Lakes shipping engaged solely in the transportation of passengers or cargo between United States ports on the Great Lakes;

(4) Specifically excluded, for the purposes of this part, are pipelines, petroleum and gas storage, agricultural food resources storage, including the cold storage of food resources, the St. Lawrence Seaway, ocean ports and Great Lakes ports and port facilities, highways, streets, roads, bridges, and related appurtenances, maintenance of inland waterways, and any transportation owned by or pre-allocated to the military.

SEC. 2103 Transportation Functions.
The Interstate Commerce Commission shall:

(1) Operational control. Develop plans with appropriate private transportation and storage organizations and associations for the coordination and direction of the use of domestic surface transportation and storage facilities for movement of passenger and freight traffic.

(2) Emergency operations. Develop and maintain necessary orders and regulations for the operation of domestic surface transport and storage industries in an emergency.

PART 22
NATIONAL AERONAUTICS AND SPACE ADMINISTRATION

SECTION 2201 Functions.
The Administrator of the National Aeronautics and Space Administration shall:

(1) Research and development. Adapt and utilize the scientific and technological capability of the National Aeronautics and

Space Administration, consistent with over-all requirements
to meet priority needs of the programs of the Federal
Government in an emergency. This will include the direction
and conduct of essential research and development activities
relating to
  (a) aircraft, spacecraft, and launch vehicles,
  (b) associated instrumentation, guidance, control and
       payload, propulsion, and communications systems,
  (c) scientific phenomena affecting both manned and
       unmanned space flights,
  (d) the life sciences (biology, medicine, and psychology)
       as they apply to aeronautics and space, and
  (e) atmospheric and geophysical sciences.
(2) Military support. Provide direct assistance as requested by
    the Department of Defense and other agencies in support of
    the military effort. This may include
  (a) undertaking urgent projects to develop superior
       aircraft, spacecraft, launch vehicles, and weapons
       systems,
  (b) developing methods to counter novel or
       revolutionary enemy weapons systems.
  (c) providing technical advice and assistance on matters
       involving air and space activities, and
  (d) furnishing personnel and facilities to assist in
       emergency repairs of equipment deficiencies and for
       other essential purposes.

PART 23
NATIONAL SCIENCE FOUNDATION

SECTION 2301 Functions.
The Director of the National Science Foundation shall:
  (1) Manpower functions. Assist the Department of Labor in
      sustaining readiness for the mobilization of civilian
      manpower by:
    (a) maintaining the Foundation's register of scientific and
         technical personnel in such form and at such
         locations as will assure maximum usefulness in an
         emergency;
    (b) being prepared for rapid expansion of the
         Foundation's current operation as a central
         clearing house for information covering all scientific

and technical personnel in the United States and its possessions; and

(c) developing, in consultation with the Department of Labor, the Selective Service System, the Department of Defense, and the Office of Science and Technology, plans and procedures to assure the most effective distribution and utilization of the Nation's scientific and engineering manpower in an emergency.

(2) Special functions.

(a) Provide leadership in developing, with the assistance of Federal and State agencies and appropriate non-governmental organizations, the ability to mobilize scientists, in consonance with over-all civilian manpower mobilization programs, to perform or assist in performance of special tasks, including the identification of and defense against unconventiona warfare;

(b) advance the national radiological defense capability by including, in consultation with appropriate agencies, pertinent scientific information and radiological defense techniques in the Foundation's scientific institute program for science, mathematics, and engineering teachers;

(c) assemble data on the location and character of major scientific research facilities, including non-governmental as well as government facilities, and their normal inventories of types of equipment and instruments which would be useful in identification and analysis of hazards to human life in the aftermath of enemy attack; and

(d) prepare to carry on necessary programs for basic research and for training of scientific manpower.

PART 24
RAILROAD RETIREMENT BOARD

SECTION 2401 Functions. The Railroad Retirement Board shall:

(1) Manpower functions. Within the framework of the over-all manpower plans and programs of the Department of Labor, assist in the mobilization of civilian manpower in an emergency by developing plans for the recruitment and referral of that segment of the Nation's manpower resources

subject to the Railroad Retirement and Railroad
Unemployment Insurance Acts.
(2) Benefit payments. Develop plans for administering, under
emergency conditions, the essential aspects of the Railroad
Retirement Act and Railroad Unemployment Insurance Act
consistent with overall Federal plans for the continuation of
benefit payments after an enemy attack.

PART 25
SECURITIES AND EXCHANGE COMMISSION

SECTION 2501 Functions.
The Securities and Exchange Commission shall collaborate with the Secretary of
the Treasury in the development of emergency financial control plans, programs,
procedures, and regulations for:
(1) Stock trading. Temporary closure of security exchanges,
suspension of redemption rights, and freezing of stock and
bond prices, if required in the interest of maintaining
economic controls.
(2) Modified trading. Development of plans designed to
reestablish and maintain a stable and orderly market
for securities when the situation permits under emergency
conditions.
(3) Protection of securities. Provision of a national records
system which will make it possible to establish current
ownership of securities in the event major trading centers and
depositories are destroyed.
(4) Flow of capital. The control of the formation and flow
of private capital as it relates to new securities offerings or
expansion of prior offerings for the purpose of establishing
or reestablishing industries in relation to the Nation's needs in
or following a national emergency.
(5) Flight of capital. The prevention of the flight of capital
outside this country, in coordination with the Secretary of
Commerce, and the impounding of securities in the hands of
enemy aliens.

PART 26
SMALL BUSINESS ADMINISTRATION

SECTION 2601 Functions.
The Administrator of the Small Business Administration shall:

(1) Prime contract authority. Develop plans to administer a program for the acquisition of prime contracts by the Administration and, in turn, for negotiating or otherwise letting of subcontracts to capable small business concerns in an emergency.

(2) Resource information. Provide data on facilities, inventories, and potential production capacity of small business concerns to all interested agencies.

(3) Procurement. Develop plans to determine jointly with Federal procurement agencies, as appropriate, which defense contracts are to go to small business concerns and to certify to the productive and financial ability of small concerns to perform specific contracts, as required.

(4) Loans for plant modernization. Develop plans for providing emergency assistance to essential individual industrial establishments through direct loans or participation loans for the financing of production facilities and equipment.

(5) Resource pools. Develop plans for encouraging and approving small business defense production and research and development pools.

(6) Financial assistance. Develop plans to make loans, directly or in participation with private lending institutions, to small business concerns and to groups or pools of such concerns, to small business investment companies, and to State and local development companies to provide them with funds for lending to small business concerns, for defense and essential civilian purposes.

Part 27
Tennessee Valley Authority

SECTION 2701 Functions.
The Board of Directors of the Tennessee Valley Authority shall:

(1) Electric power. Assist the Department of the Interior in the development of plans for the integration of the Tennessee Valley Authority power system into national emergency programs and prepare plans for the emergency management, operation, and maintenance of the system and for its essential expansion.

(2) Waterways. Assist the Interstate Commerce Commission, under the coordinating authority of the Secretary of Transportation, in the development of plans for integration and control of inland waterway transportation systems and, in

cooperation with the Department of Defense and the
Department of the Interior, prepare plans for the
management, operation, and maintenance of the river control
system in the Tennessee River and certain of its tributaries
for navigation during an emergency.

(3) Flood control. Develop plans and maintain its river control
operations for the prevention or control of floods caused
by natural phenomena or overt and covert attack affecting the
Tennessee River System and, in so doing, collaborate with
the Department of Defense with respect to the control of
water in the lower Ohio and Mississippi Rivers.

(4) Emergency health services and sanitary water supplies.
Assist the Department of Health, Education, and Welfare
in the development of plans and programs covering
emergency health services, civilian health manpower, and
health resources in the Tennessee Valley Authority area and,
in collaboration with the Department of the Interior and the
Department of Health, Education, and Welfare, prepare plans
for the management, operation and maintenance of the
Tennessee River System consistent with the needs for sanitary
public water supplies, waste disposal, and vector control.

(5) Coordination of water use. Develop plans for deter- mining
or proposing priorities for the use of water by the Tennessee
Valley Authority in the event of conflicting claims arising
from the functions listed above.

(6) Fertilizer. Assist the Department of Agriculture in the
development of plans for the distribution and claimancy
of fertilizer; assist the Department of Commerce and the
Department of Defense in the development of Tennessee
Valley Authority production quotas and any essential
expansion of production facilities, and prepare plans for the
management, operation, and maintenance of its facilities for
the manufacture of nitrogen and phosphorous fertilizers.

(7) Munitions production. Perform chemical research in
munitions as requested by the Department of Defense,
maintain standby munitions production facilities, and
develop plans for converting and utilizing fertilizer facilities
as required in support of the Department of Defense's
munitions program.

(8) Land management. Develop plans for the maintenance,
management, and utilization of Tennessee Valley Authority-
controlled lands in the interest of an emergency economy.

(9) Food and forestry. Assist the Department of Agriculture in the development of plans for the harvesting and processing of fish and game, and the Department of Commerce in the development of plans for the production and processing of forest products.

(10) Coordination with Valley States. Prepare plans and agreements with Tennessee Valley States, consistent with Federal programs, for appropriate integration of Tennessee Valley Authority and State plans for the use of available Tennessee Valley Authority resources.

PART 28
UNITED STATES CIVIL SERVICE COMMISSION

SECTION 2801 Functions.
The United States Civil Service Commission shall:

(1) Personnel system. Prepare plans for adjusting the Federal civilian personnel system to simplify administration and to meet emergency demands.

(2) Utilization. Develop policies and implementing procedures designed to assist Federal agencies in achieving the most effective utilization of the Federal Government's civilian manpower in an emergency.

(3) Manpower policies. As the representative of the Federal Government as an employer, participate, as appropriate, in the formulation of national and regional manpower policies as they affect Federal civilian personnel and establish implementing policies as necessary.

(4) Manpower administration. Prepare plans, in consonance with national manpower policies and programs, for the administration of emergency civilian manpower and employment policies within the executive branch of the Government, including the issuance and enforcement of regulations to implement such policies.

(5) Wage and salary stabilization. Participate, as appropriate, with the Office of Emergency Preparedness and the Department of Labor in the formulation of national and regional wage and salary stabilization policies as they affect Federal civilian personnel. Within the framework of such policies, prepare plans for the implementation of such policies and controls established for employees within the executive branch of the Government, including the issuance and enforcement of necessary regulations.

(6) Assistance. Develop plans for rendering personnel management and staffing assistance to new and expanding Federal agencies.

(7) Recruiting. Develop plans for the coordination and control of civilian recruiting policies and practices by all Federal agencies in order to increase the effectiveness of the total recruitment efforts during an emergency and to prevent undesirable recruitment practices.

(8) Reassignment. Develop plans to facilitate the reassignment or transfer of Federal civilian employees, including the movement of employees from one agency or location to another agency or location, in order to meet the most urgent needs of the executive branch during an emergency.

(9) Registration. Develop plans and procedures for a nationwide system of post-attack registration of Federal employees to provide a means for locating and returning to duty those employees who become physically separated from their agencies after an enemy attack, and to provide for the maximum utilization of the skills of surviving employees.

(10) Deferment. Develop plans and procedures for a system to control Government requests for the selective service deferment of employees in the executive branch of the Federal Government and in the municipal government of the District of Columbia.

(11) Investigation. Prepare plans, in coordination with agencies having responsibilities in the personnel security field, for the conduct of national agency checks and inquiries, limited suitability investigations, and full field investigations under emergency conditions.

(12) Salaries, wages, and benefits. Develop plans for operating under emergency conditions the essential aspects of salary and wage systems and such benefit systems as the Federal Employees Retirement System, the Federal Employees Group Life Insurance Program, the Federal Employees and Retired Federal Employees Health Benefits Programs, and the Federal Employees Compensation Program.

(13) Federal manpower mobilization. Assist Federal agencies in establishing manpower plans to meet their own emergency manpower requirements; identify major or special manpower problems of individual Federal agencies and the Federal Government as a whole in mobilizing a civilian work force to meet essential emergency

requirements; identify sources of emergency manpower
supply for all agencies where manpower problems are
indicated; and develop Government-wide plans for the use
of surplus Federal civilian manpower.

(14) Distribution of manpower. Participate in the formulation of
policies and decisions on the distribution of the nation's
civilian manpower resources, obtain appropriate civilian
manpower data from Federal agencies, and establish
necessary implementing policies and procedures within the
Executive Branch.

(15) Training. Develop, organize, and conduct, as appropriate,
interagency training programs in emergency personnel
management for Federal employees.

Part 29
Veterans Administration

SECTION 2901 Functions.
The Administrator of Veterans Affairs shall develop policies, plans, and
procedures for the performance of emergency functions with respect to
the continuation or restoration of authorized programs of the Veterans
Administration under all conditions of national emergency, including attack
upon the United States. These include:

(1) The emergency conduct of inpatient and outpatient care
and treatment in Veterans Administration medical facilities
and participation with the Departments of Defense and
Health, Education, and Welfare as provided for in
interagency agreements.

(2) The emergency conduct of compensation, pension,
rehabilitation, education, and insurance payments consistent
with over-all Federal plans for the continuation of Federal
benefit payments.

(3) The emergency performance of insurance and loan guaranty
functions in accordance with indirect stabilization policies
and controls designed to deal with various emergency conditions.

Part 30
General Provisions

SECTION 3001 Resource Management.
In consonance with the national preparedness, security, and mobilization
readiness plans, programs, and operations of the Office of Emergency

Preparedness under Executive Order No. 11051 of September 27, 1962, and subject to the provisions of the preceding parts, the head of each department and agency shall:

    (1) Priorities and allocations. Develop systems for the emergency application of priorities and allocations to the production, distribution, and use of resources for which he has been assigned responsibility.

    (2) Requirements. Assemble, develop as appropriate, and evaluate requirements for assigned resources, taking into account estimated needs for military, atomic energy, civilian, and foreign purposes. Such evaluation shall take into consideration geographical distribution of requirements under emergency conditions.

    (3) Evaluation. Assess assigned resources in order to estimate availability from all sources under an emergency situation, analyze resource availabilities in relation to estimated requirements, and develop appropriate recommendations and programs, including those necessary for the maintenance of an adequate mobilization base. Provide data and assistance before and after attack for national resource analysis purposes of the Office of Emergency Preparedness.

    (4) Claimancy. Prepare plans to claim from the appropriate agency supporting materials, manpower, equipment, supplies, and services which would be needed to carry out assigned responsibilities and other essential functions of his department or agency, and cooperate with other agencies in developing programs to insure availability of such resources in an emergency.

SEC. 3002 Facilities protection and warfare effects monitoring and reporting. In consonance with the national preparedness, security, and mobilization readiness plans, programs, and operations of the Office of Emergency Preparedness under Executive Order No. 11051, and with the national civil defense plans, programs, and operations of the Department of Defense under Executive Order No. 10952, the head of each department and agency shall:

    (1) Facilities protection. Provide facilities protection guidance material adapted to the needs of the facilities and services concerned and promote a national program to stimulate disaster preparedness and control in order to minimize the effects of overt and covert attack on facilities or other resources for which he has management responsibility. Guidance shall include, but not be limited to, organization

and training of facility employees, personnel shelter, evacuation plans, records protection, continuity of management, emergency repair, dispersal of facilities, and mutual aid associations for an emergency.

(2) Warfare effects monitoring and reporting. Maintain a capability, both at national and field levels, to estimate the effects of attack on assigned resources and to collaborate with and provide data to the Office of Emergency Preparedness, the Department of Defense, and other agencies, as appropriate, in verifying and updating estimates of resource status through exchanges of data and mutual assistance, and provide for the detection, identification, monitoring and reporting of such warfare effects at selected facilities under his operation or control.

(3) Salvage and rehabilitation. Develop plans for salvage, decontamination, and rehabilitation of facilities involving resources under his jurisdiction.

(4) Shelter. In conformity with national shelter policy, where authorized to engage in building construction, plan, design, and construct such buildings to protect the public to the maximum extent feasible against the hazards that could result from an attack upon the United States with nuclear weapons; and where empowered to extend Federal financial assistance, encourage recipients of such financial assistance to use standards for planning design and construction which will maximize protection for the public.

SEC. 3003 Critical skills and occupations.

(a) The Secretaries of Defense, Commerce, and Labor shall carry out the mandate of the National Security Council, dated February 15, 1968, to "maintain a continuing surveillance over the Nation's manpower needs and identify any particular occupation or skill that may warrant qualifying for deferment on a uniform national basis." In addition, the Secretaries of Defense, Commerce, Labor, and Health, Education, and Welfare shall carry out the mandate of the National Security Council to "maintain a continuing surveillance over the Nation's manpower and education needs to identify any area of graduate study that may warrant qualifying for deferment in the national interest." In carrying out these functions, the Secretaries concerned shall consult with the National Science Foundation with respect to

scientific manpower requirements.
(b) The Secretaries of Commerce and Labor shall maintain and issue, as necessary, lists of all essential activities and critical occupations that may be required for emergency preparedness purposes.

SEC. 3004 Research.
Within the framework of research policies and objectives established by the Office of Emergency Preparedness, the head of each department and agency shall supervise or conduct research in areas directly concerned with carrying out emergency preparedness responsibilities, designate representatives for necessary ad hoc or task force groups, and provide advice and assistance to other agencies in planning for research in areas involving each agency's interest.

SEC. 3005 Stockpiles.
The head of each department and agency, with appropriate emergency responsibilities, shall assist the Office of Emergency Preparedness in formulating and carrying out plans for stockpiling of strategic and critical materials, and survival items.

SEC. 3006 Direct Economic Controls.
The head of each department and agency shall cooperate with the Office of Emergency Preparedness and the Federal financial agencies in the development of emergency preparedness measures involving emergency financial and credit measures, as well as price, rent, wage and salary stabilization, and consumer rationing programs.

SEC. 3007 Financial Aid.
The head of each department and agency shall develop plans and procedures in cooperation with the Federal financial agencies for financial and credit assistance to those segments of the private sector for which he is responsible in the event such assistance is needed under emergency conditions.

SEC. 3008 Functional Guidance.
The head of each department and agency in carrying out the functions assigned to him by this order, shall be guided by the following:
(1) National program guidance. In consonance with the national preparedness, security, and mobilization readiness plans, programs, and operations of the Office of Emergency Preparedness under Executive Order No. 11051, and with the national civil defense plans, programs, and operations of

the Department of Defense, technical guidance shall be
provided to State and local governments and instrumentalities
thereof, to the end that all planning concerned with functions
assigned herein will be effectively coordinated. Relations
with the appropriate segment of the private sector shall be
maintained to foster mutual understanding of Federal
emergency plans.
(2) Interagency coordination. Emergency preparedness functions
shall be coordinated by the head of the department or agency
having primary responsibility with all other departments and
agencies having supporting functions related thereto.
(3) Emergency preparedness. Emergency plans, programs,
and an appropriate state of readiness, including
organizational readiness, shall be developed as an integral
part of the continuing activities of each department or
agency on the basis that that department or agency will have
the responsibility for carrying out such plans and programs
during an emergency. The head of each department or agency
shall be prepared to implement all appropriate plans
developed under this order. Modifications and temporary
organizational changes, based on emergency conditions, shall
be in accordance with policy determinations by the President.
(4) Professional liaison. Mutual understanding and support of
emergency preparedness activities shall be fostered, and
the National Defense Executive Reserve shall be promoted
by maintaining relations with the appropriate non-
governmental sectors.

SEC. 3009 Training.
The head of each department and agency shall develop and direct training
programs which incorporate emergency preparedness and civil defense
training and information programs necessary to insure the optimum operational
effectiveness of assigned resources, systems, and facilities.

SEC. 3010 Emergency Public Information.
In consonance with such emergency public information plans and central
program decisions of the Office of Emergency Preparedness, and with plans,
programs, and procedures established by the Department of Defense to provide
continuity of programming for the Emergency Broadcast System, the head of
each department and agency shall:
(1) Obtain and provide information as to the emergency
functions or assignments of the individual department or

agency for dissemination to the American people during the
emergency, in accordance with arrangements made by the
Office of Emergency Preparedness.

(2) Determine requirements and arrange for prerecordings to
provide continuity of program service over the Emergency
Broadcast System so that the American people can
receive information, advice, and guidance pertaining to the
implementation of the civil defense and emergency
preparedness plans or assignments of each individual
department or agency.

SEC. 3011 Emergency Actions.
This order does not confer authority to put into effect any emergency plan,
procedure, policy, program, or course of action prepared or developed pursuant
to this order. Plans so developed may be effectuated only in the event that
authority for such effectuation is provided by a law enacted by the Congress
or by an order or directive issued by the President pursuant to statutes or the
Constitution of the United States.

SEC. 3012 Redelegation.
The head of each department and agency is hereby authorized to redelegate the
functions assigned to him by this order, and to authorize

successive redelegations to agencies or instrumentalities of the United States,
and to officers and employees of the United States.

SEC. 3013 Transfer of Functions.
Any emergency preparedness function under this order, or parts thereof, may be
transferred from one department or agency to another with the consent of the
heads of the organizations involved and with the concurrence of the Director
of the Office of Emergency Preparedness. Any new emergency preparedness
function may be assigned to the head of a department or agency by the Director
of the Office of Emergency Preparedness by mutual consent.

SEC. 3014 Retention of Existing Authority.
Except as provided by Section 3015, nothing in this order shall be deemed to
derogate from any now existing assignment of functions to any department
or agency or officer thereof made by statute, Executive order, or Presidential
directives, including Memoranda.

SEC. 3015 Revoked Orders.

The following are hereby revoked:

(1) Defense Mobilization Order VI-2 of December 11, 1953.

(2) Defense Mobilization Order 1-12 of October 5, 1954.

(3) Executive Order No. 10312 of December 10, 1951.

(4) Executive Order No. 10346 of April 17, 1952.

(5) Executive Order No. 10997 of February 16, 1962.

(6) Executive Order No. 10998 of February 16, 1962.

(7) Executive Order No. 10999 of February 16, 1962.

(8) Executive Order No. 11000 of February 16, 1962.

(9) Executive Order No. 11001 of February 16, 1962.

(10) Executive Order No. 11002 of February 16, 1962.

(11) Executive Order No. 11003 of February 16, 1962.

(12) Executive Order No. 11004 of February 16, 1962.

(13) Executive Order No. 11005 of February 16, 1962.

(14) Executive Order No. 11087 of February 26, 1963.

(15) Executive Order No. 11088 of February 26, 1963.

(16) Executive Order No. 11089 of February 26, 1963.

(17) Executive Order No. 11090 of February 26, 1963.

(18) Executive Order No. 11091 of February 26, 1963.

(19) Executive Order No. 11092 of February 26, 1963.

(20) Executive Order No. 11093 of February 26, 1963.

(21) Executive Order No. 11094 of February 26, 1963.

(22) Executive Order No. 11095 of February 26, 1963.

(23) Executive Order No. 11310 of October 11, 1966.

THE WHITE HOUSE,
October 28, 1969
(signed) Richard Nixon

APPENDIX C

EXECUTIVE ORDER 12148:
FEDERAL EMERGENCY MANAGEMENT

BY THE AUTHORITY vested in me as President by the Constitution and laws of the United States of America, including the Federal Civil Defense Act of 1950, as amended (50 U.S.C. App. 2251 et seq.), the Disaster Relief Act of 1970, as amended (42 U.S.C. Chapter 58 note), the Disaster Relief Act of 1974 (88 Stat. 143; 42 U.S.C. 5121 et seq.), the Earthquake Hazards Reduction Act of 1977 (42 U.S.C. 7701 et seq.), Section 4 of Public Law 92-385 (86 Stat. 556), Section 43 of the Act of August 10, 1956, as amended (50 U.S.C. App. 2285), the National Security Act of 1947, as amended, the Defense Production Act of 1950, as amended (50 U.S.C. App. 2061 et seq.), Reorganization Plan No. 1 of 1958, Reorganization Plan No. 1 of 1973, the Strategic and Critical Materials Stock Piling Act, as amended (50 U.S.C. 98 et seq.), Section 202 of the Budget and Accounting Procedures Act of 1950 (31 U.S.C. 581c), and Section 301 of Title 3 of the United States Code, and in order to transfer emergency functions to the Federal Emergency Management Agency, it is hereby ordered as follows:

SECTION 1
TRANSFERS OR REASSIGNMENTS

1-1 Transfer or Reassignment of Existing Functions.
    1-101 All functions vested in the President that have been
        delegated or assigned to the Defense Civil Preparedness
        Agency, Department of Defense, are transferred
        or reassigned to the Director of the Federal Emergency
        Management Agency.

1-102 All functions vested in the President that have been
    delegated or assigned to the Federal Disaster Assistance
    Administration, Department of Housing and Urban
    Development, are transferred or reassigned to the Director
    of the Federal Emergency Management Agency,
    including any of those functions redelegated or reassigned
    to the Department of Commerce with respect to assistance
    to communities in the development of readiness plans for
    severe weather-related emergencies.

1-103 All functions vested in the President that have been
    delegated or assigned to the Federal Preparedness Agency,
    General Services Administration, are transferred
    or reassigned to the Director of the Federal Emergency
    Management Agency.

1-104 All functions vested in the President by the Earthquake
    Hazards Reduction Act of 1977 (42 U.S.C. 7701 et seq.),
    including those functions performed by the Office of
    Science and Technology Policy, are delegated, transferred,
    or reassigned to the Director of the Federal Emergency
    Management Agency.

1-2 Transfer or Reassignment of Resources.
    1-201 The records, property, personnel and positions, and
        unexpended balances of appropriations, available or to
        be made available, which relate to the functions
        transferred, reassigned, or redelegated by this Order are
        hereby transferred to the Director of the Federal
        Emergency Management Agency.

    1-202 The Director of the Office of Management and Budget
        shall make such determinations, issue such orders, and
        take all actions necessary or appropriate to effectuate the
        transfers or reassignments provided by this Order,
        including the transfer of funds, records, property, and
        personnel.

Section 2
Management of Emergency Planning and Assistance

2-1 General.

2-101 The Director of the Federal Emergency Management
Agency shall establish Federal policies for, and
coordinate, all civil defense and civil emergency planning,
management, mitigation, and assistance functions of
Executive agencies.

2-102 The Director shall periodically review and evaluate the
civil defense and civil emergency functions of the
Executive agencies. In order to improve the efficiency and
effectiveness of those functions, the Director shall
recommend to the President alternative methods of
providing Federal planning, management, mitigation, and
assistance.

2-103 The Director shall be responsible for the coordination of
efforts to promote dam safety, for the coordination of
natural and nuclear disaster warning systems, and for
the coordination of preparedness and planning to reduce
the consequences of major terrorist incidents.

2-104 The Director shall represent the President in working
with State and local governments and private sector to
stimulate vigorous participation in civil emergency
preparedness, mitigation, response, and recovery
programs.

2-105 The Director shall provide an annual report to the
President for subsequent transmittal to the Congress on
the functions of the Federal Emergency Management
Agency. The report shall assess the current overall state
of effectiveness of Federal civil defense and civil
emergency functions, organizations, resources, and
systems and recommend measures to be taken to improve
planning, management, assistance, and relief by all levels
of government, the private sector, and volunteer
organizations.

2-2 Implementation.

    2-201 In executing the functions under this Order, the Director shall develop policies which provide that all civil defense and civil emergency functions, resources, and systems of Executive agencies are:

      (a) founded on the use of existing organizations, resources, and systems to the maximum extent practicable;

      (b) integrated effectively with organizations, resources, and programs of State and local governments, the private sector and volunteer organizations; and

      (c) developed, tested and utilized to prepare for, mitigate, respond to and recover from the effects on the population of all forms of emergencies.

    2-202 Assignments of civil emergency functions shall, whenever possible, be based on extensions (under emergency conditions) of the regular missions of the Executive agencies.

    2-203 For purposes of this Order, 'civil emergency' means any accidental, natural, man-caused, or wartime emergency or threat thereof, which causes or may cause substantial injury or harm to the population or substantial damage to or loss of property.

    2-204 In order that civil defense planning continues to be fully compatible with the Nation's overall strategic policy, and in order to maintain an effective link between strategic nuclear planning and nuclear attack preparedness planning, the development of civil defense policies and programs by the Director of the Federal Emergency Management Agency shall be subject to oversight by the Secretary of Defense and the National Security Council.

    2-205 To the extent authorized by law and within available resources, the Secretary of Defense shall provide the Director of the Federal Emergency Management Agency with support for civil defense programs in the areas of program development and administration, technical support, research, communications, transportation, intelligence, and emergency operations.

2-206 All Executive agencies shall cooperate with and assist the Director in the performance of his functions.

2-3 Transition Provisions.

2-301 The functions which have been transferred, reassigned, or redelegated by Section 1 of this Order are recodified and revised as set forth in this Order at Section 4, and as provided by the amendments made at Section 5 to the provisions of other Orders.

2-302 Notwithstanding the revocations, revisions, codifications, and amendments made by this Order, the Director may continue to perform the functions transferred to him by Section 1 of this Order, except where they may otherwise be inconsistent with the provisions of this Order.

SECTION 3
FEDERAL EMERGENCY MANAGEMENT COUNCIL

3-1 Establishment of the Council.

3-101 There is hereby established the Emergency Managemen Council.

3-102 The Council shall be composed of the Director of the Federal Emergency Management Agency, who shall be the

Chairman, the Director of the Office of Management and Budget and such others as the President may designate.

3-2 Functions of the Council.

3-201 The Council shall advise and assist the President in the oversight and direction of Federal emergency programs and policies.

3-202 The Council shall provide guidance to the Director of the Federal Emergency Management Agency in the performance of functions vested in him.

3-3 Administrative and General Provisions.

3-301 The heads of Executive agencies shall cooperate with and assist the Council in the performance of its functions.

3-302 The Director of the Federal Emergency Management
Agency shall provide the Council with such administrative
services and support as may be necessary or appropriate.

SECTION 4
DELEGATIONS

4-1 Delegation of Functions Transferred to the President.
  4-101 The following functions were transferred to the
    Director of the Office of Defense Mobilization by Section
    2 of Reorganization Plan No. 3 of 1953 (50 U.S.C. 404
    note); they were subsequently transferred to the President
    by Section 1(a) of Reorganization Plan No. 1 of 1958,
    as amended (50 U.S.C. App. 2271 note), and they are
    hereby delegated to the Director of the Federal Emergency
    Management Agency:
      (a) The functions vested in the Secretaries of
        the Army, Navy, Air Force, and Interior
        by the Strategic and Critical Materials Stock
        Piling Act, as amended (50 U.S.C. 98 et
        seq.), including the functions vested in the
        Army and Navy Munitions Board by item (2)
        of Section 6(a) of that Act (50 U.S.C.
        98e(a)(2)), but excluding the functions
        vested in the Secretary of the Interior by
        Section 7 of that Act (50 U.S.C. 98f).
      (b) The functions vested in the Munitions Board
        of the Department of Defense by Section
        4(h) of the Commodity Credit Corporation
        Charter Act, as amended (15 U.S.C.
        714b(h)).
      (c) The function vested in the Munitions Board
        of the Department of Defense by Section
        204(f) [originally 204(e)] of the Federal
        Property and Administrative Services Act of
        1949, as amended (40 U.S.C. 485(f)).

  4-102 The functions vested in the Director of the Office of
    Defense Mobilization by Sections 103 and 303 of the
    National Security Act of 1947, as amended by Sections
    8 and 50 of the Act of September 3, 1954 (Public Law
    779; 68 Stat. 1228 and 1244) (50 U.S.C. 404 and

405), were transferred to the President by Section 1(a) of
Reorganization Plan No. 1 of 1958, as amended (50 U.S.C.
App. 2271 note), and they are hereby delegated to the Director
of the Federal Emergency Management Agency.

4-103

    (a) The functions vested in the Federal Civil Defense
    Administration or its Administrator by the Federal
    Civil Defense Act of 1950, as amended (50 U.S.C.
    App. 2251 et seq.), were transferred to the President
    by Reorganization Plan No. 1 of 1958, and they
    are hereby delegated to the Director of the Federal
    Emergency Management Agency.

    (b) Excluded from the delegation in subsection (a) is
    the function under Section 205(a)(4) of the Federal
    Civil Defense Act of 1950, as amended (50 U.S.C.
    App. 2286(a)(4)), relating to the establishment and
    maintenance of personnel standards on the merit
    basis that was delegated to the Director of the Office
    of Personnel Management by Section 1(b) of
    Executive Order No. 11589, as amended (Section 2-
    101(b) of Executive Order No. 12107).

4-104 The Director of the Federal Emergency Management
Agency is authorized to redelegate, in accord with the
provisions of Section 1(b) of Reorganization Plan No. 1
of 1958 (50 U.S.C. App. 2271 note), any of the functions
delegated by Sections 4-101, 4-102, and 4-103 of this Order.

4-105 The functions vested in the Administrator of the Federal
Civil Defense Administration by Section 43 of the Act
of August 10, 1956 (70A Stat. 636) were transferred to
the President by Reorganization Plan No. 1 of 1958,
as amended (50 U.S.C. App. 2271 note), were
subsequently revested in the Director of the Office of
Civil and Defense Mobilization by Section 512 of Public
Law 86-500 (50 U.S.C. App. 2285) [the office was
changed to Office of Emergency Planning by Public
Law 87-296 (75 Stat. 630) and then to the Office of
Emergency Preparedness by Section 402 of Public Law
90- 608 (82 Stat. 1194)], were again transferred to the
President by Section 1 of Reorganization Plan No. 1 of

1973 (50 U.S.C. App. 2271 note), and they are hereby delegated to the Director of the Federal Emergency Management Agency.

4-106 The functions vested in the Director of the Office of Emergency Preparedness by Section 16 of the Act of September 23, 1950, as amended (20 U.S.C. 646), and by Section 7 of the Act of September 30, 1950, as amended (20 U.S.C. 241-1), were transferred to the President by Section 1 of Reorganization Plan No. 1 of 1973 (50 U.S.C. App. 2271 note), and they are hereby delegated to the Director of the Federal Emergency Management Agency.

4-107 That function vested in the Director of the Office of Emergency Preparedness by Section 762(a) of the Higher Education Act of 1965, as added by Section 161(a) of the Education Amendments of 1972, and as further amended (20 U.S.C. 1132d-1(a)), to the extent transferred to the President by Reorganization Plan No. 1 of 1973 (50 U.S.C. App. 2271 note), is hereby delegated to the Director of the Federal Emergency Management Agency.

4-2 Delegation of Functions Vested in the President.
  4-201 The functions vested in the President by the Disaster Relief Act of 1970, as amended (42 U.S.C. Chapter 58 note), are hereby delegated to the Director of the Federal Emergency Management Agency.

  4-202 The functions (related to grants for damages resulting from hurricane and tropical storm Agnes) vested in the President by Section 4 of Public Law 92-385 (86 Stat. 556) are hereby delegated to the Director of the Federal Emergency Management Agency.

  4-203 The functions vested in the President by the Disaster Relief Act of 1974 (88 Stat. 143; 42 U.S.C. 5121 et seq.), except those functions vested in the President by Sections 301 (relating to the declaration of emergencies and major disasters), 401 (relating to the repair, reconstruction, restoration, or replacement of Federal facilities), and 409 (relating to food coupons and surplus commodities), are hereby delegated to the Director of the Federal Emergency Management Agency.

4-204 The functions vested in the President by the Earthquake Hazards Reduction Act of 1977 (91 Stat. 1098; 42 U.S.C. 7701 et seq.) are hereby delegated to the Director of the Federal Emergency Management Agency.

Section 5
Other Executive Orders

5-1 Revocations.

5-101 Executive Order No. 10242, as amended, entitled 'Prescribing Regulations Governing the Exercise by the Federal Civil Defense Administrator of Certain Administrative Authority Granted by the Federal Civil Defense Act of 1950', is revoked.

5-102 Sections 1 and 2 of Executive Order No. 10296, as amended, entitled 'Providing for the Performance of Certain Defense Housing and Community Facilities and Service Functions', are revoked.

5-103 Executive Order No. 10494, as amended, relating to the disposition of remaining functions, is revoked.

5-104 Executive Order No. 10529, as amended, relating to federal employee participation in State and local civil defense programs, is revoked.

5-105 Section 3 of Executive Order No. 10601, as amended, which concerns the Commodity Set Aside, is revoked.

5-106 Executive Order No. 10634, as amended, relating to loans for facilities destroyed or damaged by a major disaster, is revoked.

5-107 Section 4(d)(2) of Executive Order No. 10900, as amended, which concerns foreign currencies made available to make purchases for the supplemental stockpile, is revoked.

5-108 Executive Order No. 10952, as amended, entitled 'Assigning Civil Defense Responsibilities to the Secretary of Defense and Others', is revoked.

5-109 Executive Order No. 11051, as amended, relating to responsibilities of the Office of Emergency Preparedness, is revoked.

5-110 Executive Order No. 11415, as amended, relating to the Health Resources Advisory Committee, is revoked.

5-111 Executive Order No. 11795, as amended, entitled 'Delegating Disaster Relief Functions Pursuant to the Disaster Relief Act of 1974', is revoked, except for Section 3 thereof.

5-112 Executive Order No. 11725, as amended, entitled 'Transfer of Certain Functions of the Office of Emergency Preparedness', is revoked.

5-113 Executive Order No. 11749, as amended, entitled 'Consolidating Disaster Relief Functions Assigned to the Secretary of Housing and Urban Development' is revoked.

5-2 Amendments.

5-201 Executive Order No. 10421, as amended, relating to physical security of defense facilities is further amended by (a) substituting the 'Director of the Federal Emergency Management Agency' for 'Director of the Office of Emergency Planning' in Sections 1(a), 1(c), and 6(b); and, (b) substituting 'Federal Emergency Management Agency' for 'Office of Emergency Planning' in Sections 6(b) and 7(b).

5-202 Executive Order No. 10480, as amended, is further amended by (a) substituting 'Director of the Federal Emergency Management Agency' for 'Director of the Office of Emergency Planning' in Sections 101(a), 101(b), 201(a), 201(b), 301, 304, 307, 308, 310(b), 311(b), 312, 313, 401(b), 401(e), and 605; and, (b) substituting 'Director of the Federal Emergency Management Agency' for 'Administrator of General Services' in Section 610.

5-203 Section 3(d) of Executive Order No. 10582, as amended, which relates to determinations under the Buy American Act is amended by deleting 'Director of the Office of Emergency Planning' and substituting therefore 'Director of the Federal Emergency Management Agency'.

5-204 Paragraph 21 of Executive Order No. 10789, as amended, is further amended by adding 'The Federal Emergency Management Agency' after 'Government Printing Office'.

5-205 Executive Order No. 11179, as amended, concerning the National Defense Executive Reserve, is further amended by deleting 'Director of the Office of Emergency Planning' in Section 2 and substituting therefore 'Director of the Federal Emergency Management Agency'.

5-206 Section 7 of Executive Order No. 11912, as amended, concerning energy policy and conservation, is further amended by deleting 'Administrator of General Services' and substituting therefore 'Director of the Federal Emergency Management Agency'.

5-207 Section 2(d) of Executive Order No. 11988 entitled 'Floodplain Management' is amended by deleting 'Federal Insurance Administration' and substituting therefore 'Director of the Federal Emergency Management Agency'.

5-208 Section 5-3 of Executive Order No. 12046 of March 29, 1978, is amended by deleting 'General Services Administration' and substituting therefore 'Federal Emergency Management Agency' and by deleting 'Administrator of General Services' and substituting therefore 'Director of the Federal Emergency Management Agency'.

5-209 Section 1-201 of Executive Order No. 12065 is amended by adding 'The Director of the Federal Emergency Management Agency' after 'The Administrator, National Aeronautics and Space Administration' and by deleting 'Director, Federal Preparedness Agency and to the' from the parentheses after 'The Administrator of General Services'.

5-210 Section 1-102 of Executive Order No. 12075 of August
      16, 1978, is amended by adding in alphabetical order '(p)
      Federal Emergency Management Agency'.

5-211 Section 1-102 of Executive Order No. 12083 of September
      27, 1978 is amended by adding in alphabetical order '(x)
      the Director of the Federal Emergency Management
      Agency'.

5-212 Section 9.11(b) of Civil Service Rule IX (5 CFR Part 9)
      is amended by deleting 'the Defense Civil Preparedness
      Agency and'.

5-213 Section 3(2) of each of the following described Executive
      orders is amended by adding 'Federal Emergency
      Management Agency' immediately after 'Department of
      Transportation'.
      (a) Executive Order No. 11331 establishing the
          Pacific Northwest River Basins Commission.
      (b) Executive Order No. 11345, as amended,
          establishing the Great Lakes Basin
          Commission.
      (c) Executive Order No. 11371, as amended,
          establishing the New England River Basins
          Commission.
      (d) Executive Order No. 11578, as amended,
          establishing the Ohio River Basin
          Commission.
      (e) Executive Order No. 11658, as amended,
          establishing the Missouri River Basin
          Commission.
      (f) Executive Order No. 11659, as amended,
          establishing the Upper Mississippi River
          Basin Commission.

5-214 Executive Order No. 11490, as amended, is further
      amended as follows:
      (a) Delete the last sentence of Section 102(a) and
          substitute therefore the following: 'The activities
          undertaken by the departments and agencies pursuant
          to this Order, except as provided in Section 3003,
          shall be in accordance with guidance provided by,

and subject to, evaluation by the Director of the
Federal Emergency Management Agency.'.
(b) Delete Section 103 entitled 'Presidential Assistance'
and substitute the following new Section 103:
'Sec. 103 General Coordination. The Director of
the Federal Emergency Management Agency
(FEMA) shall determine national preparedness goals
and policies for the performance of functions under
this Order and coordinate the performance of such
functions with the total national preparedness
programs.'.
(c) Delete the portion of the first sentence of Section
401 prior to the colon and insert the following:
'The Secretary of Defense shall perform the
following emergency preparedness functions'.
(d) Delete 'Director of the Federal Preparedness Agency
(GSA)' or 'the Federal Preparedness Agency (GSA)'
and substitute therefore 'Director, FEMA', in Sections
401(3), 401(4), 401(5), 401(9), 401(10), 401(14),
401(15), 401(16), 401(19), 401(21), 401(22), 501(8),
601(2), 904(2), 1102(2), 1204(2), 1401(a), 1701,
1702, 2003, 2004, 2801(5), 3001, 3002(2), 3004,
3005, 3006, 3008, 3010, and 3013.
(e) The number assigned to this Order shall be
substituted for '11051 of September 27, 1962' in
Section 3001, and for '11051' in Sections 1802,
2002(3), 3002 and 3008(1).
(f) The number assigned to this Order shall be
substituted for '10952' in Sections 1103, 1104, 1205,
and 3002.
(g) Delete 'Department of Defense' in Sections 502,
601(1), 804, 905, 1103, 1104, 1106(4), 1205, 2002(8),
the first sentence of Section 3002, and Sections
3008(1) and 3010 and substitute therefore 'Director of
the Federal Emergency Management Agency.'.

SECTION 6
This Order is effective July 15, 1979.

THE WHITE HOUSE
July 20, 1979
(signed) Jimmy Carter